SECRET SOLDIERS OF
THE REVOLUTION

Recent Titles in
Contributions in Military Studies

Secret Soldiers of the Revolution

Soviet Military Intelligence, 1918–1933

Raymond W. Leonard

Contributions in Military Studies,
Number 183

GREENWOOD PRESS
Westport, Connecticut • London

Library of Congress Cataloging-in-Publication Data

Leonard, Raymond W.
   Secret soldiers of the revolution : Soviet military intelligence,
   1918–1933 / Raymond W. Leonard.
      p.   cm — (Contributions in military studies, ISSN 0883–6884
; no. 183)
   Includes bibliographical references (p.   ).
   ISBN 0–313–30990–6 (alk. paper)
      1. Military intelligence—Soviet Union—History.   2. Soviet Union.
Glavnoe razvedyvatel 'noe upravlenie—History.   I. Title.
II. Series.
UB251.R8L46   1999
327.1247´0904—dc21   99–32003

British Library Cataloguing in Publication Data is available.

Library of Congress Catalog Card Number: 99–32003
ISBN: 0–313–30990–6
ISSN: 0883–6884

First published in 1999

Greenwood Press, 88 Post Road West, Westport, CT 06881
An imprint of Greenwood Publishing Group, Inc.
www.greenwood.com

Printed in the United States of America

The paper used in this book complies with the
Permanent Paper Standard issued by the National
Information Standards Organization (Z39.48–1984).

10 9 8 7 6 5 4 3 2 1

Contents

Abbreviations and Glossary

Amtorg	*Amerikanskaia torgovaia*, the American Trading Organization, Soviet trade concession and front for covert operations headquartered in New York City
Arcos	All-Russian Cooperative Society, Soviet trade concession and front for covert operations headquartered in London
BB	*Betriebs Berichterstatter*, "Worker-correspondents" (German)
CCP	Chinese Communist Party
CER	Chinese Eastern Railroad
Cheka	*Chrezvychainaia komissiia po borbe s kontrrevoliutsiei, spekuliatsiei, sabotazhem i prestupleniiamai po dolzhnosti*, the "Extraordinary Commission for Combating Counterrevolution, Speculation, Sabotage and Misconduct in Office" (first Soviet secret police)
Comintern	Communist International
CPGB	Communist Party of Great Britain
CPSU	Communist Party of the Soviet Union
CPUSA	Communist Party of the United States
FBI	Federal Bureau of Investigation
Fourth Department	Red Army Intelligence Directorate (RU, *Registraupr, Razvedupr*)
Front	(Military) army group
GC & CS	Government Code and Cypher School (British signals intelligence)

GKO   *Gosudarstvennaia komissiia oborony*, "State Defense Committee"

GPU   *Gosudarstvennoe politicheskoe upravlenie*, "State Political Directorate" (secret police; successor to the OGPU)

GRU   *Glavnoe razvedyvatelnoe upravlenie*, "Main Intelligence Directorate" of the Red Army (successor to RU)

INO   *Inostranny otdel*, "Foreign Department" of the State Security organ (Cheka, OGPU, NKVD)

JCP   Japanese Communist party

KPD   *Kommunistische Partei Deutschlands*, "German Communist party"

Kuomintang   Chinese Nationalist party

MI1c   British foreign intelligence service (predecessor of MI6)

MI5   British security service

MI6   British foreign intelligence service (successor to MI1c)

M-Apparat   *Militärische*-apparatus, KPD section responsible for liaison with the Red Army

N-Apparat   *Nachtrichtungsdienst*-apparatus, "Secret Service" (KPD's illegal espionage organization subordinate to RU through OMS)

Narkomindel *Narodnyi komissariat inostrannykh del*, "People's Commissariat of Foreign Affairs"

NKVD   *Narodnyi komissariat vnutrennikh del*, "People's Commissariat of Internal Affairs" (secret police; successor to GPU)

OGPU   *Obedinennoe gosudarstvennoe politicheskoe upravlenie*, "United State Political Directorate" (secret police; successor to the Cheka)

OMS   *Otdel mezhdunarodnykh svyazai*, "Department of International Liaison" (Comintern's clandestine service)

OO   *Osoby otdel*, "Special Department" (secret police security and punitive sections attached to Red Army units)

PCF   *Parti Communiste Français*, French Communist Party

PMC   Peking Military Center

Rabkor   *Rabochii korespondent*, "Worker correspondent" (Russian)

Razvedupr   *Razvedyvatelnoe upravlenie*, "Intelligence Directorate," Red Army Intelligence, 1921–1941 (see also Fourth Department, RU, *Registraupr*)

Registraupr *Registratsie upravlenie*, "Registration Directorate," Red Army Intelligence, 1918–1921 (see also Fourth Department, RU, *Razvedupr*)

RKKA   *Raboche-Krestianskaia Krasnaia Armiia*, Workers' and Peasants' Red Army

RU   *Razvedyvatelnoe upravlenie*, Intelligence Directorate of the Red Army, 1918–1941 (see also Fourth Department, *Registraupr, Razvedupr*)

Sigint   Signals Intelligence (decryption and/or analysis of radio communications)

Spets otdel   "Special Department" (Soviet signals intelligence)

Sûreté   French security service

T-Apparat   *Terroristiche*-apparatus, KPD section responsible for carrying out sabotage and assassinations; formed in preparation for Hamburg Uprising

Tokubetsu Kotoka   "Thought Police" (Japanese security police)

TsGASA   *Tsentral'nyi Gosudarstvennyi Arkhiv Krasnoi Armii*, Central State Archives of the Soviet Army

Z-Apparat   see *T-Apparat*

Introduction

In the 1920s, it organized revolutionary insurrection from Europe to China. In the 1930s, it was directing and supporting the Republican forces fighting Franco, Hitler, and Mussolini in Spain. And in 1941, it provided Stalin with advanced warning about both the German invasion of the Soviet Union, "Operation Barbarossa," and the Japanese decision to attack the United States. During World War II, it provided Lavrenti Beria, director of the Soviet atomic research program and head of the secret police, with critical information about American and British atomic research, including the Manhattan Project. All the while, it ran clandestine networks composed of hundreds of agents, some of whom managed to penetrate the highest levels of foreign governments, including Great Britain, Germany, and the United States. For much of the last seventy years, it was the largest and best funded intelligence organization in the world. Yet it is virtually unknown, even by those who study intelligence and espionage. Indeed, few have ever heard of the Red Army Intelligence Directorate, known since World War II as the *Glavnoe Razvedyvatelnoe Upravlenie* (Main Intelligence Directorate), or GRU.

The Soviet state security organs, the Cheka (*Chrezvychainaia Komissiia po borbe s Kontrrevoliutsiei, Spekuliatsiei, Sabotazhem i Prestupleniiamai po Dolzhnosti* [Extraordinary Commission for Combating Counter-revolution, Speculation, Sabotage and Misconduct in Office]), and its successors, including the OGPU, NKVD, and KGB, have been the subject of numerous studies since 1970. Yet aside from a few peripheral paragraphs here and there, the history of the GRU, especially for the years before 1945, has all but been ignored.[1]

What could possibly explain this immense gap in our understanding of Soviet intelligence history? Perhaps the most important reason is simple ignorance. Until recently, little in the way of documentary evidence has been available on the history of Soviet military intelligence, especially for the years preceding World War II. Furthermore, the West's understanding of the relationship between the various Soviet security and espionage organs over the years was and remains tenuous, as demonstrated by the fact that journalists and historians all continue to make the same mistakes, like equating "SMERSH" (the NKVD-directed unit of Red Army counterespionage during World War II) with the KGB. Further confusing matters is the fact that the GRU, like the KGB, has also been known by a variety of names over the decades. Almost no one (at least those writing in open sources) has made the connection between the *Registraupr*, *Razvedupr*, RU, Third Department, Fourth Department, "Intelligence Service," "Military Intelligence," and GRU, all of which are the same entity.[2]

Another explanation lies in the realm of national security. The Soviets obviously preferred to have their clandestine services remain as nebulous as possible in the eyes of western counterintelligence agencies, and for similar reasons the latter no doubt chose to encourage Moscow's belief that it had succeeded in doing so. There may indeed exist detailed histories of the GRU buried in the musty archives of the GRU, KGB, and Kremlin, not to mention the *Sûreté*, MI5, and FBI. This, however, does us historians who must ponder our subjects in the open press little good.

Nevertheless, these explanations are still insufficient to fully explain the lack of serious study of the GRU. Documents clearly identifying the Red Army Intelligence Directorate and distinguishing it from the security organs have been available in open sources since at least 1928 or 1929, following a raid by the Chinese police on a major Soviet espionage center in Peking. The first published OGPU defector, Georges Agabekov, also mentioned the military intelligence directorate in his 1931 memoir, *OGPU: The Russian Secret Terror*, and Walter Krivitsky, the most senior Red Army intelligence officer ever to defect, described in detail the organization in which he spent most of his professional career in his 1939 autobiography, *I Was Stalin's Agent*.[3] In the late 1940s, intelligence documents on the GRU also figured prominently in the controversy surrounding charges that Whittaker Chambers, Alger Hiss, Noel Field, Agnes Smedley, and others were Soviet agents. By 1955, enough was known about Red Army espionage for it to be described at length by David J. Dallin in *Soviet Espionage*.[4] And since the 1950s, several former GRU operatives have published their memoirs, including Hede Massing, Elisabeth Poretsky, Aino Kuusinen, Leopold Trepper, Ismail Akhmedov, and Ruth Werner.[5] Yet this study, based on research conducted in the early and mid- 1990s, represents the first attempt to seriously analyze this body of work and the organization at its center.

This leads us to another possible explanation: academic fashion. Historians of Soviet intelligence tend to fall into one of two categories. On the one hand are those drawn to the subject by the bloody legacy of the Cheka and its successors. Always at the pinnacle of Soviet power, and a symbol of all that went wrong with the Soviet experiment, the security organs continue to monopolize serious scholarship in this field. On the other hand are scholars whose primary interest is military history, and they tend to focus almost exclusively on the "conventional" military intelligence mission of the GRU in the Great Patriotic War.[6]

Finally, the historical study of Soviet military intelligence may be simply, perhaps even subliminally, politically unpopular, at least among American historians. The remarkably consistent and unflattering picture of American communists and communist sympathizers now emerging does little to bolster their "traditional" image as heroic representatives of American radicalism victimized by "right-wing" zealots. The evidence is out and the jury is in: Whittaker Chambers was indeed right about Alger Hiss.

Whatever the reasons in the past for ignoring the GRU, continuing to do so now significantly undermines our understanding of the Soviet past and the Russian present. It is clear that the part played by the GRU in the course of events since 1918 has simply been far too great to remain unexamined. And although I do not share the belief of many of my colleagues that in order for a historical study to be justified, it must have some contemporary relevance—this frequently leads to wild leaps of causality and hasty generalizations that often become mainstream "interpretations" with little or no debate—I will nonetheless offer the following caution: the GRU is still around; it is still huge; it still carries out clandestine operations on a global scale; it still shapes the Kremlin's foreign and military policies; and, as the situation of the Russian army becomes more precarious, its political potential remains both imponderable and menacing.

This study focuses on the early years of Red Army Intelligence, from 1918 to 1933. The year 1933 seems a most logical and convenient ending point for a first volume, for that is the year in which Adolf Hitler became chancellor of Germany, Franklin Roosevelt became president of the United States, and the long slide toward World War II began in earnest. The fundamental orientation of GRU threat assessment and espionage changed dramatically after 1933, as the growing menace of Germany in Europe and Japan in the Far East replaced the Soviet fixation on a possible attack by Poland and the other states bordering its western frontier.

The period from 1918 through 1933 witnessed the maturation of the GRU into a professional intelligence organization, albeit one whose roots were never far from revolution. In these years Red Army Intelligence was born, experienced its baptism of fire in the Civil and Soviet-Polish wars, and, as part of the struggle for control of the Communist Party of the Soviet Union (CPSU) that followed the death of Lenin, attempted to spread the workers' revolution through armed insurrection. Meanwhile, the GRU also established a worldwide system of intelligence-gathering networks that expanded in size and ambition as the Soviet Union achieved widespread diplomatic representation. By the early 1920s, the GRU had already clearly emerged as the preeminent foreign intelligence organization of the USSR, a status that remained unchallenged until after World War II.

The nature of the subject, combined with the chronological and ethnic diversity of the sources, has forced me to adopt some simple, if crude, conventions to avoid complete chaos. The true identities of many of the people who appear in this narrative remain unknown even today. To maintain some degree of consistency, quotation marks (" ") indicate that the name I use is the only identification I could find. On those occasions when two or more aliases are known, I provide these after what seems to be the most commonly used name with the appellation "a.k.a." (also known as). There were similar problems with transliterations. Some sources had been translated from three or more languages by the time I saw them. In these cases I have no idea what the original version looked like. I therefore have deemed it best to go with the exact transliteration used by the source in which I found it. Similarly, I have decided to use the Wade-Giles system of Chinese transliteration in preference to Pinyin, since I do not read the language and most of the sources I used follow the older form. I apologize for any confusion resulting from these decisions.

In an article published in 1992, I suggested that a useful history of the GRU would demand the skills of the biographer, intellectual historian, organizational historian, and military historian.[7] To these, I would now add the diplomatic historian. No one has since embarked upon this enterprise, and I certainly do not possess all of these abilities. What I have attempted here should therefore be regarded as a beginning, and is in no measure definitive. In the same article I observed that the first order of business for serious study of the Red Army Intelligence Directorate was for someone to "bring together the information now available into some coherent, if preliminary, narrative of the GRU . . . since 1918," in order to "clarify further lines of inquiry and to offer scholars working in related fields some access to the material."[8] This volume is meant to be the first step in the first attempt to do this.

It is my hope that *Secret Soldiers of the Revolution* will provide a foundation for further work, and, perhaps by demonstrating how much we already know, help scholars to gain further access to classified material from the 1920s, 1930s, and 1940s still ludicrously locked away in the archives in London, Washington, Paris, and Moscow. There is no doubt that such material will enable future historians to find connections and patterns that have eluded me, and will contribute even more to our understanding of the turbulent course of the last seventy years.

NOTES

1. To date only two published narratives have meaningfully addressed this subject, one by the French journalist Pierre de Villemarest, and another by GRU defector Vladimir B. Rezoun, a.k.a. "Viktor Suvorov." See Pierre de Villemarest, *GRU: Le plus secret des services sovietiques, 1918–1988* (Paris: Editions Stock, 1988); Viktor Suvorov, *Inside Soviet Military Intelligence* (New York: Macmillan, 1984). Villemarest's work is poorly documented and analytically shallow, focuses on Cold War espionage, and is heavily derived from Suvorov. And although Suvorov provides the most extensive historical background on the origins and early history of the GRU thus far, he still devotes no more than twenty-five pages to the entire period from 1918 to 1945.

Other western sources have attempted to describe the early organization of the RU, none with complete accuracy. One of the best accounts is in Heinz Höhne, *Codeword Direktor* (New York: Berkley, 1970), pp. 34–36. This description is based on a variety of secondary sources and one poorly described document in the archives of *Der Spiegel*, and the documents in TsGASA demonstrate that Höhne's discussion is erroneous in a number of significant ways.

For a full discussion of the value of works on the KGB for researching the GRU, see Raymond W. Leonard, "Studying the Kremlin's Secret Soldiers: A Historiographical Essay on the GRU, 1918–1945," *The Journal of Military History* 56, no. 3 (July 1992): 411–412.

2. This is why I have chosen to use all of these terms interchangeably. It is my intention to get the reader accustomed to equating them, so that if they should appear in another context the reader may have some sense of their true significance.

3. Georges Agabekov, *OGPU: The Russian Secret Terror*, trans. from the French by Henry Bunn (New York: Brentano's, 1931); Walter Krivitsky, *I Was Stalin's Agent* (London: The Right Book Club, 1940).

4. David J. Dallin, *Soviet Espionage* (New Haven: Yale University Press, 1955). I rely on Dallin extensively, for it contains much crucial information available nowhere else. It therefore merits comment. This remarkable work was based on interviews of members of western intelligence agencies as well as Soviet and eastern bloc defectors conducted by Dallin and his wife in the late 1940s and early 1950s. He cites this material as the "D-Papers." In a number of places, his information is confirmed or supported by other material, and I discovered nothing in the primary sources that fundamentally disputes Dallin's account or conclusions. In fact, the only major problem with this work, aside from its age, is that it frequently fails to clearly distinguish between the Comintern, KGB, and GRU. I have sought to remedy this by sorting out Dallin's account and including the material referring to Red Army Intelligence.

I am grateful for the assistance of Dr. Alexander Dallin, David Dallin's son, who provided me with a brief summary of the "D-Papers" project. The description here, however, is, like any errors therein, entirely my own.

5. Hede Massing, *This Deception* (New York: Duell, Sloan and Pearce, 1951); Elisabeth Poretsky, *Our Own People: A Memoir of 'Ignace Reiss' and His Friends* (London: Oxford University Press, 1969); Aino Kuusinen, *Before and after Stalin: A Personal Account of Soviet Russia from the 1920s to the 1960s* (London: Michael Joseph, 1974); Leopold Trepper, *The Great Game: Memoirs of the Spy Hitler Couldn't Silence* (New York: McGraw-Hill, 1977); Ismail Akhmedov, *In and out of Stalin's GRU: A Tatar's Escape from Red Army Intelligence* (Frederick, Md.: University

Publications of America, 1984); and Ruth Werner, *Sonya's Report*, trans. by Renate Simpson (London: Chatto & Windus, 1991).

6. Outstanding examples of the former "school" include Christopher Andrew, John Dziak, Amy Knight, and George Leggett. The military side of the equation has been impressively explored in the work of Col. David Glantz.

7. Leonard, "Studying the Kremlin's Secret Soldiers," p. 405.

8. Ibid., p. 420.

CHAPTER 1

The Origins of Red Army Intelligence

> We Communists are different. Our intelligence must be different. It must be more active, stronger. [Capitalist intelligence officers] are technicians. We are revolutionaries.
>
> —General Minzakir Absalyamov[1]

The Red Army Intelligence Directorate was forged in the fires of revolution and civil war. Yet it did not spring from these sources alone; influential historical traditions, both intellectual and imperial, also played an important part. The resulting institution was unique in its combination of personnel, methods, and objectives.

RUSSIAN MILITARY INTELLIGENCE: THE TSARIST LEGACY

The creation of the Red Army Intelligence Directorate is shrouded in myth and misperception. The prevailing notion is that this organ essentially came into existence out of "thin air," created in a vacuum by the necessities of civil war.[2] In fact, like the Red Army itself, Soviet military intelligence owed much to its imperial predecessor.[3]

The Russian military leadership had recognized the need for a central office for coordinating and interpreting intelligence at the general staff level at least as early as 1863. Trying to come to grips with its embarrassing performances in the Crimean War, on the Central Asian steppes, and in suppressing rebellion, the Russian army experienced a period of reform under the direction of the energetic and able minister for war, D. A. Miliutin. A modern general staff, the GUGSh, was established for the Russian army that year. This body was subordinate to the Quartermaster General, and included a section for gathering intelligence.[4] The GUGSh was later called the Main Staff; it continued to undergo periodic restructuring thereafter, usually after poor performance in the field.

By the 1880s, the military-technological revolution that was industrializing warfare had made the Napoleonic ideal of a general staff obsolete. Based largely on the Prussian model that had emerged victorious from the German wars of unification, the new concept of a general staff as a body composed of specialized and highly trained experts was soon adopted by industrialized armies around the globe. In 1903, the Main Staff of the Russian army was reorganized yet again, this time along the lines suggested in the mid-1880s by its chief at the time, N. N. Obruchev. The new Main Staff included five main directorates: First and Second Quartermaster General; Adjutant General; Military Communications; and Military Topography. The Second Quartermaster General Directorate was divided into two sections, one responsible for mobilization, and the other for "military statistics" and intelligence.[5]

Throughout the late nineteenth and early twentieth centuries, espionage became for the Russian army an increasingly important source of intelligence about potential enemies, especially Austro-Hungary, Germany, and Turkey. The Russians regarded espionage to be a key "tool with which to compensate for Russia's backwardness."[6] The Russian army emphasized quantity over quality in the recruiting of agents, much as the Soviets did in later years. This policy resulted partly from the scattered distribution of miserly resources to individual intelligence officers assigned to recruit agents, and partly from the disorganized structure of Russian intelligence gathering and analysis.[7]

By the late nineteenth century, the Russian Main Staff possessed, at least on paper, a central clearing house for intelligence. This was the Military Education Committee, which was supposed to receive all reports of "military significance" and then forward them to the chief of the Main Staff. By the early twentieth century, however, the disorganization of Nicholas II's government meant that intelligence gathering and analysis was increasingly dispersed among many tenuously connected agencies and organizations. Frequently there was little or no communication, let alone cooperation, between the different offices responsible for reporting and analyzing information. An especially telling example was the poor intelligence coordination between the military attachés and the diplomatic corps.[8]

In 1905, following another and even more disastrous defeat, this time at the hands of Imperial Japan, the Main Staff, once more called GUGSh, was reorganized yet again. The GUGSh was separated into three main directorates, the most important of which was the Quartermaster General. This directorate included the First Over Quartermaster subdivision, which was responsible for war planning, troop mobilization and movements, fortresses, and intelligence.[9]

From 1909 to 1914, Iu. N. Danilov commanded the Intelligence Section. It had at its disposal three intelligence-gathering mechanisms: a system of military attachés; the intelligence departments of the various military districts, most importantly those along the western frontier; and a limited number of officers and assets directly subordinate to the Intelligence Section.[10]

The Intelligence Section forwarded information gathered from espionage and open sources through the chain of command. Occasionally, the GUGSh would disseminate the findings of its analyses in secret reports for use by the high command. Beginning in 1909, a top-secret journal containing articles about foreign military developments was also published, called *Sbornik glavnogo upravleniia general'nogo shtaba.*[11] By August 1914, sixty-two issues had been produced. The Red Army Intelligence Directorate later published a similar journal (see chapter 7).

The conceptual development of military intelligence took an important step forward in 1912 with the publication of "Instructions for Field Service of the Russian Army." Reflecting both the German service manual published four years previously, upon which it was largely modeled, as well as the traditional Russian penchant for regarding military theory as a natural science, the new Russian regulations sought to provide a more sophisticated context for military operations.[12]

The German publication stressed the importance of clearly delineated roles for various intelligence-gathering means, and defined intelligence tasks in terms of the broad goal of determining the operations and strength of the enemy. The most important method for achieving this goal was the correct employment of cavalry.[13] The Russian manual incorporated all of this, but went much further in developing the theoretical role of military *razvedka* (a Russian term combining the concepts of espionage, reconnaissance, and intelligence operations in general).

In Article 53, the Field Regulation described two general categories of intelligence data: information about the terrain on which military operations were likely to be conducted, and intelligence about the enemy's "disposition and activities." Intelligence sources were identified as interrogations of prisoners of war, deserters, and local inhabitants; eavesdropping on enemy telephone and telegraph communications; the deployment of spies and agent networks; and analysis of captured papers and publically available literature about the enemy.[14]

Organizationally, all intelligence was to be channeled to special units and "subunits." Interestingly, "balloon sections" were also incorporated, in one of the first examples of organic aerial reconnaissance detachments. Intelligence staffs of approximately four men each were now posted permanently to every rifle company and cavalry squadron, although similar ad hoc intelligence detachments had appeared in cavalry units as early as 1891, and in infantry units in 1908. In 1907, again reflecting lessons learned in the Russo-Japanese War, artillery batteries began to include organic intelligence sections of approximately twelve men; "artillery reconnaissance" would eventually become one of the most important sources of tactical intelligence for both the Russian and the Red armies.[15]

Despite its theoretical sophistication, however, Russian military intelligence suffered from major flaws in the years immediately preceding World War I. Bureaucratic infighting, both within the army and between rival government departments, continued to get worse. The army and the Ministry of Foreign Affairs conducted their business in almost complete isolation from each other.[16]

Although the GUGSh obtained excellent information about Austro-Hungarian capabilities, largely supplied by the notorious spy Col. Alfred Redl, intelligence on German and Turkish capabilities, and indeed even those of their French allies, remained poor.[17] Furthermore, Russian analysis of enemy (and allied) intentions derived from long-standing assumptions, many of which proved to be tragically mistaken.[18] In both respects, the Russians were not alone. Aggravating these problems, however, was the fact that the General Staff's intelligence section was severely undermanned, underequipped, underpaid, and overworked.[19]

World War I immediately exposed the inability of the Russian army to realize the promise of prewar theory and organization. Intelligence failures were frequent, often contributing to or even precipitating disastrous results, like the Russian invasion of East Prussia in August 1914 which culminated in the humiliating defeats at Tannenberg and the Masurian Lakes.[20] The changes eventually adopted by the Russian army indicate that the most fundamental reasons for intelligence problems were, first, an amazingly inefficient system for channeling the flow of crucial information; and second, a serious shortage of trained and competent officers and men capable of doing intelligence work. The General Staff tried two solutions: increasingly rigid centralization of intelligence processing; and adoption of clearly defined doctrine.

By 1916, many of the most serious problems had been remedied, and Soviet historians regarded the *razvedka* effort associated with the Brusilov Offensive of that summer to be a success on many levels. A major reason for this was the fact that, possibly for the first time, each participating *front* (army group) had its own *razvedka* staff that collected and coordinated the intelligence gathered by its subordinate corps and divisions.[21] The successful intelligence efforts in this offensive soon led to their widespread adoption throughout the Russian army.

By 1917, doctrine defined the principal types of intelligence as troop reconnaissance (*voiskovaya*); and engineering, artillery, aerial, radio-telegraph, telephone, eavesdropping (*podslushivanie*), photographic, and agent *razvedka*. Strategic reconnaissance was the responsibility of the cavalry.[22] The trend toward centralization and rationalization of intelligence methods continued right up to the Bolshevik Revolution. The Intelligence Sections of the individual field armies emerged as the focal points for these efforts. These sections were in turn accountable to the Intelligence Department of the Supreme Command. *Razvedka* assets of field armies were also at the disposal of their superior *fronts*; likewise, subordinate corps commanded the Intelligence Sections of their divisions, and so on, down through battalion level. In addition, companies generally had one specially assigned intelligence officer, probably for duties like prisoner interrogation and identifying and forwarding captured documents.

The increasing centralization of intelligence processing, however, inevitably interfered with dissemination of information at lower levels. The General Staff tried to compensate by encouraging headquarters staffs and their intelligence departments to strive for timely interaction between intelligence assessment and active operations. A 1917 manual stressed the importance of "frequent individual contact between all the organs of intelligence . . . [and] connection and coordination with operational units."[23] Whether or not these guidelines effectively addressed the problem is unknown.

Clearly, however, by the time the Red Army Intelligence Directorate was established in the fall of 1918, there existed in Russia a sophisticated organizational and theoretical framework for military intelligence. Given Commissar for War Lev Trotsky's preference for using "military specialists" (i.e., former tsarist officers) for the leadership of the new Red Army, it was only natural that the new Bolshevik military intelligence organization would bear more than a passing resemblance to its imperial predecessor.

THE "REGISTRATION DEPARTMENT"

Little information is available about the precise circumstances surrounding the original establishment of the Red Army Intelligence Directorate, and in fact the early history of the RU remains shrouded in mystery. The most commonly cited account relies on British Capt. George Hill's contention that he "helped the Bolshevik military headquarters to organize an Intelligence Section for the purpose of identifying German units on the Russian front and for keeping the troop movements under close observation." Hill went on to claim that "within several days" this section had organized networks of agents throughout the "Eastern territories occupied by the Austro-German army," and that he also set up a "Bolshevik counter-espionage section to spy on the German secret service and [diplomatic] Missions in Petrograd and Moscow."[24]

This story has been uncritically accepted by most western sources.[25] Yet even superficially it seems to contradict what we know about Russian military history, the personalities of the Bolshevik leaders, and the nature of the threat confronting them in the fall of 1918. The assumption that a man like Trotsky would need a foreign secret agent to tell him how to organize and conduct military intelligence borders on the absurd. British Intelligence was, as Trotsky well knew, even at that very moment being thoroughly duped by the Bolsheviks.[26] Furthermore, the Bolshevik leadership almost universally mistrusted the British.[27] And by the summer of 1918, the Germans were far less of a threat to the revolutionary regime than the various White Guard armies attacking from practically all directions. Finally, it is highly unlikely that agent networks could be assembled at all, let alone on such a sweeping scale, within "several days."

The most persuasive account of the origins of the Red Army Intelligence Directorate comes from GRU defector V. Rezoun, a.k.a. Viktor Suvorov.[28] According to Suvorov, like early Cheka formations, Bolshevik military intelligence units initially were formed at a variety of command levels in response to immediate necessity. As the Red Army took shape throughout the spring and summer of 1918, commanders of major units (corps, armies, and *fronts*), usually former tsarist officers, needed information, and began to organize ad hoc intelligence sections. The increasingly urgent need to coordinate partisan and antipartisan operations throughout the depth of the various combat areas gave additional impetus to the creation of a general staff–level organ.

In June 1918, the first Bolshevik army group, the Eastern *Front*, was organized with the first "registrational department" as part of its staff. It was composed of the chiefs of the Intelligence Sections of the *front*'s subordinate armies and the Volga Flotilla. This Registration Department was not only responsible for coordinating intelligence gathering by the *front*'s *razvedka* sections, but also for aerial reconnaissance, for which purpose a few aircraft were permanently attached to the department, and for organizing and running agent networks in the *front*'s area of operations. The latter were originally primarily intended to be used for gathering information; in practice, however, they were frequently employed in what the Soviets would later call "active measures": sabotage, propaganda, subversion, and paramilitary operations.[29]

In this respect the Red Army Intelligence Sections differed greatly from their tsarist predecessors. The Imperial Army also made use of agent networks, but conceptually their role was much more conventional, being primarily to supply intelligence through espionage. It took the Bolsheviks with their background in conspiracy, revolution, and partisan warfare to fully exploit the potential of agents deployed deep in the enemy rear. Indeed, the Bolshevik unification of these concepts figured prominently in the development of Soviet operational art in the 1920s and 1930s.

By the fall of 1918, a system of intelligence sections had been created from the ground up at virtually all levels of the Red Army except for the General Staff. They were known as ROs (*razvedyvatelnye otdely*, reconnaissance sections), and became the "nervous system" of the General Staff's Intelligence Directorate. According to Suvorov, the decision to establish an intelligence service at the general staff level owed more to political intrigue between Trotsky and Feliks Dzerzhinsky about jurisdiction over operating agent networks than it did to military necessity. Lenin, Suvorov maintains, ultimately agreed to Trotsky's desire to establish such a service in order that it might serve as a counterweight to the Dzerzhinsky's Cheka.[30]

It is certainly true that eventually great animosity existed between the state security organs and military intelligence. Nevertheless, it is at least as likely that the Red Army intelligence service was created in response to the increasingly critical necessity to coordinate intelligence efforts. The serious military situation faced by the Bolsheviks in the fall of 1918 led them to adopt radical and bloody measures, including an intensification of "war communism" and Red Terror. There is no need to look beyond this very real crisis for an explanation for the creation of the Intelligence Directorate, especially when we also bear in mind that Trotsky's "military specialists" (the former tsarist officers) were the products of a military organization that had included an intelligence department at the general staff level.

Lenin signed a decree on 21 October 1918 that formally created the Registration Directorate (*Registrupravlenie*, or RU).[31] As originally established, the Registration Department was not directly subordinate to the General Staff (at the time called the Red Army Field Staff—*Polevoi Shtab*). Administratively, it was the Third Department of the Field Staff's Operations Directorate.[32] In July 1920, the RU was made the second of four main departments in the Operations Directorate.[33] Until 1921, it was usually called the *Registraupr* (Registration Department). That year, following the Soviet-Polish War, it was elevated in status to become the Second (Intelligence) Directorate of the Red Army Staff, and was thereafter known as the *Razvedupr*. This probably resulted from its new primary peacetime responsibilities as the main source of foreign intelligence for the Soviet leadership. As part of a major re-organization of the Red Army, sometime in 1925 or 1926 the RU became the Fourth (Intelligence) Directorate of the Red Army Staff, and was thereafter also known simply as the "Fourth Department."[34] Throughout most of the interwar period, the men and women who worked for Red Army Intelligence called it either the Fourth Department, the Intelligence Service, the *Razvedupr*, or the RU.[35]

From its inception, the Red Army Intelligence Directorate was intended to be the "central organ for land and naval intelligence."[36] It remained so, despite periodic attempts at co-option by the Cheka and its successors, the OGPU, NKVD, and KGB, into the Cold War and beyond. In practice, however, at least until 1921, the RU was directly subordinate to the Military Revolutionary Committee of the Soviet Republic (*Revvoensovet Respubliki*, or RVSR), and then probably to the Red Army Staff until 1926. As a result of the re-organization that year, carried out in part to break up Trotsky's hold on the army, the Fourth Department seems to have been placed directly under the control of the State Defense Council (*Gosudarstvennaia komissiia oborony*, or GKO), the successor of the RVSR. Thereafter its analysis and reports went directly to the GKO and Politburo, even apparently bypassing the Red Army Staff.[37]

The initial organization of the RU reflected both its tsarist heritage and the revolutionary nature of the Red Army. Conceptually more complex than Russian Imperial Intelligence, the RU combined traditional military intelligence missions with a variety of political and security tasks that reflected Bolshevik ideology and the RU's strong maternal ties to the Cheka.

The Registration Department, as originally established in 1918, was composed of three main departments, seven independent bureaus, and several subordinate sections.[38] The three main departments were the Department of Military Inspection, the Agent Department, and the Military-Censorship Department. The Military Inspection Department was probably responsible for administrative monitoring of the RU, and the duties of the Military-Censorship Department are self-explanatory. The heart of the *Registraupr* was the Agent Department, which included the Chancellery (administration), the Agent Section (recruitment and management of agents and networks), and the Training Section ("courses in intelligence and military direction").[39]

The first section probably maintained and updated files and paperwork on the case officers and agents fielded by the directorate. In addition, the Administration Section may have been responsible for paying salaries; if so, other financial matters were probably handled through the Treasury Section.[40] The Agent Section is described at length below. The third section, training and control, ran a series of schools for covert and partisan operations, and may also have been the forerunner of what Cold War–era GRU officers called the "Aquarium," the main training academy for officers destined for clandestine assignments.[41]

The seven independent sections were directly subordinate to the chief of the RU:

Section One: The Common Office in the Structure of the Administrative Command Section. This was probably responsible for liaison with other directorates and departments of the Red Army, as well as with the civilian government and security organs.

Section Two: The Organizational-Inspectorate. The precise function of this section is unclear; perhaps it was charged with internal auditing or security, or alternatively with providing support services to the rest of the directorate.

Section Three: The Active Section. Traditionally, in Soviet espionage organs this has been the name given to departments responsible for clandestine operations, including sabotage, assassinations, *maskirovka* (camouflage and deception), and *disinformatsiya* (disinformation).

Section Four: The Registration Section. This was the analysis and threat assessment branch of the RU, and was responsible for producing threat assessments for the Red Army Staff and the RVSR (see chapter 7). If the Agent Section can be regarded as the heart of the RU, the Registration Section was its brain. This section also oversaw bureaus responsible for "registration" (analysis), "permits" (*propuska*—admissions and personal documents), a photography lab, and an investigative office (perhaps responsible for internal security). Some time before 1926, the Registration Section became known as the "Third Section."

Section Five: The Treasury Section. This section arranged financing for RU operations, probably including dispersal of money for agent payments and other clandestine activities.

Section Six: The Printing Bureau. It is interesting to note that an entirely separate bureau was set up to carry out "printing." This probably reflected traditional Bolshevik reliance on underground presses as a tool for mobilizing the masses and coordinating Party activities, and demonstrated the regime's revolutionary expectations. The Printing Bureau prepared a range of documents, from revolutionary placards and leaflets to forgeries and counterfeit money. It may also have provided translators, and was probably closely linked to underground Comintern printing operations like the *Pass-Apparat* described in chapter 6.[42]

Section Seven: The Naval Intelligence Section. From the very beginning, the RU maintained a separate section responsible for gathering intelligence of all types about naval operations, including enemy strength and capabilities, and the terrain, weather, and currents of likely areas of operations. Eventually, the Naval Intelligence Section resembled a miniature RU, with its own agent networks, diversionary operations, and units of special designation (*spetsnazi*).

Considered in its entirety, even in its nascent form, the Red Army Intelligence Directorate displayed remarkable theoretical sophistication and combined an impressive array of intelligence responsibilities and resources under one umbrella. Nevertheless, as we shall see, this potential frequently exceeded the practical.

The structure of the RU underwent periodic alterations over the following years. But the major principles expressed during its organization in October 1918—equivalent emphasis on both agent and combat intelligence, an administrative structure requiring a strictly hierarchical flow of information, a highly centralized command that nevertheless left considerable responsibility for *razvedka* operations in the hands of subordinates, and an obsession with security—were to remain constant up to and beyond the Great Patriotic War.

A Red Army Staff directive dated 21 June 1919 called for a significant reorganization of the RU, the basic effect of which was to improve agent *razvedka* capabilities. This may have been prompted by recent reversals on the northern and eastern fronts in the Civil War. The Agent Department was split into two parts, with Department I assuming responsibility for all "ground agent" operations, and Department II becoming solely responsible for naval agent *razvedka*. Department II was divided into four geographical sections: North, West, Near East, and Far East.[43] Under Y. K. Berzin's direction, in the late 1920s, the Agent Department underwent further restructuring. Administration of agent operations became more tightly organized. They varied over time; generally, however, there emerged major sections for Europe (sometimes divided between eastern and western sections), North America, the Far East, and the Middle East (including India).[44] The actual designations of these sections also changed over the years; for example, one source identifies the Western European section as Section I (One), while another refers to it as the Third Section.[45]

COMMANDERS OF THE "INVISIBLE FRONT": RU CHIEFS, 1918–1933

There were important links at the highest command levels between the Cheka and military intelligence throughout the interwar period. This was a deliberate policy fostered by the Communist Party of the Soviet Union (CPSU) leadership as a means of facilitating Party control over military *razvedka*, much as the Cheka's OOs (*Osoby Otdely*, special sections) likewise kept the army under tight Cheka, and therefore Party, control.[46] Cheka domination of the Red Army Intelligence Directorate was theoretically achieved by the practice of appointing senior members of the security organ to the directorship of the *Razvedupr*. According to Suvorov, the CPSU further hoped that this arrangement would keep the Cheka, Red Army, and RU at odds with one another and thus ensure the primacy of the Party.[47] In reality, however, and especially during the tenure of Yan Berzin, military intelligence chiefs tended to identify their interests with those of the Red Army. This situation was reflected in the ongoing antagonism between the RU and the chekists, and in the efforts of the latter to subordinate or completely eliminate their Red Army rivals.

The first chief of the RU was an experienced, high-ranking Cheka officer, Simon Ivanovich Aralov (December 1880–May 1969).[48] A founding member of the VeCheka, in January 1918 he became head of the Operational Department of the Moscow Military District. In the spring of 1918, Trotsky dispatched him to negotiate with the Czech Legion in Siberia.[49] By September he was a member of the Military Revolutionary Committee in which capacity and on Trotsky's direction he was responsible for carrying out the "Hostage Policy," reprisals against Red Army officers (and their families) who were suspected of treason.

In late December, as chief of the RU, Aralov joined with Trotsky and Joachim Vatsetis, first commander in chief of the Red Army and former commander of the Latvian Rifles, elite units originally organized in 1916 as part of the Russian army that subsequently became the shock troops of the Bolshevik Revolution, to form the Executive Bureau of the Defense Council.[50] Aralov served as RU chief until July 1920, when another Latvian, Oskar Ansovich Stigga, replaced him just before the Polish army's counteroffensive near Warsaw. During Aralov's tenure, partisan operations, including agent *razvedka* (intelligence operations), especially crucial in the Civil War, became a major priority of the *Registraupr*.

Aralov remained an important figure in Red Army Intelligence for much of the rest of his life, holding a variety of posts within the Fourth Department, including chief of the 12th Army RO and commander of the Intelligence

Section of the South West *Front*. From 1921 to 1927, Aralov also served as a principal deputy to succeeding chiefs of the RU, and he frequently served abroad under diplomatic cover, helping to establish RU residencies. Between 1921 and 1925, for example, he carried out this assignment while officially serving at one time or another as Soviet ambassador to Turkey, Latvia, and Lithuania. At the end of 1926, Moscow posted him as ambassador to Chiang Kai-shek's Nationalist (Kuomintang) government in China. After the split with the Kuomintang, he served as a Fourth Department "trouble-shooter," again under diplomatic cover, in the United States, Germany, and Japan.[51]

Oskar Stigga was another Latvian who rose to prominence in the Latvian Rifles and went on to hold key posts in the Cheka and Fourth Department. Stigga, however, remains otherwise obscure. Suvorov maintains that he served in Lenin's personal bodyguard. He became the deputy chief of the RU at its creation in October 1918, and, Suvorov claims, "immediately moved as an illegal [an intelligence officer without diplomatic cover] into Poland, Lithuania and Latvia." This was part of a pattern in the RU's early history in which the deputy director was frequently responsible for overseeing agent operations.[52]

In Stigga's case, this assignment also reflected the course of the Revolution, which by late 1918 seemed to be headed west toward Germany. Stigga's initial task was to organize partisan operations that would facilitate the Red Army's advance into the Baltic states. Sometime in 1919, he was appointed chief of the Western *Front*'s Intelligence Section (RO). In August 1920, he became head of the RU. Two years later, Stigga was reassigned to the Deputy Directorship and the even more mysterious A. M. Nikonov became RU chief. Thereafter, like Aralov, Stigga remained with the *Razvedupr*, overseeing covert work overseas. We know that as late as the mid-1930s, he continued to play an important role in the Fourth Department, heading the western European bureau of the Agent Department. He was shot in 1938.[53]

Almost nothing is known of Nikonov. Even Suvorov is uncertain of the precise length of his directorship, other than that he commanded the RU after Stigga. Nikonov was succeeded as director of the Intelligence Directorate in the spring of 1921 by Yan Berzin. Nikonov also remained with the RU, and spent much of the next decade in charge of its Third Section, the department responsible for research and analysis. There he was a key force in Soviet analysis and threat assessment, and contributed to many publications prepared by the Third Section, including *The Future War*.

Yan Karlovich Berzin was the most important figure in the history of Red Army Intelligence, and partly as a result of this fact much more biographical information exists about him than any of his predecessors (or indeed, his successors). Born Peter Kyuzis in Latvia in 1889, as a youth he aspired to be a teacher, a common calling at that time and a place for idealistic young nationalists. As a student at a teaching seminary, in 1904 he became involved with a revolutionary socialist group that eventually became the Latvian Social

Democracy Party (LSDP). The following year, Kyuzis actively participated in the partisan uprisings in Latvia that were associated with the disturbances sweeping the Russian Empire—collectively known as the Revolution of 1905. Over the course of almost a decade of partisan activity, Kyuzis was repeatedly beaten and arrested, and twice shot. He had one death sentence commuted on account of his youth, but was later captured and exiled to Siberia in 1910. In mid-1914, he escaped and made his way back to Riga, where, to honor his older brother and grandfather, he assumed the name of Yan Karlovich Berzin.[54]

On the orders of the Latvian Social Democrats (the Bolshevik-affiliated successor to the LSDP), in 1914 Berzin joined the Russian army in order to proselytize among the troops. By 1916 he was in a Latvian Rifles regiment. Pursued for his revolutionary activities by the tsar's secret police, the *Okhrana*, Berzin once again fled to Riga, where he went underground and became a prominent member of the most radical wing of the Bolshevik party, the Vyborg Bolshevik Committee. Thereafter, he took part in most of the dramatic events surrounding the October Revolution. Along the way, he attracted the attention and patronage of several leading Bolsheviks, including Trotsky, Vatsetis, V. I. Lenin, and Feliks Dzerzhinsky, the founder and first chief of the Cheka.

In December 1917, probably at Dzerzhinsky's request, Berzin joined the Cheka, and during the summer of 1918 he played a major role in carrying out the "Red Terror," most notably following the Bolshevik recapture of Yaroslavl.[55] His service in the Red Army began as a political commissar in December 1918. Soon thereafter, he was the commissar for internal affairs in the short-lived Latvian Socialist Republic. Following the re-occupation of Latvia by German and nationalist Latvian troops, Berzin became an OO chief—first of a rifle division, and then, by August 1919, of the Fifteenth Army.

Berzin's duties as OO chief of the Fifteenth Army may also have included some intelligence work. But it was almost certainly his experience in partisan warfare, and his background as a trusted chekist, that led Dzerzhinsky to recommend his appointment in April 1921 as deputy director of the *Registraupr*.[56] For the next few years Berzin was intimately involved with the organization and operations of the RU's Agent Department. Within two years he was chief of Red Army Intelligence, and for much of the intervening period he may have functioned as its real head.[57] As a key player in the shadowy world of intelligence, he thereafter became a "nonperson," and as a result, with the exception of his service in Spain as the chief Soviet advisor to the Republicans, biographical information about him all but vanishes after 1922.

Berzin remained director of the RU until 1935, when Stalin briefly appointed him deputy commander of the Special Far Eastern Military District, where he may have been charged with carrying out a bloody purge of the local OGPU.[58] A little over a year later, the Politburo dispatched him to Spain, where he was known as "General Grishin."[59] Late in 1937, as Stalin's purge of the Red Army high command began to gather momentum, Berzin became chief of the Fourth Department once again. The following year, however, his luck—or, more probably, his usefulness—finally ran out, and he was shot in December 1938.

PARTISAN OPERATIONS AND THE CIVIL WAR

Following the outbreak of Civil War in the spring of 1918, a variety of irregular, loosely organized forces sprang up throughout the former Tsarist Empire, from Poland to the Far East. Most of these partisan bands owed at least tentative allegiance to one of the two main factions in the war, the Reds and the Whites. Many of them, however, also switched sides or declared neutrality as necessity required or as opportunity for profit appeared. Others remained resolutely above the ideological fray, setting up independent fiefdoms in remote and virtually inaccessible areas.[60] In a war with few real front lines, a shortage of regular forces, and primitive communications, partisan warfare was both inevitable and highly effective. Attempting to control and use what was, in effect, a force already in being made good military sense to the Bolshevik leadership. Partisans were efficient combat units, needing relatively little external support. They lived off the land and knew the terrain well; they could move with much greater speed than regular units; and no other force available at the time had the potential to inflict such disproportionate damage in the enemy's rear areas. Partisans seemed to be the perfect weapon for an impoverished and besieged regime.

Early on, however, the Bolshevik leadership sensed even greater potential in this type of warfare. It is important to remember that the leadership of the Red Army and the Bolshevik party approached partisan warfare in 1917–18 in the context of the expected world revolution. Many prominent Bolsheviks, including Berzin, had as revolutionary activists extensive personal experience in guerrilla operations going back to at least 1905. Partisan units, as envisioned by the Bolsheviks, represented a concrete manifestation of the class struggle. Furthermore, the nature of partisan warfare, and, equally important, the responses it tended to provoke from the enemy (i.e., reprisals), served to very effectively mobilize the "class consciousness" of the workers and peasants in the surrounding towns and fields. Partisan warfare was, in other words, revolutionary warfare.

It should come as no surprise, therefore, that although partisan operations are as old as war itself, the Red Army approached them with a fundamentally different understanding. From the Bolshevik perspective, partisans traditionally suffered from several liabilities. Historically, they had always been organized haphazardly, in *response* to foreign occupation or brutalization by local authorities. In the past, partisans had operated on a strictly local basis, remaining almost completely autonomous from the national government or regular army. They possessed a very narrow strategic vision, and their operations were coordinated—at most—only with regular forces in the same area. Even more ominously, successful partisan leaders were notoriously independent, frequently to the point of treason. For the Bolsheviks, this was the most serious concern.

Red Army leaders sought to magnify the advantages of partisans while neutralizing their disadvantages. The most important measure was to centralize and rationalize partisan operations as much as possible. In addition to trying to extend Bolshevik authority to those bands that sprang up independently, from the very beginning of the Civil War both the *Registraupr* and Cheka also set out to create tailor-made partisan units. These were provided with trained, politically reliable, and, whenever possible, experienced leadership cadres. Their actions were designed from their inception to be coordinated with larger operational and strategic operations.

Whether this meant partisans were primarily a defensive weapon (as M. V. Frunze, one of the early supporters of this idea, maintained) or one of offense (in Mikhail Tukhachevsky's view) remained a matter of debate throughout the 1920s. But in either case, partisans gave the Red Army the potential to operate throughout the depth of an enemy's defenses—a depth that by the mid-1920s was defined both geographically and conceptually as extending even into the enemy's homeland—and it therefore was crucial to the theoretical development of Soviet operational art ("Deep Battle") in the 1930s. For the Red Army, the idea of "partisan operations" eventually came to embrace almost every kind of clandestine activity, from infiltrating individual operatives behind enemy lines to organizing large-scale armed insurrection. The connection between revolution and partisan warfare remained the basis for much of Soviet foreign policy, and Fourth Department operations, up to World War II and beyond.

Not surprisingly, given many of their personal backgrounds, the Bolsheviks sought to organize and use partisan forces at the very outset of the Civil War. Both the *Registraupr* and the Cheka organized partisan units. The first incarnation of the Red Army Staff's Operational Department included a Central Staff of Partisan Detachments. It was already "inserting and controlling partisan units in the rear of the Central Powers forces" by December 1917. By early 1918, the Central Staff was subordinate to the Registration Department, and was run directly by Aralov.[61]

In response to the German army's continued advance into Ukraine in the winter of 1917–18, the Central Staff of Partisan Detachments selected qualified officers and men from the Red Army, gave them brief training in such skills as demolitions and camouflage, and deployed them in the rear of the German lines. Their initial task was to mobilize effective partisan units, organize and train them, and cache weapons and supplies in well-camouflaged, secret dumps. They also carried out limited active operations, like raiding enemy supply dumps and garrisons and disrupting enemy lines of communication.[62]

In addition to those officers who served as cadres for locally organized partisan units, a few regular Red Army units were assigned to partisan work under the direction of the RU. These were elite engineer regiments and companies, which were soon employed by the Red Army in a variety of roles associated with the penetration and disruption of enemy rear areas. Successful officers and enlisted men from the Red Army Engineers later rose to become the cream of the leadership of the units of special designation (*spetsnazi*).[63]

Following the signing of the Treaty of Brest-Litovsk in March 1918, Aralov's Central Staff began to organize partisan bands all along the western frontier, as well as across the border in parts of Poland, Romania, and the Baltic states.[64] These units had limited success at best; the most effective partisans during the Civil War were usually those fighting against the Reds. With the outbreak of war with Poland in February 1919, however, Aralov's partisans made a significant contribution to Soviet offensive operations.

As tensions between Warsaw and Moscow increased in early 1920, the RU and Cheka organized more partisan units behind Polish lines in Ukraine, Belorussia, and Poland. Their mission was to gather intelligence and prepare for active operations. The pattern of their deployment probably reflected successful intelligence assessments of the planned initial Polish lines of advance.[65] By the time the Red Army went over to the offensive, they had managed to successfully penetrate "the police force, the church, and the Jewish community."[66] During Tukhachevsky's drive into Poland, RU partisans operated in the Polish rear in direct support of the Soviet advance. Bolshevik leaders were now able to put their theories about revolutionary warfare to the test on the field of battle.

Many men and women who later rose to prominence in Red Army Intelligence carried out their first missions for the *Registraupr* during the Soviet-Polish War, including Walter Krivitsky and Ignace Poretsky. Krivitsky was originally recruited into an OMS (*Otdel mezhdunarodnoi svyazi*, the "International Liaison Department," the Comintern's secret service) network in 1919 by the network's chief, a Comintern operative identified only as "the Baron." Through the OMS, the Red Army assigned this network intelligence-gathering and sabotage missions. Sometime later that year, the Baron died while playing golf, and his network of Polish agents was taken over directly by the RU.[67]

In 1920, Red Army Intelligence assigned Krivitsky and his group to Stigga's Western *Front* RO to support Tukhachevsky's drive into Poland. Krivitsky explained that the mission of the *front* RO was to operate secretly behind the Polish lines, "to create diversions, to sabotage the shipment of munitions, to shatter the morale of the Polish Army by propaganda, and to furnish the general staff of the Red Army with military and political information."[68] Krivitsky and his associates were also responsible for conducting various political operations, including encouraging Polish workers to strike or otherwise block the flow of material to the front, and publishing and distributing a "revolutionary newspaper" called *Svit* (Dawn).[69] Ignace Poretsky carried out similar tasks, although through a more indirect chain of command which ran from the Polish Communist Workers Party to the OMS and thence to the Red Army. In addition to the future stars of Red Army Intelligence, several other senior Red Army leaders participated in or relied heavily upon partisan operations during the Civil War and the war with Poland, including Trotsky, Tukhachevsky, Frunze, and K. E. Voroshilov. Frunze was in fact responsible for reorganizing many of the locally formed partisan bands and bringing them under direct Red Army command.[70]

Although the Civil War technically ended with the Treaty of Riga in March 1921, Soviet partisans continued to operate on foreign soil. Red Army Intelligence and the Cheka both maintained partisan units, many of which were now based on underground cells, in Ukraine, Belorussia, Lithuania, and eastern Poland until as late as 1925. Their activities included sabotage, assassinations, robbing trains and train stations, and "executing spies."[71] There were frequent skirmishes with the Polish police and military. Eventually a combination of circumstances led the Bolshevik leadership to end support for these partisan operations. Many of the abandoned partisans, now completely at the mercy of the Polish authorities, sought refuge in the Soviet Union and the RU.[72]

Following the Civil War, the conceptual importance of partisan operations in the enemy's rear only increased. Initially this was primarily in an offensive sense, as the dangerously weak Bolshevik regime sought security in a desperate series of attempts to bring about the increasingly elusive world revolution. The RU, manned and led by veterans of partisan warfare, was charged with carrying out this strategy for the next six years.

With the failure of these efforts, the Red Army was forced to prepare for war against what RU threat assessment from the mid-1920s identified as the "coalition of western bordering states" (Poland, Romania, the Baltic states, and Finland). Until the industrial and military might of the USSR could be drastically increased, this would of necessity be a defensive war, fought at least in its first phase on Soviet soil. Under these circumstances, partisan operations would again prove immensely valuable. Consequently, as we shall see, throughout the late 1920s and into the early 1930s, the Red Army invested immense effort and considerable resources into creating a series of partisan bases and units stationed along the USSR's western frontier that had the mission of slowing down attacking forces and preparing for the Red Army's eventual transition over to offensive operations.

As Soviet military capabilities grew, and Red Army leaders became increasingly committed to operational and strategic level offensive operations, partisans remained an important weapon for causing political and military disruption in the heart of the enemy's rear areas. This sophisticated view of partisan warfare that emerged in Soviet military doctrine and operational art by the mid-1930s was a direct result of the RU's experiences in the Civil and Soviet-Polish wars.

THE COMINTERN CONNECTION

By the end of the Soviet-Polish War, the Registration Department had recruited agents and set up networks throughout Central and Eastern Europe, and in the various bordering regions later absorbed into the Soviet Union. Within a few more years, an RU presence of some sort was established in every major nation from Great Britain to China. Through the auspices of the Comintern and OMS, foreign communist parties provided a ready-made source of ideologically dedicated agents. In the years immediately following World War I, the Soviets also successfully capitalized on the war's legacy of cynicism in the West to recruit supporters around the world. One early RU manual on agent recruiting, for example, suggested that if intelligence officers needed "a facilities agent (a radio operator, owner of a safe house or transmission point), find a tall handsome man who has lost a leg or arm in the war."[73]

From the moment of its creation in March 1919, the Third Communist International, or Comintern, was closely tied to Soviet foreign policy.[74] The Comintern proved to be an important resource not only for Soviet foreign policy, but also for the Fourth Department.[75] Many of the great RU intelligence officers and agents of the interwar years got their start in the Comintern, including, in addition to Krivitsky and Poretsky, Richard Sorge and Leopold Trepper.[76]

The Comintern directed its clandestine operations through the OMS. As we shall see, however, after a series of Comintern failures, in 1924 the OMS was put under the direction of Red Army Intelligence and the GPU, the successor to the Cheka. In effect this basically built on well-established precedent, for, as noted earlier, the *Registraupr* had been running networks under OMS cover since the Civil War.[77]

The division between "agent" and "intelligence officer" was often cloudy in those confused early years. Generally speaking, an officer had official military rank in the Red Army and worked directly for the RU. Nevertheless, it was unusual for even senior RU officers to have corresponding military rank before World War II. Walter Krivitsky and Ignace Reiss, both occupying command-level positions in the RU, each had the official rank and pay of captains, but otherwise the status of civilians. Two other prominent officers, Alfred Tilton (the chief of the Fourth Department's residency in the United States from 1929 to 1933) and Alex Borovich (military advisor to Karl Radek at the Sun Yat Sen School in Moscow) had the military rank of colonel.[78] An agent, in contrast, was a source recruited by another agent or intelligence officer. He or she was usually a member of the local communist party. Agents ran the gamut from short-term sources of mediocre information to long-term penetration agents, called "moles" in the West. Arthur Koestler is a good example of the former type of agent, and John H. King of the latter.

Compounding the problem of identifying individual Soviet operatives is the fact that throughout much of the 1920s there was a great deal of personnel cross-over between the RU, the Cheka, and the Comintern. Even Red Army intelligence officers serving at the time recalled much organizational confusion.[79] Between 1919 and 1922, people frequently moved back and forth between the *Razvedupr* and Comintern. During the Civil War and the war with Poland, Comintern operatives tended to be assigned directly or indirectly to Red Army Intelligence, while the rest of the time they usually remained subordinate to the OMS, except for those who as a result of their wartime service were recruited outright into the RU.[80] Some were, with their knowledge, recommended to the RU by the OMS (and so were "conscious" agents); others were passed over unaware to Fourth Department handlers (and thus were "unconscious" agents). On rare occasions, the RU directly recruited individuals from the Comintern without the approval or knowledge of the OMS itself, as apparently happened with Aino Kuusinen.

Until 1922, however, the standard procedure seems to have been that the OMS would first assign subordinate Communist party members to work on behalf of the Red Army, and then the RU would eventually recruit selected operatives from these ranks to be officers and "conscious" agents and officers. Once co-opted by military intelligence, foreign communists were usually, but not always, ordered to immediately resign so as to distance themselves from their own party for security reasons. As we shall see, these procedures achieved some measure of regularity following the crises of 1924 and 1927.

The close relationship between the Third International and the *Razvedupr* is well illustrated by the fact that one of the Comintern's founding members, the Finnish communist Otto Kuusinen, while serving as the acting executive director of the Comintern in the mid- and late 1920s, was also married to one of RU Chief Berzin's most important field agents, Aino Kuusinen.[81] In fact, Otto Kuusinen was himself "closely linked" with the RU from 1921 on, and became its deputy director in the mid-1930s.[82] More to the point, the close working relationship between the two organizations is highlighted by the fact that every member party in the Comintern was required to have its own military intelligence section that was ultimately subordinate to the RU.[83]

In the heady, early years following the October Revolution, there was no shortage of capable people willing to work enthusiastically on behalf of the world revolution, either in the Comintern or Red Army Intelligence. In contrast, those who worked for the Cheka were almost universally despised by the ranks of the OMS and the RU, who regarded the *chekisti* as little more than ignorant thugs continuing the brutal traditions of the tsarist gendarmes.[84] The *Razvedupr* was therefore, as compared to the Cheka, an uncharacteristically cosmopolitan organization, with members from almost every ethnic background. Many of them were highly educated, and from middle- or upper-class families. This was especially notable when compared to the frequently humble origins of the chekists.[85]

This cosmopolitan membership had important consequences. The RU's leadership and field cadres were dominated by non-Russians, particularly Poles, Germans, and, of course, Latvians like Stigga and Berzin.[86] This enhanced its ability to successfully operate on a global scale. The relative sophistication of the RU's officers and agents also gave them access to the aristocratic circles of Western Europe in a way that was impossible for the Cheka.[87] This predictably exacerbated the rivalry between the two organizations.

In fact, conflict between the Cheka and Red Army Intelligence existed throughout the history of the Soviet Union. In the early months of the Bolshevik regime, this hostility, exemplified by the OOs, took the form of frequent and bloody jurisdictional disputes over partisan operations.[88] From the mid-1920s on the chekists took ever greater pains to undermine their Red Army rivals, trying everything from encouraging Fourth Department officers to defect to the INO, to repeatedly petitioning the Central Committee and Politburo for the complete abolition of the *Razvedupr*.[89] In addition, from the beginning the Cheka, reacting to the disparity in the caliber of personnel, "made strenuous efforts to recruit personnel from the Fourth Department and the Comintern," although until the mid-1930s these efforts rarely succeeded. The Cheka finally won this battle, however, when, in the wake of Stalin's purge of the Red Army and its intelligence service in the late 1930s, it took over many of the Fourth Department's officers and networks. Indeed, the purges themselves were in part a reflection of Stalin's paranoid suspicions of both the Red Army and the concentration of foreigners in the ranks of its Intelligence Directorate.

THE *RAZVEDUPR* AFTER THE CIVIL WAR

The overall results of the intelligence effort during the Soviet-Polish War were something less than spectacular, especially in terms of operational level analysis. In particular, Red Army Intelligence seems to have completely failed to predict the timing, objectives, or even possibility of Polish commander Jozef Pilsudski's decisive counterattack in mid-August 1920. The resources to acquire such information were available, but the focus on partisan operations overrode analysis.

Nevertheless, there is no doubt that the *Razvedupr* emerged from the Civil and Soviet-Polish wars as the most important intelligence-gathering organ of Soviet Russia, a status it retained throughout the interwar period. The Cheka, including its foreign intelligence section, the INO (*Inostrannyi Otdel*, the Foreign Department), as well as its successors, the GPU, OGPU, and NKVD, focused primarily on combating counter-revolution, both real and imagined, at home and abroad. An official history prepared in 1980 by the

KGB's First Chief Directorate, the section responsible for foreign intelligence operations, noted that "until the 1930s the OGPU's main foreign target remained the White Guard movement centered on the headquarters of the ROVS (Russian Combined Services Union) in Paris."[90]

Following the Soviet-Polish War, the Fourth Department directed its efforts abroad toward the pursuit of two fundamental objectives: subversion of foreign governments in preparation for the coming revolution, and espionage. There was no real conceptual distinction between these goals from the Soviet point of view, however, since they furthered the same ideological vision.

NOTES

1. Ismail Akhmedov, *In and out of Stalin's GRU: A Tatar's Escape from Red Army Intelligence* (Frederick, Md.: University Publications of America, 1984), p. 79.

2. See Viktor Suvorov, *Inside Soviet Military Intelligence* (New York: Macmillan, 1984), pp. 6–13; John Dziak, *Chekisty: A History of the KGB* (New York: Ivy Books, 1988), p. 17; George Leggett, *The Cheka: Lenin's Political Police* (Oxford: Clarendon Press, 1981), p. 301; John Barron, *KGB: The Secret Work of Soviet Secret Agents* (New York: Bantam Books, 1974), pp. 463–464; and Pierre de Villemarest, *GRU: Le plus secret des services sovietiques, 1918–1988* (Paris: Editions Stock, 1988), pp. 99–101 (which is based on Suvorov).

3. This was also true of the Cheka, which took over several *Okhrana* networks intact and ran the former tsarist agents as its own. William R. Corson and Robert T. Crowley, *The New KGB: Engine of Soviet Power* (New York: William Morrow and Company, 1985), p. 51.

4. Bruce W. Menning, *Bayonets before Bullets: The Russian Imperial Army, 1861–1914* (Bloomington: Indiana University Press, 1992), pp. 16–17.

5. Ibid., pp. 97–98.

6. William C. Fuller, *Strategy and Power in Russia, 1600–1914* (New York: The Free Press, 1992), p. 344.

7. Ibid.

8. Ibid., pp. 344–35; William C. Fuller, "The Russian Empire," in *Knowing One's Enemies: Intelligence Assessment before the Two World Wars*, ed. by Ernest R. May (Princeton: Princeton University Press, 1984), pp. 107, 124.

9. Fuller, *Strategy and Power*, p. 218. For a brief discussion of failed intelligence operations in the Russo-Japanese War, see L. Korzun, "*Razvedka v russkoi armii v pervoi mirovoi voine*," *Voennoe istoricheskiy Zhurnal*, no. 4 (April 1981): p. 60.

10. See Fuller's discussion in "Russian Empire," pp. 104–107.

11. Ibid., p. 107.

12. This question is discussed in its broadest context in Menning, *Bayonets*.

13. Korzun, "*Razvedka*," p. 60.

14. Ibid., pp. 60–61.

15. Ibid., p. 61.

16. Fuller, "Russian Empire," pp. 98–102.

17. For more on Redl, see ibid., p. 115.

18. Ibid., pp. 109–123.

19. Ibid., pp. 105–107.

20. Indeed, poor Russian radio security, combined with German successes in decryption, gave the Germans thorough advanced knowledge about Russian operations, and contributed significantly to the disasters in East Prussia; see David Kahn, *The Code-Breakers* (London: Sphere Books, 1973), pp. 344–349.

21. Korzun, "*Razvedka*," pp. 61–62.

22. Ibid., pp. 62–63.

23. Ibid., pp. 64–65.

24. Captain George A. Hill, *Go Spy the Land: Being the Adventures of I.K.8 of the British Secret Service* (London: Cassell and Company, 1936), p. 193. Captain Hill was an officer of MI1c, the predecessor of MI6 (Secret Service).

25. See for example Leggett, *Cheka*, p. 301, and Richard Deacon, *A History of the Russian Secret Service* (London: Frederick Muller, 1972), p. 224. However, Christopher Andrew and Oleg Gordievsky in *KGB: The Inside Story of Its Foreign Operations from Lenin to Gorbachev* (New York: Harper Collins, 1990), do challenge Hill's claims (pp. 54–55).

26. The most notorious example of this was of course the "Lockhart" or "Ambassadors'" Plot. See Leggett, *Cheka*, pp. 280–284; Dziak, *Chekisty*, pp. 46–48; and R. H. Bruce Lockhart, *Memoirs of a British Agent* (London: MacMillan London, 1974), pp. 314–316.

27. Deacon implicitly acknowledges this argument when he claims that Dzerzhinsky's realization that a British intelligence officer had helped create Trotsky's intelligence directorate prompted the Cheka chief to suspect some foreign plot (p. 224).

28. Suvorov, *Inside Soviet Military Intelligence*, pp. 6–9.

29. Ibid., p. 7. On "active measures," see, for example, Walter Krivitsky, *I Was Stalin's Agent* (London: The Right Book Club, 1940), pp. 46–47.

30. Suvorov, *Inside Soviet Military Intelligence*, pp. 7–9.

31. Ibid., p. 9.

32. See for example the chart following p. 320 in S. M. Klyatsin, *Na zashchite Oktyabrya: organizatsiya regulyarnoi armii i militsionnoe stroitel'stvo v Sovetskoi Respublike, 1917–1920* (Moscow: "Nauka," 1965).

33. "*Polevoi shtab RVSR*" (Field Staff of the RVSR), TsGASA, f. 6, op. 1, l. 7–9.

34. Suvorov, *Inside Soviet Military Intelligence*, p. 10; Dziak, *Chekisty*, p. 200. The exact date of the transition from the Second Department of the Operations Directorate to the Fourth Chief Directorate of the Red Army Staff is unknown. Dziak gives the year as 1925 in *Chekisty*. John Erickson implies that the RU became the Fourth Directorate as the result of the major reorganization of the Red Army Staff in 12 July 1926; see John Erickson, *The Soviet High Command, a Military-Political History* (London: St. Martin's Press, 1962), pp. 203, 794.

There is also disagreement over when the RU became the GRU. Dziak maintains that this re-designation happened in 1942 in *Chekisty*, p. 200. In John Costello, *Mask of Treachery: Spies, Lies and Betrayal* (New York: Warner Books, 1989), Costello implies that it occurred at some undesignated point around 1930 (second "document" in "Documents" section following p. 598). Akhmedov, *In and out of Stalin's*, p. 213, more or less agrees with Dziak, asserting that the RU became the GRU "at the beginning of" World War II. Given Dziak's verified accuracy on this issue, I am inclined to accept his chronology.

35. For example, see Poretsky, *Our Own People, passim. Razvedupr* was the name by which German counterintelligence officials knew it; Heinz Höhne, *Codeword Direktor* (New York: Berkley, 1970), p. 33.

36. *"Polevoi shtab RVSR,"* TsGASA, l. 7–9, 11–12.

37. This amazing detail has only recently come to light; see Lennart Samuelson, *Soviet Defence Industry Planning: Tukhachevskii and Military-Industrial Mobilisation, 1926–1937* (Stockholm: Stockholm Institute of East European Economies, 1996), p. 73.

38. The Russian words for department, directorate, office, section, and bureau somewhat overlap. For the purposes of this discussion, I will use the following translations: *otdel*—department; *otdelenie*—section; *byuro*—bureau; and *stol*—office.

39. Unless otherwise noted, all information on the organization of the RU between 1918–1920 comes from *"Polevoi shtab RVSR,"* TsGASA, 1, l. 7–12.

40. This was the case with the Administration Department of the Comintern; see Aino Kuusinen, *Before and after Stalin: A Personal Account of Soviet Russia from the 1920s to the 1960s* (London: Michael Joseph, 1974), p. 43.

41. Elisabeth Poretsky, whose husband Ignace was a prominent officer in the Fourth Department, maintains that there "were no 'schools for agents', as certain romantically inclined writers would have us believe"; Elisabeth Poretsky, *Our Own People: A Memoir of 'Ignace Reiss' and His Friends* (London: Oxford University Press, 1969), p. 70. This may, however, have referred only to agents recruited in the field as opposed to Red Army officers assigned to the Intelligence Directorate, who would have been the ones to go through the Training and Control Section. There is overwhelming evidence for the early existence of schools for active measures; see for example the discussion in chapter 2.

42. The "Press Department" of the Comintern was responsible for supplying translators for a variety of foreign languages; see Kuusinen, *Before and after Stalin*, p. 41.

43. *"Polevoi shtab RVSR,"* TsGASA, l. 7–12.

44. Höhne, *Codeword Direktor*, p. 34.

45. Ibid.; Krivitsky, *I Was Stalin's Agent*, p. 53.

46. The OOs were Cheka security and counterintelligence sections attached to all Red Army formations from *front* level down through regiment as of January 1919. They were primarily responsible for ensuring the loyalty of the army's officer cadres through terror. The OOs remained a source of friction between the Red Army and the Cheka for decades; see Leggett, *Cheka*, pp. 205–208; Corson and Crowley, *New KGB*, pp. 39–40; and Dziak, *Chekisty*, p. 4.

47. Suvorov, *Inside Soviet Military Intelligence*, pp. 10–11.

48. Ibid., p. 176.

49. Leon Trotsky, *How the Revolution Armed: The Military Writings and Speeches of Leon Trotsky*, Vol. 1, *The Year 1918*, trans. and annotated by Brian Pearce (London: New Park Publications, 1979), p. 278.

50. Ibid., pp. 469–470. For more on the Latvian Rifles, see Ya. P. Krastynya, ed., *Istoria latyskskikh strelkov* (Riga: Izdatl'stvo "Zinatne," 1972); Uldis Germanis, *Oberst Vacietis und die lettischen Schuetzen im Weltkrieg und in der Oktoberrevolution* (Stockholm: Almquist & Wiksell, 1974); and Visvaldis Mangulis, *Latvia in the Wars of the 20th Century* (Princeton Junction, N.J.: Cognition Books, 1983).

51. Suvorov, *Inside Soviet Military Intelligence*, p. 176; Lars T. Lih, Oleg V. Naumov, and Oleg V. Khlevniuk, eds., *Stalin's Letters to Molotov, 1925–1936*, trans. by Catherine A. Fitzpatrick (New Haven: Yale University Press, 1995), Letter 22, p. 117, also p. 252.

Arrested during the purges, Aralov survived the Gulag and the Great Patriotic War to briefly serve again in Red Army Intelligence in 1945–46. Arrested again in 1946, he spent the next ten years in a labor camp, following which he was again posted to the GRU, this time as its deputy chief. He was purged once more in 1957, but this time went into a relatively comfortable retirement. Aralov died in 1969; Suvorov, *Inside Soviet Military Intelligence*, p. 176. He also wrote at least one book: *V. I. Lenin i Krasnaya Armiya* (published in 1959; see Klyatsin, *Na zashchite*, p. 20 n. 35). His longevity was almost miraculous for a high-ranking Soviet intelligence officer from the interwar years.

52. Suvorov, *Inside Soviet Military Intelligence*, p. 176.

53. Ibid.; Leopold Trepper, *The Great Game: Memoirs of the Spy Hitler Couldn't Silence* (New York: McGraw-Hill, 1977), pp. 77–78.

54. Unless otherwise indicated, biographical information on Berzin's life comes from the following sources: Ovidii Gorchakov, "*V golovnom dozore RKKA*," in *Vstretimsya posle zadaniya* (Moscow: Izdatel'stvo DOSAAF, 1973), pp. 11–35; M. Kolesnikov, "*Yan Karlovich Berzin*," in *Soldaty nevidimykh srazhenii: rasskazy o podvigakh chekistov*, ed. by I. I. Shumelev (Moscow: Voennoe izdatel'stvo Ministerstva Oborony SSSR, 1968), pp. 81–92; G. Solonitsyn, "*Nachal'nik sovetskoi razvedki*," *Voennoe istoricheskiy Zhurnal*, no. 11 (November, 1979): 92–94; S. Golyakov and V. Ponizovskii, "*Nachal'nik razvedki*," *Komsomol'skaya pravda* (13 November 1964): 4; and V. Ponizovskii, "*Starik*," in *Soldatskoe pole: geroicheskie biografii* (Moscow: Izdatel'stvo vsesoyuznovo ordena krasnovo znameni dobrovol'novo obshchestvo sodeistviya armii, aviatsii i flotu, 1971), pp. 105–120.

55. Information on Berzin's role in the Red Terror comes from Suvorov, *Inside Soviet Military Intelligence*, p. 177.

56. According to most Soviet sources, Berzin was appointed chief of an unspecified *Razvedupr* department in December 1920; see, for example, Gorchakov, "*V golovnom.*" However, the only date all of the sources agree on is March 1924 for Berzin's appointment as chief of the RU.

Suvorov contends that Berzin played a bloody role in the suppression of the Kronstadt Mutiny, and that he "particularly distinguished himself in the course of the pursuit and liquidation of captured sailors"; *Inside Soviet Military Intelligence*, p. 117.

57. Ibid., p. 177.

58. Suvorov contends that Berzin led a Fourth Department purge of the "leading illegals" of the OGPU in the Far East on Stalin's orders; ibid., pp. 21–22.

59. For Berzin's work in Spain, see Ovidii Gorchakov, "*Yan Berzin: sud'ba komandarma nevidimovo fronta*," *Novaya i noveishaya istoriya*, no. 2 (March–April 1989: 131–159.

60. See Robert Suggs's background chapter in Colonel I. G. Starinov, *Over the Abyss: My Life in Soviet Special Operations*, trans. by Robert Suggs (New York: Ivy Books, 1995), pp. 4–5; also see Erickson, *Soviet High Command*, p. 86 fn.

61. Suggs, in Starinov, *Over the Abyss*, pp. 2–3.

62. Ibid.

63. Examples include S. V. Vaupshasov and I. G. Starinov. For more on Vaupshasov, see his memoirs, *Na trevozhnykh perekrestkakh. Zapiski chekista* (Moscow: Politizdat, 1971).

64. For Red Partisan operations during the Civil War, see Erickson, *Soviet High Command*, pp. 64–65.

65. Suggs, in Starinova, *Over the Abyss*, pp. 7–8.

66. Ibid., p. 8.

67. Poretsky, *Our Own People*, pp. 53–54.

68. Krivitsky, *I Was Stalin's Agent*, p. 46.

69. Ibid., pp. 46–48.

70. Viktor Suvorov, *Spetsnaz: The Inside Story of the Soviet Special Forces*, trans. by David Floyd (New York: W. W. Norton & Company; 1987), pp. 13–14; also, see Suggs, in Starinov, *Over the Abyss*, p. 11.

71. Suggs, in Starinov, *Over the Abyss*, p. 9.

72. Ibid.

73. Suvorov, *Inside Soviet Military Intelligence*, p. 13.

74. An early attempt to view Comintern operations in the context of the overall Soviet intelligence effort is included in Gunther Nollau's *International Communism and World Revolution: History and Methods*, foreword by Leonard Shapiro (London: Hollis & Carter, 1961), pp. 177–183. Also useful, although with a much different focus, are Stephan Koch, *Double Lives: Spies and Writers in the Secret Soviet War of Ideas against the West* (New York: The Free Press, 1994), and Harvey Klehr, John Earl Haynes, and Fridrikh Igorevich Firsov, *The Secret World of American Communism* (New Haven: Yale University Press, 1995).

The Communist International formed in March of 1919 was also known as the "Third International," that is, the Third International Working Men's Association. The first was organized by Karl Marx in 1866. The Second International was formed in Paris in 1889. Nollau, *International Communism*, pp. 9–38.

75. Several authors, notably Volkogonov and Corson and Crowley, make numerous errors in their discussion of the Comintern and Soviet covert operations. For more details, the reader is referred to Raymond W. Leonard, *The Kremlin's Secret Soldiers: Soviet Military Intelligence, 1918–1933*, Ph.D. dissertation (Lawrence, Kans.: University of Kansas, 1997).

76. Suvorov, *Inside Soviet Military Intelligence*, p. 12.

77. Andrew and Gordievsky, *KGB*, p. 93; Kuusinen, *Before and after Stalin*, p. 51; Poretsky, *Our Own People*, p. 53.

78. Poretsky, *Our Own People*, p. 185.

79. An excellent firsthand description of this confusion can be found in Poretsky, *Our Own People*, pp. 53–55.

80. See ibid., pp. 41–43.

81. On Otto Kuusinen's role in the founding of the Comintern, see Branko Lazitch and Milorad M. Drachkovitch, *Lenin and the Comintern*, vol. 1 (Stanford: Hoover Institution Press, 1972), pp. 67, 79–80. Aino Turtiainen married Otto Kuusinen in 1922; see Kuusinen, *Before and after Stalin*, pp. 22–25.

82. Suvorov, *Spetsnaz*, p. 17.

83. Poretsky, *Our Own People*, p. 54.

84. Ibid., pp. 54–55.

85. Corson and Crowley, *New KGB*, p. 28.

86. Poretsky, *Our Own People*, p. 81.

87. Richard Sorge, for example, moved quite freely among the German aristocracy (see chapter 5). Other RU officers with aristocratic or upper-middle-class backgrounds included Aino Kuusinen and Ruth Werner.

88. Suvorov, *Inside Soviet Military Intelligence*, pp. 8–12. Indeed, Suvorov contends that the entire intelligence section of the Eastern *Front,* along with its commander, M. A. Muraviev, was shot by the Cheka in July 1918, in a dispute over jurisdiction. Other sources, however, indicate that Muraviev defected to the Whites, and even attempted to kidnap Tukhachevsky; see Erickson, *Soviet High Command*, p. 54. Muraviev apparently had a history of this sort of behavior, fortuitously joining whichever side appeared to him to be winning; see Erich Wollenberg, *The Red Army: A Study in the Growth of Soviet Imperialism* (London: Seeker & Warburg, 1940), pp. 67–68.

89. Georges Agabekov, *OGPU: The Russian Secret Terror*, trans. from the French by Henry Bunn (New York: Brentano's, 1931), p. 275. Agabekov was a chekist who served as chief of the INO's Eastern Section and OGPU resident in Constantinople until his defection in 1930.

90. Cited by Andrew and Gordievsky, *KGB*, p. 150.

CHAPTER 2

Exporting the Revolution: Insurrection and Partisan Warfare, 1923–1927

Out of the ruins of the Communist revolution we built in Germany for Soviet Russia a brilliant intelligence service, the envy of every other nation.

—Walter Krivitsky[1]

Lenin died on 21 January 1924. For the next four years, the Bolshevik leadership struggled for control of the CPSU. This conflict focused on the nature of the world revolution. Until 1923, there was no real disagreement that a world, or at least European, revolution was both imminent and necessary for the practical survival of the first workers' state. Lenin was a strong proponent of this view, and he enthusiastically called for and approved the expenditure of vast sums, including significant amounts of Russia's precious gold reserves, on behalf of the revolution. At a Comintern budget meeting in March 1922, 5,536,400 gold rubles were earmarked for distribution to various Comintern member parties and organizations. This "river of gold for [the] Comintern" amounted to three times the sum spent to combat the famine in Russia during that entire year.[2]

Following Lenin's death, however, disputes over the question of "continuing revolution" dominated the Party leadership. One faction, led by Trotsky and the chairman of the Comintern, Grigorii E. Zinoviev, argued that the wisest course was to continue to support policies likely to lead to further revolutions. They were opposed by those who argued that the Party's first priority should be to ensure the survival of Soviet Russia by consolidating political control of the state and concentrating resources on industrialization.

The Fourth Department quickly found itself at the center of this dangerous political whirlwind, because it was the only organization capable of organizing armed insurrection abroad. Consequently, Zinoviev repeatedly called upon it to try and achieve for him the revolutionary success abroad that would translate into political advantage at home. For Red Army Intelligence, these operations were viewed as conceptually akin to the "partisan warfare" of the Civil War, and they played an important part in the Red Army's increasingly sophisticated approach to modern warfare.

GERMANY

In the early 1920s, political violence and economic crisis rocked the fragile Weimar Republic. In 1923, hyperinflation threatened to finally topple the new regime. Attempting to collect by force the reparations that were their due under the terms of the Versailles Treaty, and, not incidentally, seeking to penalize Weimar for showing dangerous independence in dealing with Moscow, in January 1923 France and Belgium sent troops to occupy the Ruhr, the industrial heart of Germany. This led to a series of protests and strikes, passive resistance, and, ultimately, two major attempts at insurrection. The Moscow-sponsored "Hamburg Uprising" occurred in October 1923; a month later, Adolf Hitler's National Socialists and their allies staged the notorious "Beer Hall Putsch" in Munich.

The background for the decision to foster revolution in Germany remains a matter of debate. Krivitsky observed that the Ruhr crisis led Moscow to conclude that "the French occupation would open the way for a renewed Comintern drive in Germany."[3] A German diplomat serving in Moscow, Gustav Hilger, concluded that the Soviets saw in the French move "a threat to [their] own security."[4] A prominent German communist who participated in these events, Ruth Fischer, maintained that the idea of sponsoring a revolution was fueled by a power struggle between CPSU factions, led on the one hand by Stalin, who counseled against it, and on the other by Zinoviev, chairman of the Comintern, and Trotsky, who both firmly believed that a revolutionary situation existed in Germany.[5] Meanwhile, in the "spirit of Rapallo," Soviet representatives repeatedly assured the German government of Moscow's support in its confrontation with France. Earlier, in December 1922, Trotsky had even informed the German representative in Moscow, Count Ulrich von Brockdorff-Rantzau, that the Red Army would prevent a Polish advance into German Silesia in the event of a Franco-Belgian invasion of the Ruhr.[6]

By early October 1923, after months of argument and tentative preparations, and a failed attempt at sparking revolution in Bulgaria (see below), the Soviet leadership finally agreed that the situation in Germany was, indeed, ripe for staging an uprising. Many leaders of the German Communist Party (KPD) had advocated this move for several months. Now, through the direction of the Comintern, the more cautious and reluctant German communists, including the chief of the KPD Politburo, Heinrich Brandler, were persuaded to support a revolt.[7]

The Hamburg Uprising has been well described elsewhere.[8] This discussion will focus on the role played in it by the RU. The highest echelons of the Soviet leadership not only approved the idea, but supervised its planning and execution. The "revolution" was essentially a Comintern operation carried out by the KPD with *Razvedupr* leadership and material.[9] Zinoviev had the authority to issue the order for the insurrection to commence, and together with Karl Radek was most responsible for its failure.[10] In September 1923, Iosef Unshlikht, Dzerzhinsky's second-in-command in the Cheka and one of Stalin's close allies, became Berzin's deputy at the RU. From Moscow, Unshlikht probably served as the commander of the Fourth Department's partisan operations in Germany.[11]

Within days of the French occupation, the RU infiltrated six high-ranking officers, including Krivitsky, into Germany. Their mission was to gather intelligence and "to forge the weapons for an uprising when the proper moment arrived."[12] Once the Soviet Politburo, and through it the Comintern, decided to proceed with an uprising, Krivitsky and the other five RU officers were directed to help organize the KPD for carrying it out.

The German comrades were instructed to create six "military-political commands" corresponding to the six divisional military districts of the *Reichswehr*. Each of these commands had a political secretary, a military-political secretary (probably corresponding to what Krivitsky referred to as the "Party Intelligence Service"), and an RU advisor, whom the Germans called a "Soviet general."[13] The evidence suggests that the six "Soviet generals" were in fact the six Fourth Department officers sent to Germany earlier. In the North-West Command (also known as the "Seaboard" Command), which centered on the port of Hamburg, the political secretary was Hugo Urbahns, the military-political secretary was Albert Schreiner, and the RU "general" was Moishe Stern.[14]

Unshlikht's RU advisors produced a scheme for creating a workers' army that would first carry out the insurrection, and then serve as a basis for the German "Red Army." On paper, this was a very impressive organization. The workers were to be assembled into hundred-man units, called "Proletarian Hundreds" (or "Unshlikht's Hundreds"), based on the factories where they worked or the neighborhoods in which they lived.[15] A "technical staff" was organized and was composed of combat veterans and communications workers.[16] Some of them underwent further training in Russia, probably at early versions of what would come to be known as the "special partisan schools."[17] Units composed of women trained for medical duties were also created.[18]

In command of this nascent German "Red Army" was Peter Aleksandrovich Skoblevsky, the chief of Soviet Red Army advisor operations in Germany.[19] To lead them, the RU "generals," in consultation with the six

military-political secretaries, drew up lists of communists who were also veterans of World War I. At a major conference in Moscow that finalized plans
for the revolt, Bolshevik leaders also decided to supplement the German
communist "officers" with "several hundred" Red Army officers who were
assigned to command the most capable German units.[20]

In reality, however, the measures undertaken to prepare a "proletarian
army" proved to be not only inadequate, but also quite amateurish. Although
the KPD had access to arms, its leadership was concerned that training with
weapons would attract the unwelcome attention of the authorities, and consequently the German "Red Army" had little training in their use. The
weapons were for the most part hidden away under tight security. The KPD
not only had to be wary of German police, but also of officers of the Allied
Control Commission enforcing the Versailles Treaty. The police were occasionally tipped off by the underground arms dealers with whom the communists dealt, and in some instances the arms sellers themselves sold the KPD
cases of weapons that turned out to be "full of stones."[21]

The result was that the would-be vanguard of the German Red Army was
forced to drill, on those rare occasions when it could, "in factory grounds and
on open spaces," "armed only with sticks and clubs." When Hans Kippenberger, chief of one of the "Proletarian Hundreds" units in Hamburg, tried to
train his men in the woods nearby with a few old pistols and shotguns, he was
(briefly) relieved by the Seaboard Sector Party leadership.[22] The opinion of
the Fourth Department advisors about this situation is unknown, although
Krivitsky, assigned to the West Sector, claims that in apparent violation of security restrictions the RU officers personally supervised some military training in the wooded areas near Solingen, a town in the Rhineland.[23]

The Fourth Department advisors also supervised the KPD's organization
of the *Zersetzungsdienst*, a section devoted to directing propaganda and psy-
chological warfare against the *Reichswehr* and the police. In addition to the
Zersetzungsdienst, the *Razvedupr* set up teams of saboteurs and assassins
called "T-units" (a measure that became standard in RU preparations for insurrection). The task of the T-units was to demoralize the army and police
through acts of terror. In anticipation of the imminent revolution, they carried out political murders in major German cities at least as early as
September 1923. Their targets included the *Reichswehr* chief, Gen. Hans von
Seeckt, and industrialists Conrad von Borsig and Hugo Stinnes.[24] According
to Ruth Fischer, another section of the RU operation in Germany was responsible for liaison to oppositionist officers in the German army.[25] No other
source mentions this, but it seems credible. The Red Army had had rather
cordial relations with the *Reichswehr* since at least the Rapallo agreements of
1922. At the same time, this pointedly demonstrates the typically surreal position the Red Army found itself in as it pursued ever closer military and economic ties with the Weimar government while simultaneously organizing
efforts to subvert and topple it.

When Zinoviev ordered the start of the uprising in September, it was almost immediately cancelled in a pattern repeated on numerous occasions over the next several weeks.[26] After the government of President Friedrich Ebert established martial law throughout central Germany in the second week of October, Zinoviev and Radek sent couriers to all the communist cells throughout Germany, once again ordering them to prepare for the revolt. As before, it was postponed, and more couriers went out to inform the commands. Unfortunately, the courier sent to the Seaboard Command arrived too late.[27] The Hamburg communists, subordinate to the Seaboard Command, consequently staged their uprising on schedule at dawn on the morning of 23 October 1923.[28]

According to both Krivitsky and Erich Wollenberg, a German communist who joined the RU after the insurrection, for all practical purposes it was Kippenberger who led the Hamburg Uprising. His role in this episode was described in heroic terms by Larrisa Reissner.[29] Before the uprising, he had managed on his own to recruit networks of sympathizers and informants from the ranks of the workers, police, and army, and even far-right political organizations like the *Wehrwolf*, the *Stahlhelm*, and the Nazis.

The insurrection was almost entirely limited to Hamburg's Barmbeck district, primarily a residential area for shipworkers. Kippenberger had no idea how many men he had, or what the situation was in greater Hamburg, much less in Germany as a whole. Kippenberger's "Proletarian Hundreds" only had enough food for two days, and although the Party and the RU had supposedly stashed away large caches of arms and ammunition, the rebels were very poorly armed. Kippenberger had at his disposal nineteen rifles and twenty-seven pistols. One group of fifty men had between them a total of three revolvers and two rifles.[30]

Although Kippenberger's men managed to hold out against the police and army for three days, the end was inevitable, and the uprising was predictably a disaster.[31] Casualties among the workers were surprisingly light, although many subsequently received prison sentences.[32] But the KPD was thoroughly discredited, and the uprising contributed to a far-right backlash that produced a favorable climate for, among other things, Adolf Hitler's "Pütsch" the following month in Munich. The Soviet leadership blamed the fiasco on the leader of the German communists, Heinrich Brandler. He and his faction were soon replaced by Ruth Fischer, Ernst Thaelmann, and Arkadi Maslow.[33]

There were also consequences for the USSR. Moscow's support for the insurrection threatened to wreck the fragile German-Soviet rapprochement begun at Rapallo. German authorities were well aware of Soviet Russia's involvement in this episode. Following her ouster from the KPD on Moscow's orders, Fischer made public documents that showed the "extent to which Russian emissaries had participated in the attempts at communist revolt."[34] That same month, German authorities expelled a Soviet "military agent" (a Frenchman known as "Petrov"). In the spring of 1925, Skoblevsky himself was tried in Leipzig by the German Supreme Court. In preparation for his inevitable conviction, the Cheka framed two inexperienced German entrepreneurs and some high-level diplomatic personnel in the German Embassy in Moscow on charges of plotting to kill Stalin and Trotsky, in a clumsy scheme to trade them for Skoblevsky. This caused another crisis in German-Soviet relations that lasted until August.[35] Although both Moscow and Berlin quickly returned to the policies of cooperation characteristic of Rapallo, "the scars made by the events of October, 1923, could never be removed."[36] For the next ten years, the Soviets continued to follow a duplicitous policy of pursuing closer relations with the Weimar Republic while simultaneously fostering subversion there.

The failure of the German revolution was also a major setback for Zinoviev and the Comintern, although many in Moscow retained hope that a revolution could still somehow be nursed into existence under the right circumstances. For the Fourth Department, however, there was an unexpected silver lining. Although an unknown but probably small number of RU officers were captured (including Skoblevsky), Krivitsky noted that if the German adventure achieved nothing else, it allowed the *Razvedupr* to absorb into its ranks the best people from the KPD. "Out of the ruins of the Communist revolution we built in Germany for Soviet Russia a brilliant intelligence service, the envy of every other nation."[37] Most of these "new recruits" had already been de facto agents of the RU in the German Communist party, and "almost all of those who worked in the military apparatus [of the KPD] under the supervision of the Fourth Department wound up as members of it."[38] These new acquisitions included Kippenberger, Wilhelm Zaisser (who would later spearhead RU operations in France, China, and the U.S.), Nikolai Krebs (a.k.a. Nikolai Rakov and Felix Wolf), and Arthur Illner (a.k.a. Richard Stahlmann).[39]

After the failure of the uprising, although a significant RU presence remained in Germany, operating out of fronts like the *Handelsvertretung*, much of the Fourth Department *apparat* (organization of residencies and agent networks) was relocated to Vienna. The Vienna post thereafter became the center not only for the RU's efforts directed at Germany, but for operations in the Balkans as well.[40]

BULGARIA

Even while the Comintern and Red Army Intelligence planned for revolution in Germany, they prepared a similar operation in Bulgaria. Unlike Germany, however, Bulgaria was not a target for ideological reasons. Traditional Russian concerns about access to the eastern Mediterranean and the balance of power in the Balkans were exacerbated by the Bulgarian monarchy's recent apparent diplomatic shift toward Great Britain.[41]

Political instability had plagued Bulgaria ever since it surrendered to the Allies in 1918. By 1923, elections had established the Bulgarian National

Agrarian Party's (BNAP) control of a government led by Alexander Stamboliiski.[42] Although not radical by Bolshevik standards, the BNAP's program of land redistribution and selective nationalization of industries, together with its close association, both perceived and actual, with the more radical parties on the Left, soon inspired an organized right-wing opposition that became known as the "National Alliance." The National Alliance staged a coup against Stamboliiski in June 1923, and led by Alexander Tsankov, it installed a new, reactionary government decidedly hostile to parties of the Left, particularly the Bulgarian Communist Party (BCP), as well as Soviet Russia.[43]

Meanwhile, Bulgarian communists, despite pleas for unity from other leftist parties, remained resolutely aloof from the power struggle on orders from the Comintern, which had decided at its Fourth World Congress in 1922 that member parties should stay out of domestic political squabbles (except, of course, when the Soviets wanted them to get involved). This policy was heartily endorsed by the leader of the BCP, Georgi Dimitrov.

The repression unleashed upon opponents of the new regime, especially the communists, reinforced the perception in Moscow that the British were somehow behind the coup. At about the same time, skillful British diplomacy succeeded in wrecking a possible reconciliation between Turkey and Soviet Russia. In both events the Soviets saw a growing British menace in the Balkans and Mediterranean. The decision to intervene in Bulgaria therefore represented "not the beginning of a new European wave of Communist revolution but a prop to Russian influence in the Balkans."[44]

At the same conference in Moscow in June 1923 at which they decided upon staging revolution in Germany, the Comintern and Politburo resolved that the BCP should also launch an uprising as soon as possible. The fact that Tsankov's coup had only occurred earlier that same month indicates that the Soviet decision was primarily dictated by opportunism. The objective was not to create a Bulgarian socialist republic, but to replace Tsankov's regime with one led again by the relatively popular and pro-Soviet Agrarian party, which naturally would thereby be indebted to Dimitrov's communists.[45] Later in June, the RU infiltrated a group of "military advisors" into Bulgaria, and the Politburo provided through the Comintern a small "war chest" to finance the operation.[46] In northwest Bulgaria, Dimitrov, Vasil Kolarov, and the *Razvedupr* advisors mapped out the strategy for the uprising.[47]

It began on 23 September. It was a complete disaster from the start. Even more poorly organized and led than their counterparts in Hamburg, the Bulgarian revolutionaries also faced a much more ruthless and united opposition.[48] The rebels held out for barely two days. By early morning on the 26th, Dimitrov, Kolarov, and the other Bulgarian and Red Army officers were forced to evacuate their "command post" in Mihailovgrad and scamper for the Yugoslav border.[49]

Tsankov unleashed a wave of terror in the wake of the failed uprising; as many as 20,000 people may have died. Most of the remnants of the Bulgarian

Communist Party either fled the country, including about a thousand who crossed into Yugoslavia, or were killed or imprisoned.[50] Far from toppling Tsankov, the revolt vastly strengthened his hand and unleashed the forces of reaction throughout the Balkans. There was no "silver lining" for the RU this time. Red Army Intelligence was unable to salvage anything from the meager resources and organization created for the revolt. Ironically, one of the only communists to emerge with his status and reputation more or less intact was Dimitrov, who, as one of the few surviving BCP leaders, and, more importantly, a man clearly willing to blindly follow Moscow's directives, eventually climbed through the ranks of the Comintern as it was decimated by purges. He later gained a very public and international notoriety during the Reichstag Fire trial, and went on to become the Comintern's last secretary-general, from 1935–43, and Stalin's hand-picked ruler of Bulgaria after World War II.[51]

ESTONIA

Soon after Lenin's death in January 1924, the Comintern leadership came to believe that a revolutionary situation was developing in Estonia. The disaster in Hamburg was still fresh on the minds of many in the Comintern and *Razvedupr*. The CPSU leadership, and that of the Comintern, as well, following the fiascos in Germany and Bulgaria, seemed to agree that deliberate attempts to spark the international revolution should be abandoned. Lenin's death, however, disrupted this tentative consensus.

For Zinoviev and his supporters, it now seemed imperative in this power vacuum to demonstrate the revolutionary potential and ideological leadership of the Comintern by producing a victory, and quickly. Further evidence of his growing desperation lies in the fact that Zinoviev seems to have convinced himself that a successful revolt in Estonia just might trigger the world revolution that was supposed to have begun in Germany the previous October.[52]

Once again Zinoviev relied on Red Army Intelligence to execute his scheme. He probably outlined the plan to Berzin sometime in April 1924.[53] Abandoning any pretense of ideological justification for such an act, Zinoviev, reflecting upon the failures in Germany and Bulgaria, concluded that the major problem in both instances was that the authorities had too much warning, and therefore the forces of reaction were given too much time to respond. This time, he suggested to Berzin, there should be no large-scale strikes, public demonstrations, or other public Party activity—that is, any activity commonly understood as indicative of a revolutionary situation. The Comintern would rely instead on careful preparation of underground cells of revolutionary fighters, trained and equipped by the RU, and the revolt would rely on surprise for success. In other words, a general uprising was to be abandoned this time in favor of a coup d'etat. So much for Marx.

Berzin's personal opinion about this plan is unknown. Krivitsky, writing with the benefit of hindsight, implied that Berzin participated in this scheme not out of shared enthusiasm for its prospects, but only because he was ordered to by Zinoviev and the Politburo.[54] Given the losses and defeats his organization had recently suffered in what were, by comparison, much more promising circumstances, Berzin could have entertained little hope that an attempted uprising in Estonia could achieve at best more than local and temporary success.

Estonia in 1924 was a small but politically stable nation, with an overwhelmingly agrarian economy. The peasantry had been largely satisfied by the newly independent regime's land-redistribution policies in 1919–20. There were three main political parties, none of which could have in any meaningful sense been described as "radical." What little industry there was employed relatively few workers and they, for the most part, had little sympathy for the communists. Estonians viewed their larger Soviet neighbor with the reserved suspicion one would expect from a people who until recently had been occupied by a foreign power. The dominant sentiment in the young and culturally homogenous state was nationalism.[55]

There was a small but "very militant" Estonian Communist Party (ECP). By early 1924, the party had 2,000 members, 500 of them in the capital city of Reval. Its small size led it to cooperate with the agricultural and trade union political movements (according to official Comintern policy for small and weak communist parties). Nevertheless, its agitational activities, which appeared more ominous to the Estonian authorities following the Soviet/Comintern adventures in Germany and Bulgaria, led the Estonian authorities to launch a crackdown on the ECP in the spring of 1924; 250 communists were arrested. This was followed by a "show trial" of 149 of them.[56]

Zinoviev probably saw in these events a low-risk opportunity with great promise. If by some stroke of good fortune the small and battered Estonian Communist party could really pull off a coup, then he would gain considerable political capital. Zinoviev may have also won Politburo approval for this plan by arguing that if the whole enterprise collapsed, then the Comintern would still have suffered no great loss; after all, the Estonian authorities were on the brink of destroying the ECP anyway.

The timely connection between the repression of the Estonian communists and Zinoviev's actions is the key to understanding the immediate background for the uprising, for, despite subsequent Soviet claims to the contrary, there was no objective evidence that anything remotely like a "revolutionary situation" existed in Estonia in the fall of 1924. Aino Kuusinen, privy to the innermost Comintern deliberations through her husband, Otto, recalled his opinion that Estonia "certainly did not fulfil Lenin's conditions for revolution: it was politically and economically on the up grade [*sic*], and there was no question of an internal crisis."[57]

Sixty RU officers were dispatched to Reval sometime in the spring of 1924 to organize the uprising. According to Krivitsky, these men were under the command of a Civil War hero named "Zhibur."[58] Unshlikht may again also have been involved; we do know that he later supervised the preparation of the *Razvedupr*'s assessment of the operation.[59] The RU "advisors" in Estonia had meager resources at their disposal. Krivitsky recalled that some 200 men were available.[60] Unshlikht's summary mentioned three "battalions" organized in Reval: the 1st Battalion had 170 men, the 2d Battalion 120, and the 3d Battalion 110, for a total of about 400 men. Some of them had at least basic military training, but the vast majority were almost completely ignorant about arms and tactics, to say nothing of discipline. Little could be done about this, however, given the need to ensure surprise, which was the only effective weapon the RU officers believed the rebels would have.[61]

In late November 1924, at about the same time the "Trial of the 149" concluded, Moscow decided to launch the uprising on 1 December. Badly outnumbered, poorly prepared, and poorly led, the unfortunate revolutionaries quickly ran out of enthusiasm after suffering early reverses. Indeed, if it were not for its tragic aftermath, the Reval Uprising might be remembered primarily as low comedy. Small groups of rebels chased half-dressed police and militia around barracks; others threw grenades without pulling the pins first, or stole tanks only to find that the exits of the tank garages were blocked.[62]

One small group of "rebels," breaking into the barracks of a battalion of garrison troops, tried to persuade the sleepy soldiers that the revolution had come and that they should all join. Peering out into the darkness (it was about 5:30 in the morning), the troops saw no crowds, heard no gunfire, and saw no evidence of revolution. After thoughtfully considering the suggestion of the communists, the soldiers resolved to remain neutral, and went back to bed.[63] The actions of that particular garrison unit were indicative of the response of the people of Reval as a whole: unable to see any sign of a revolution, they also decided to "remain neutral," and went back to bed.

The communists predictably suffered heavy casualties. Various sources claim that somewhere between 150 and 500 were killed during the course of the insurrection. Hundreds, perhaps thousands more, most of whom probably had nothing to do with the attempted coup, were imprisoned or shot over the next few years. Most of the Fourth Department officers, however, seem once again to have escaped to the Soviet Union, including Zhibur, who quietly "reappeared at his desk in the offices of the General Staff."[64]

If, indeed, Zinoviev really assumed that the USSR had nothing to lose from a failed attempt at revolution in Estonia, he was soon proved to be seriously mistaken. Coming at the end of a year filled with diplomatic faux pas and espionage scandals, the Reval Uprising threatened to unravel the tentative progress the USSR was making toward normalizing relations with the rest of the world. The view of many in Moscow following the Reval Uprising was that "Russia was struggling too hard to rearrange her economic and diplomatic relations with the world to be yet further burdened with this Comintern business."[65]

For Zinoviev personally, the Reval Uprising proved costly, especially coming as it did on the heels of the "Zinoviev Letter" scandal in Great Britain (see chapter 3). His stock in the Comintern, which had been steadily dropping since the Hamburg debacle, now fell even more precipitously. By the time of the Fourteenth Party Congress in April 1925, Zinoviev's authority in the Comintern was reduced to that of a figurehead. GPU officers loyal to Stalin had so thoroughly infiltrated the Executive Committee of the Comintern that Zinoviev even found it difficult to communicate with his supporters abroad. Even more ominous for his future, the combination of Comintern fiascos (which were of course really CPSU fiascos) in Germany, Bulgaria, and Estonia provided Stalin with ample ammunition for an attack on Zinoviev and his supporters at the Fourteenth Congress.[66] Stalin argued that Zinoviev's revolutionary adventures were evidence of what Lenin called the "infantile disorder" of "left-wing deviationism." In July 1926, Zinoviev was expelled from the Politburo; by October, Bukharin had replaced him as chairman of the Third International, and Zinoviev had been defeated as a serious rival to Stalin once and for all.[67]

To defeat Trotsky, however, Stalin needed more than a failed coup d'etat in Estonia. With the emergence in the Politburo of a major ideological dispute over Soviet policy in China, the issue of Moscow's support for foreign revolution came to occupy center stage in the intensifying battle for control of the CPSU.

CHINA

Much more significant for the struggle between Stalin and Trotsky than the adventures in the Baltic was the complicated Soviet involvement in China.[68] Throughout the 1920s, the Soviet leadership pursued a policy toward China designed to both normalize diplomatic and economic relations and foster the growth of Soviet influence in the region. The latter objective was to be achieved by influencing key political movements, encouraging the growth and spread of revolutionary ideas and organizations, and, in Mongolia, outright military conquest.

In China, the brief experiment in "republican" government that followed the 1911 revolution against the last imperial dynasty, the Manchus, had collapsed by 1917. Out of the ruins rose dozens of regional "warlords," with power bases rooted in provincial politics and personal armies, who vied for control of what had once been the Chinese Empire with each other and with the remnants of the republican government, the Nationalist party (Kuomintang, or KMT) led by Sun Yat Sen.[69] Isolated diplomatically from the West, Sun saw in Soviet Russia a possible ally and counterweight to "foreign imperialism" in Asia, as well as a possible source of military support against his rivals.[70] Many Bolsheviks, including Lenin, likewise regarded the movement led by the charismatic Sun to be "progressive," if not by any stretch of the imagination "socialist." Some Soviet leaders also envisaged a great, anti-British revolutionary union between Soviet Russia, China, Japan, India, and the rest of "oppressed" Asia.[71]

With the failure of the last major Comintern efforts to bring about revolution in Europe, in China the Politburo saw opportunities it could not ignore. Furthermore, China seemed the perfect base from which to undermine British power in Asia. Many in the Soviet leadership, including Stalin, Zinoviev, and Trotsky, also convinced themselves that if only they could fathom the right approach, they might yet be able to start the world revolution there. Lenin himself argued that a Chinese "nationalist" revolution, directed against the imperialist occupiers (primarily Britain) could trigger similar nationalist uprisings throughout Asia, thereby ultimately contributing to the collapse and destruction of the capitalist empires in Europe.[72] The mistrust and hatred of the British shared by Lenin and Sun was not the only reason for Soviet cooperation with this "bourgeois" Chinese leader. The Chinese Communist Party (CCP) had not been founded until 1921; by 1924 it was still quite small, numbering its members in the hundreds.[73] In contrast, the Kuomintang was large and growing, controlled much of southern China, and had bona fide revolutionary credentials.

An argument soon developed among the Soviet leadership over the role the Chinese communists should play in China. Trotsky argued that the CCP must remain separate from the Kuomintang, that cooperation with this "bourgeois-nationalist party" would fatally compromise the communists, and therefore that the Politburo should build up the forces for social revolution exclusively through the Chinese communists. Stalin, on the other hand, argued that the prospects for a socialist revolution in China in the foreseeable future were unrealistic, and that the Soviets should therefore support the one effective "revolutionary" force in China, the Kuomintang. Stalin's position won out by 1923, although Trotsky continued to oppose it.

By autumn 1923, the Soviet government and the Comintern became effectively allied with the KMT.[74] Sun's chief lieutenant, Chiang Kai-shek, went to Moscow to establish more extensive contacts, and to study at the Frunze Military Academy.[75] In September, Russian "advisors" under the command of Mikhail Borodin began pouring into Kuomintang-controlled southern China. The chief Soviet military advisor was General V. Blücher. Borodin had operational command of the most important advisor groups, while Blücher spent most of his time advising Chiang.[76] The Politburo established a special "Chinese Commission" to supervise and monitor Soviet-Chinese relations. Although technically subordinate to the Comintern, this commission was actually headed by Stalin, through the Central Committee of the CPSU. The executive director of the Chinese Commission was the ubiquitous Iosef Unshlikht, who reported directly to Stalin.[77] The growing size of the mission and the ongoing interdepartmental fighting led the Red Army command in

1925 to establish the "Peking Military Center" (PMC—see chapter 3). These measures did little to end the bickering but at least they brought coherence to Soviet operations in China.

By 1926, relations between Moscow and the Kuomintang were severely strained and getting worse. Sun had died in March 1925. In the struggle for power that followed, Chiang defeated most of his KMT rivals, and in early 1926, in accordance with plans worked out in Moscow, and accompanied by his Red Army advisor, Blücher, began the "Northern Expedition," a series of military operations to expand KMT control to the rest of China. Chiang had been attentive to the conversations that went on around him when he was in Moscow, and had no illusions about the long-term fidelity of either the Russians or the CCP. From 1925 on, KMT security forces began to arrest, interrogate, and torture Chinese communists, in some cases at the very moment Chiang's representatives were being feted by Soviet and Comintern officials in Moscow.[78]

Meanwhile, the Comintern believed Chinese workers were becoming increasingly radicalized. In major industrial centers like Shanghai and Canton, the CCP indeed began growing rapidly in membership and political significance.[79] By July 1925, the Chinese communists managed to take over the local KMT organization in Canton. Ambassador L. Karakhan's warnings to Moscow about Chiang's likely response were rejected; in September, Stalin went so far as to assert that "Karakhan will never understand that Hankow [part of the Wuhan urban complex] will soon become the Chinese Moscow."[80] In March 1926, however, Chiang sent troops into the city who executed several prominent communists.

Stalin's China strategy thereafter came under increasing attack in the Politburo. In May, Zinoviev called for the Chinese communists to quit the Kuomintang.[81] Nevertheless, still publically committed to a policy of total support for Chiang, Moscow suppressed news of Chiang's attacks on the CCP, and upheld the long-standing policy of requiring it to virtually surrender all autonomy to the KMT and follow its directives without question.[82]

As Chiang redirected his efforts once more to the conquest of the northern provinces, the CCP reported to Moscow considerably exaggerated, if not downright falsified, assessments of the growth of revolutionary sentiment. In fact, large disturbances did take place in Shanghai, which had also been the scene of bloody uprisings in October 1926 and February and March 1927.[83] Partly in response to these developments, with Borodin's support, the CCP together with the leftists in the KMT decided in February to establish the seat of Chinese government in Wuchang. Chiang, however, in April declared the new capital to be Nanking, where his headquarters were. His newly organized government significantly failed to include any communists. This was ominous, for the Chinese communists had always held at least one prominent position in the KMT government since the 1922 agreements between Sun and Moscow.

Clearly, Chiang had resolved to rid himself once and for all of the communist albatross around his neck. His security forces began rounding up communists in the north while other troops moved toward CCP strongholds in his rear. Moscow was caught by surprise; too late Soviet and Comintern officials finally saw the writing on the wall, and began denouncing Chiang as a traitor to the revolution.[84] Stalin, amazingly, still refused to admit that his policy in China had been a failure.[85] By now, this had become far more than a matter of personal ego, for his struggle with Trotsky for control of the CPSU had become encapsulated in the argument over Soviet strategy in China. With such high stakes, much like Zinoviev in Estonia, Stalin concluded that there was nothing to lose by trying to force a revolution. Red Army Intelligence was again called upon to organize and prepare an insurrection in a most unlikely place.

It is important to realize the context of Stalin's decision. The year 1927 had not been good for the Soviet Union. In April, Chinese police raided the PMC, seizing thousands of incriminating documents. Diplomatic fiascos involving both the RU and the GPU in Great Britain and France had led those nations to the brink of severing diplomatic relations with Moscow; Britain finally did so in May, and France threatened to do so in June. Similar intrigues threatened the otherwise smooth course of Soviet-German relations, and in July 700 communists were arrested in Berlin. Shortly before in Warsaw, the Soviet ambassador, Pyotr Voikov, an alleged participant in the murders of the tsar and his family, was assassinated by a Russian monarchist. These events led to a "war scare" in Moscow and other European capitals (see chapter 4).[86]

Recently published documents demonstrate that Stalin's first response to the Chinese crisis in the spring of 1927 was, incredibly, to advocate that Moscow sponsor the Wuhan "government" in a military expedition of its own against Chiang. He was willing to provide up to five million rubles for this purpose.[87] As late as July, Stalin continued to hold out hopes that this scheme might save the day. This idea, however, seems to have been opposed even by some of his staunchest supporters, including Voroshilov, and Stalin was eventually forced to consider an alternative.[88]

Furthermore, he also seems to have convinced himself that in China by the summer of 1927 there existed the possibility that a revolution could manipulate the "correlation of forces" (the Marxist-Leninist calculation of the relative global geopolitical strengths of "progressive" and "reactionary" forces) in favor of world socialism. Such a strategy would have the additional benefit of undermining the main enemy, Great Britain. Moreover, the failure of Stalin's policy of supporting Chiang, heavily criticized from the start by Trotsky and Zinoviev, left Stalin politically vulnerable. Even if moving against Chiang did not actually lead to revolution, it would allow Stalin to lay the blame for the failure of his policy on the Chinese communists.[89]

In August and September 1927, Moscow Center sent several more RU officers into China, including Heinz Neumann (a veteran of the Hamburg

Uprising) and Ho Chi Minh.[90] There they joined other Soviet RU and Comintern agents, including Gerhard Eisler and Earl Browder, and set about trying to organize an uprising in Canton, the city in which the CCP and leftist elements of the KMT were strongest.[91] Stalin rationalized that since Canton had a radicalized proletariat, it was possible that a successful uprising there, although led at first perhaps only by relatively weak communist elements, could quickly receive widespread support from oppressed workers in other cities, and even spark mutinies among some of Chiang's troops.[92]

Using an organization similar to that adopted for the uprisings in Europe, the Fourth Department officers together with the communist Kwantung Provincial Committee divided the province into ten "military districts," each with its own command structure, Red Army advisor, and sections for intelligence, agitation, and terrorism. "Red Guard" units, organized in cells of ten men, were subordinate to the military commander in each district until about two weeks before the insurrection, when they were theoretically organized into larger units under specially appointed "military leaders." The total number of men available to start the revolution in Canton was about 3,200.[93]

The Comintern and RU advisors faced some familiar problems in Canton: a serious shortage of weapons, inadequate training, and poor leadership. "The Red Guard hardly had any weapons at all. In the whole of Canton, it had only 29 Mausers and 200 grenades; not a single rifle."[94] The lack of military experience and training was in part a reflection of the usual demands of conspiratorial operations. In this case, however, the situation was aggravated by the fact that few Chinese, especially urban workers, had any military training or experience at all. The *Razvedupr* summary of the Canton insurrection explained that in China "there is no compulsory military service; all Chinese armies are mercenary armies. The Chinese people has a genuine hatred of soldiers. . . . The workers do not go into the army. For this reason, the Chinese working class hardly has any chance to learn the art of war by legal means." This problem also extended to the Red Guard commanders, a particularly ironic situation considering the fact that for years Red Army advisors had been training the elite military cadre of the Kuomintang, which supervised the suppress of the insurrection."[95] Given the scarcity of arms and ammunition, and the strength of the opposition, it seems impossible that even 2,000 hardened veterans of World War I could have succeeded. Chiang and the Kuomintang had some 10,000 troops in and around Canton, and another 50,000 men within two or three days march of the city.[96]

The Chinese communist leadership, in consultation with their *Razvedupr* advisors, decided to strike at 3:30 AM on 11 December 1927. The revolt was to be carried out in three stages. The first was the most crucial: the neutralization of the armed opposition in Canton proper, together with the seizure and distribution of all the weapons stored in the city. Revolutionary cadres would simultaneously proclaim the establishment of the "Canton Commune," and rally and arm the "masses." The second and third stages called for spreading the revolution beyond Canton.

The insurrection began as planned, and at first went surprisingly well. The rebels captured several arms depots, as well as key government buildings and offices, including police stations. Some of the local opposing forces were persuaded to join, or at least remain neutral, and in several pitched battles, the poorly armed and led Chinese revolutionaries initially managed to hold their own. Nevertheless, like all the previous uprisings, this one was doomed from the start. The weapons seized from captured arsenals did not make it into the hands of the perhaps 20,000 workers who expressed sympathy for the rebels; few of them would have known how to use them anyway. A combination of poor leadership and inexperience meant that initial tactical successes could not be exploited or even sustained. Most importantly, however, Chiang's forces, perhaps anticipating the CCP's plans (Chiang had an excellent intelligence network of his own), moved with speed and overwhelming force to crush the rebels. The revolt was soon put down, although isolated resistance continued until the evening of 13 December.

The Fourth Department analysis of the uprising episode claimed that some 1,500 men managed to escape (including apparently, once again, all of the Comintern and *Razvedupr* operatives). Thousands more were not so fortunate. At least 4,000 people were killed within days in a subsequent wave of repression unleashed by Chiang in and around Canton.[97] Stalin, predictably, held the survivors of the CCP responsible for the failure of the "revolution," and the leadership of the party was purged.[98] The way was now cleared for the rise of the next generation of Chinese communist leaders, including Mao Tse-tung and Chou En-lai.

The failure of Stalin's policy in China made Trotsky even more of a threat; "so long as Soviet policy in China had been successful, . . . Trotsky could be tolerated [by Stalin]. . . . Now, when everything collapsed, Trotsky could no longer be put up with. His mere presence was a reproach."[99] In November 1927, almost a month before the climax of Stalin's Chinese policy in the Canton Insurrection, Trotsky was exiled to Kazakhstan. He would never see Moscow again.

Stalin, therefore, managed to turn this crushing defeat into a personal triumph. He now insisted that Party unity in the face of the onslaught of international capitalism was essential. The failure of Soviet strategy in China, combined with the "war scare" and the "threat" of a Trotskyite "conspiracy of the left," paved the way for Stalin's policy of building "socialism in one country" through the collectivization of agriculture, an all-out centrally directed program for rapid industrialization, and major efforts to acquire foreign military and industrial technology by any means possible.[100] These objectives soon found expression in the first Five Year Plan.

The Canton Insurrection had an important impact on the Fourth Department, as well. It was the last time before World War II that the Red Army

Intelligence Directorate became involved in trying to sponsor armed rebellion.[101] The Comintern twice more attempted to start the revolution: in Britain in 1927–28, through the trade unions, and in Germany in the early 1930s, through the German Communist Party. Neither of these efforts, however, involved insurrection; they instead relied on the manipulation of the legitimate political processes of each nation. The Comintern, by the end of the 1920s, had become irrelevant in the power structure of the Soviet Union, and was even more subservient to the *Razvedupr*, and, in some cases, the GPU. A close relationship between the Fourth Department and the Comintern continued. But for the rest of the interwar period, the Red Army used the Comintern, especially the OMS, primarily for agent support and as a source of recruits for its own purposes.

ADVENTURE IN AFGHANISTAN

For several years after the 1920 Treaty of Riga, active military operations continued along the eastern and southern periphery of Soviet Russia, where the Bolsheviks pursued the traditional Russian objectives of subduing the peoples of Central Asia and opposing Great Britain at every opportunity. Red Army troops, in conjunction with the Cheka and *Razvedupr*, fought a series of small but bloody battles against many of the same peoples who had been subdued by the tsars during the previous two centuries. Moscow also cast a covetous eye on Afghanistan and even India, the "jewel in the crown" of the British Empire and the center of British power in the Near East. Both seemed promising new targets in the wake of the Bolshevik Revolution. Indeed, Soviet meddling in India, mostly organized by the notorious Comintern agent Manabendra Roy, proved to be a particularly sensitive issue with the British government and public. Nevertheless, Moscow's schemes in India produced little in the way of concrete results until the 1950s. In Afghanistan, however, the Fourth Department almost succeeded in creating the first Soviet client state.

Soviet encroachment on Afghan territory must be understood first of all in the context of Russian history, including the rivalry in the Near and Far East between Russia and Great Britain that had developed during the nineteenth century. Bolshevik aggression against Kabul began in 1924, when Soviet troops disguised in civilian clothes seized control of an Afghan island in the Amu Daria River, which constitutes much of the border between the USSR and Afghanistan.[102] The Red Army promptly fortified the island, and it almost certainly served as a major staging area for clandestine operations in Afghanistan thereafter. This annexation also prompted intense anti-Soviet feelings throughout the country, particularly in Kabul.

A few years later, a series of revolts broke out among the various Afghan tribes when the Amir, Amanullah, after visiting both London and Moscow, resolved in 1928 to embark on a course of westernization that included both legal and parliamentary reforms. In the south, clans hostile to Amanullah seized upon this as a pretext for rebellion. At about the same time, a peasant uprising further north began under the leadership of a charismatic deserter from the Afghan Army called Batcha Sakao (the "Water Carrier").

According to OGPU defector G. S. Agabekov, a dispute broke out in Moscow between the INO and the Commissariat for Foreign Affairs over which faction to support. The chekists argued that backing the "proletarian" Batcha Sakao was a means toward establishing communist power in Kabul (thereby, incidentally, demonstrating their imperfect mastery of Marxism). The Bolshevik diplomats, however, many of whom came from the prewar aristocracy and still tended to view international affairs as a "Great Game" between competing powers, advocated supporting the Amir as the surest way of striking a blow at British imperialism. The Amir, they believed, was predisposed to meddle with the anti-British populace of northwestern India; this in turn would cause many headaches in London.

Something about the Byzantine nature of the *Narkomindel*'s view must have appealed to Stalin, for he supported the Commissariat of Foreign Affairs.[103] Consequently, Stalin personally directed the *Razvedupr* to subdue Sakao's rebellion and restore the lawful, pro-British monarch, Amanullah, to the throne. The Fourth Department organized a small force in Turkestan of about 800 men from "the best units of Tashkent" (probably partisan cadres). These troops were liberally supplied with machine guns and supported by artillery and aircraft. The military attaché in Kabul, an RU officer named "Primakov," was in command. To give the expedition some appearance of legitimacy, the Amir's representative in Moscow, Goulam Nahi Khan, was made the nominal leader of the expedition.

Sometime in the spring or early summer of 1928, Primakov's column, disguised in Afghan army uniforms, crossed into Afghanistan. Their abundant firepower allowed them to defeat Batcha Sakao's forces, which were encountered in detail, with little difficulty; the combination of machine guns, artillery, and aircraft worked great slaughter among the tribal warriors. The climax of the campaign occurred in a battle fought near the town of Tashkurgan in which Sakao's forces were routed; Agabekov claims 3,000 of them were killed. Primakov and Goulam paused to consolidate their position and reorganize for the final march on Kabul.

Meanwhile, Moscow discovered that the Amir, apparently possessing little faith in Soviet good intentions, had fled to India. The Soviets also learned, mostly from radio decryptions provided by the joint OGPU/RU signals intelligence unit, the *Spets otdel* (see chapter 4), that their attempt to disguise the RU expedition as an Afghan force had fooled no one. Moscow began to sense a propaganda disaster in the making, not to mention a possible confrontation with the British. Primakov, with Kabul in his grasp, was ordered to return to Turkestan, and it was Batcha Sakao who marched triumphantly into Kabul after all. His "reign" as the new king of Afghanistan was short lived, however. Within the year Kabul fell to forces led by Nadir Khan, the former Afghan minister to Paris. Nadir captured the "Water Carrier" and had him promptly executed.[104]

The USSR was, as the Commissariat of Foreign Affairs had predicted, briefly the target of bad publicity; much of the international community denounced the immense hypocrisy of the "workers' state" attempting to destroy a peasant revolt by restoring a monarch to power. On the whole, however, other than reinforcing Afghan loathing for the Russians, Moscow suffered little long-term damage to its interests in the region. Indeed, the Red Army gained priceless experience in the use of small covert expeditions to achieve strategic objectives, which would prove very valuable in the years to come.

LEARNING FROM FAILURE: *ARMED INSURRECTION* AND PARTISAN WARFARE

In 1928, following the last gasp of the policy of promoting armed revolution in China, the Red Army General Staff commissioned a collection of essays on the insurrections of the previous five years. An earlier, smaller monograph, called *The Road to Victory: The Art of Armed Insurrection*, was already being used in Red Army and Comintern schools. O. Piatnitsky, head of the OMS, explained to *Razvedupr* officer Erich Wollenberg, who was charged with editing the planned collection, that "now was the right moment to publish a popular work on armed insurrection, aimed at a wider public of communists and sympathizers."[105] The timing also coincided with the growth of special partisan schools.

The completed work combined analytical essays with carefully edited RU after-action reports and was entitled *Armed Insurrection*. It contained accounts written by firsthand participants, including Unshlikht, Wollenberg, Kippenberger, and Ho Chi Minh. Taken as a whole, the essays are remarkably straightforward and objective, even to the point of occasionally criticizing Stalin's policies, for example, those on China.[106] The fact that they were originally published in German not only demonstrates once more the prevelance of native speakers of that tongue among RU cadres, but also shows the continuing importance of Germany for the international revolution.[107]

Armed Insurrection also contained an essay by Mikhail Tukhachevsky, "Field Regulations for Armed Insurrection." Tukhachevsky had long been involved in the theoretical development of revolutionary warfare, at least as early as the Soviet-Polish War. In 1920–21, he had pressed the Red Army General Staff to create an "International Communist General Staff" (the proposal was rejected). The offensive possibilities of partisan warfare grew in importance in response to the increased capability of the Red Army to conduct sustained offensive operations. Subsequently, the development of the operational concept of "Deep Battle," expressed in its mature form in the *Provisional Field*

Regulations of the RKKA [the Worker's and Peasants' Red Army] for 1936, called for a sophisticated assault on a potential enemy's "rear area," including sabotage, assassinations, propaganda, and the promotion of class warfare—that is, fostering revolution. Indeed, Soviet military doctrine eventually defined victory in terms of social revolution in the enemy state.[108]

By the late 1920s, Moscow's attempts to carry the revolution beyond the first workers' state had clearly failed. Meanwhile, old foes along the borders, particularly Poland, continued to grow in strength. RU threat assessments repeatedly focused on the danger of war with the "coalition of western bordering states," a war that would, until the Red Army substantially increased in size and technological capabilities, almost certainly be fought in its initial phase on Soviet soil. The prospects for and likely course of this conflict were most fully described by the RU assessment published in 1928 known as *The Future War* (see chapter 7). This view led the Red Army to reassess its conceptions about war and revolution in the enemy's rear. In a real sense, what emerged from the mid-1920s was a partisan strategy that was basically defensive, reflecting the increasing if unwelcome consensus that the world revolution was not after all destined to happen in the foreseeable future.

Consequently, starting in 1926, engineering units, technical troops, and security units from the RU and Cheka were placed at the disposal of the Intelligence Sections (ROs) of the Ukrainian, Leningrad, and Belorussian Military Districts (MDs). In each MD, preparations for active partisan operations seem to have been supervised by commissions chaired by Fourth Department partisan specialists who, in turn, answered directly to the district commander.[109] The task of these commissions was to prepare for war in the rear areas of an invading army.[110] In practice, this involved a wide range of measures, including recruiting, organizing, and training partisan cadres from the local villages, and building, stocking, and camouflaging numerous caches of arms, ammunition, medicine, food, and clothing. These efforts were undertaken not only in the military districts themselves, but also along the frontiers of adjacent countries, including Poland, the Baltic states, and Romania, and reflected the fact that by 1928, RU analysts had concluded that the western coalition's most likely axis of attack would be a combined thrust by the main body of the Polish and Romanian armies south of the Pripyet Marshes into Ukraine.[111]

These preparations were essentially complete by 1933. A total of around 9,000 men and women were organized into detachments led by Red Army officers in staffs modeled on those used for the insurrections in Germany, Bulgaria, Estonia, and China of conventional army and corps-level field headquarters.[112] In some areas, more arms and supplies were cached than "the partisans in those areas actually received during all of World War II."[113] In Ukraine, partisan cadres were also organized into "a significant number of smaller, highly maneuverable detachments and sabotage groups," reflecting Red Army plans to coordinate operational maneuvering abilities with partisan attacks, much as Tukhachevsky sought to do during his advance on Warsaw in 1920.[114] Extensive preparations were also made for conducting "barrier operations," designed to slow an enemy's advance and channel it into specially prepared "killing zones," and establishing special teams of railroad saboteurs prepared to disrupt rail lines to a depth of (in the Ukrainian MD) 180 to 200 kilometers from the border.[115]

In the judgment of one of their architects, I. G. Starinov, if these preparations made in the years between 1928 and 1931 had been maintained and supported until June 1941, the Nazi invasion would have been all but strangled in its infancy.[116] This, however, was not meant to be. Even as they neared completion, they ran head on into Stalin's more immediate objective of collectivizing agriculture and crushing the "kulaks." Soon thereafter, Stalin's paranoia led to the effective dismantling of most of what was still left in the course of his purge of the Red Army. The "kulaks," in effect the bulk of the productive peasantry, were not coincidentally also the backbone of the partisan cadres, and their destruction meant the virtual end of any effective prepared partisan organization, as well.[117]

Theoretical development and training for partisan warfare progressed considerably in the 1920s. By 1928, the OGPU and RU had each established a number of "special covert partisan schools" throughout the Soviet Union. These schools relied on expert Red Army instructors who were veterans of partisan warfare and all aspects of covert operations.[118] Most of the graduates were assigned to the partisan "maneuver groups" or underground cadres being organized in the border military districts. Some of them, however, went on to become Red Army intelligence officers and agents, serving throughout Europe and the Near and Far East.

Except for the major Fourth Department training center in Moscow, the schools were all quite small. The OGPU schools usually processed between five and twelve students at a time, and Red Army schools trained between thirty and thirty-five.[119] There were two basic types of schools, those that prepared cadres for underground, covert, and sabotage operations; and those that trained personnel for "partisan maneuver detachments." These were partisan bands assigned to operate in the rear of the enemy but in close cooperation with regular Red Army forces. Both the OGPU and the RU operated the former type, although the second was probably exclusively used by the Red Army. Although some of the smaller underground schools may have trained foreign communists destined to carry out covert work in their own countries, most of the foreign cadres seem to have been trained at the prestigious Swierczewski School in Moscow. The students at the smaller underground sabotage schools were chosen almost exclusively from the ranks of the CPSU or the *Komsomol.*

The Swierczewski School in Moscow was named after its founder and long-time director, Karol Swierczewski, a Polish Red Army Intelligence veteran known for his success as a Red partisan commander in the Civil War.

Students at this school included prominent figures in the international communist movement, such as Wilhelm Pieck, Palmiro Togliatti, and Maurice Thorez, as well as several members of the Chinese Communist party. Lecturers at this center were some of the most senior and experienced officers in the Red Army, including Berzin and Blücher.[120]

CONCLUSION

The pursuit of armed insurrection as a mechanism for "jump starting" national or even regional revolution was a strategy of desperation resulting from the internal political struggle in the CPSU and ideological myopia. Its chief advocate, Grigorii Zinoviev, was destroyed by its failure in Germany, Bulgaria, and Estonia, just as surely as Trotsky, even though opposed to the Soviet China policy, was destroyed by its failure there. In their defeat, Stalin triumphed.

Red Army Intelligence, on balance, emerged stronger from these adventures, as well. The intense organizational effort required to prepare for insurrection produced networks and leaders well suited for the RU's other clandestine missions. And almost all of the casualties were suffered by the hapless indigenous forces and civilians who bore the brunt of the fighting and the inevitable reprisals.

The RU also learned much about partisan warfare. By observing firsthand its strengths and weaknesses under the severest circumstances, Red Army leaders enhanced their appreciation of the strategic potential of deep operations in the enemy's rear areas. This was of immediate relevance to their defensive preparations for repelling the anticipated capitalist onslaught on its western borders. But it also proved of immense value in other situations to follow, including the Spanish Civil War, the Great Patriotic War, and the Cold War.

NOTES

1. Krivitsky, *I Was Stalin's Agent*, p. 64.

2. Dmitri Volkogonov, *Lenin: A New Biography*, ed. and trans. by Harold Shukman (New York: The Free Press, 1994), pp. 399–400.

3. Krivitsky, *I Was Stalin's Agent*, p. 55.

4. Gustav Hilger and Alfred G. Meyer, *The Incompatible Allies: A Memoir of German-Soviet Relations, 1918–1941* (New York: MacMillan, 1953), p. 121.

5. Ruth Fischer, *Stalin and German Communism: A Study in the Origins of the State Party*, preface by Sidney B. Fay (Cambridge: Harvard University Press, 1948), pp. 305–306, 311–313.

6. Hilger and Meyer, *Incompatible Allies*, p. 120.

7. Ibid., pp. 312–313.

8. Although she was not an actual eyewitness, Larissa Reissner provides the most colorful, and one of the more accurate, accounts in *Hamburg at the Barricades, and*

Other Writings on Weimar Germany, trans. and ed. by Richard Chappell (London: Pluto Press, 1977). See also Richard Krebs [Jan Valtin], *Out of the Night* (New York: Alliance Book Corporation, 1940); Werner T. Angress, *Stillborn Revolution: The Communist Bid for Power in Germany, 1921–1923* (Princeton: Princeton University Press, 1963); and A. Neuberg, *Armed Insurrection*, trans. by Quintin Hoare (London: NLB, 1970), chap. 4 (although this essay was written by a participant).

9. For the Comintern's role in the Hamburg Uprising, see Neuberg, *Armed Insurrection*, pp. 12–18, chap. 4.

10. Krivitsky, *I Was Stalin's Agent*, p. 61.

11. Suvorov, *Spetsnaz*, p. 15. Suvorov cites as a source for this contention B. Bazhanov, "Memoirs of a Secretary to Stalin," *Tretya volna* (1980): 67–69.

Most sources either claim that Unshlikht was a chekist throughout his career or are uncertain about when he made the crossover to Red Army Intelligence; see, for example, Leggett, *Cheka*, p. 273. Suvorov, however, clearly states that Unshlikht was Berzin's deputy director as of 1923. Unshlikht's membership in the *Razvedupr* is also supported by the context of remarks by Elisabeth Poretsky, *Our Own People* (e.g., p. 75).

12. The specifics on the RU's involvement in the Hamburg Uprising are, except when otherwise noted, from Krivitsky, *I Was Stalin's Agent*, pp. 55–64.

13. This "Intelligence Section" was probably the organization required by the OMS to be present in every Communist party for liaison work with the Red Army.

14. Stern later served in Spain as "Emilio Kleber" under Berzin in command of an international brigade. He was murdered during the purges; see Neuberg, *Armed Insurrection*, p. 16.

15. Neuberg, *Armed Insurrection*, p. 13; Suvorov, *Spetsnaz*, p. 15.

16. Krivitsky, *I Was Stalin's Agent*, pp. 60–61.

17. Fischer, *Stalin*, p. 319.

18. Krivitsky, *I Was Stalin's Agent*, pp. 60–61.

19. Dallin, *Soviet Espionage*, p. 73.

20. There were also plans for trying to recruit or otherwise use defecting *Reichswehr* officers; see Fischer, *Stalin*, pp. 319, 321.

21. Poretsky, *Our Own People*, p. 57.

22. Neuberg, *Armed Insurrection*, p. 13.

23. Krivitsky, *I Was Stalin's Agent*, p. 61.

24. Ibid., pp. 60–61; Hilger and Meyer, *Incompatible Allies*, p. 140. Apparently no serious attempts were made on the lives of these three men.

25. Fischer, *Stalin*, p. 320.

26. Krivitsky, *I Was Stalin's Agent*, p. 61.

27. For a summary of the likely reasons for Remmele's delay, see Angress, *Stillborn Revolution*, pp. 444–446 fn. 57.

28. Neuberg, *Armed Insurrection*, p. 13 fn. 9.

29. Reissner, *Hamburg*, pp. 11–12; Neuberg, *Armed Insurrection*, p. 12.

30. Fischer, *Stalin*, p. 339.

31. Neuberg, *Armed Insurrection*, p. 12, also see chap. 4.

32. See Angress, *Stillborn Revolution*, pp. 450–451 fn. 60.

33. Krivitsky, *I Was Stalin's Agent*, pp. 62–63.

34. Hilger and Meyer, *Incompatible Allies*, p. 124.

35. Ibid., pp. 138–144.

36. Ibid., p. 124.

37. Krivitsky, *I Was Stalin's Agent*, p. 64.

38. Poretsky, *Our Own People*, p. 58.

39. Nollau, *International Communism*, p. 86.

40. Poretsky, *Our Own People*, pp. 57–59.

41. Fischer, *Stalin*, pp. 309–310. There is for all intents and purposes no western scholarship on the Bulgarian Uprising of 1923.

42. Robert J. McIntyre, *Bulgaria: Politics, Economics and Society* (London: Pinter Publishers, 1988), pp. 29–37.

43. Ibid., pp. 36–37.

44. Fischer, *Stalin*, pp. 307–311.

45. Ibid., p. 311.

46. One of these RU officers may have been Ignace Reiss. This is suggested by the context of his widow's description of a Fourth Department source in Bulgaria, Dr. Alexander Lykov; see Poretsky, *Our Own People*, p. 66.

47. Fischer, *Stalin*, p. 317.

48. Although they apparently did have a few field pieces, see Ivan Andreyev, "In the Centre of the September Uprising," in *Memories of Georgi Dimitrov* (Sofia: Sofia Press, 1972), p. 58.

49. Ibid.

50. McIntyre, *Bulgaria*, p. 39.

51. There is some evidence that Fourth Department officers may have been involved in the notorious bombing of the Svetya Nedelya Cathedral in Sofia on 16 April 1925. See Fischer, *Stalin*, pp. 465–470; Krivitsky, *I Was Stalin's Agent*, p. 66; and Suvorov, *Spetsnaz*, pp. 16–17. If so, it is possible they may have had some connection to the mysterious RU operative "Boris," who directed "terroristic acts" and assassinations in Bulgaria in 1922 under the cover of the Soviet Red Cross Mission; see Corson and Crowley, *New KGB*, p. 296.

52. Fischer, *Stalin*, p. 463; Krivitsky, *I Was Stalin's Agent*, pp. 64–65; and Neuberg *Armed Insurrection*, p. 11.

53. Unshlikht noted that in April 1924 the Central Committee of the CPSU decided "to orient itself towards the preparation of an armed insurrection [in Estonia]." Unshlikht, "The Reval Uprising," in Neuberg, *Armed Insurrection*, p. 63.

54. Krivitsky, *I Was Stalin's Agent*, p. 65.

55. Fischer, *Stalin*, p. 464. The Reval/Talinin Uprising has been all but ignored by western scholars; indeed, as is the case for Bulgaria, little academic literature, at least in English, exists on this period of Estonian history.

56. Fischer, *Stalin*, p. 464; Neuberg, *Armed Insurrection*, p. 61 fn. 1-C, and p. 63.

57. Kuusinen, *Before and after Stalin*, p. 66; Neuberg, *Armed Insurrection*, p. 11.

58. Krivitsky, *I Was Stalin's Agent*, p. 65.

59. Neuberg, *Armed Insurrection*, p. 11.

60. Krivitsky, *I Was Stalin's Agent*, p. 65.

61. Neuberg, *Armed Insurrection*, pp. 64, 66.

62. Ibid., pp. 70–71, 77–78.

63. Ibid., pp. 74–75.

64. Krivitsky, *I Was Stalin's Agent*, p. 64.

65. Fischer, *Stalin*, p. 465.

66. Ibid., p. 439; Nollau, *International Communisim*, p. 180.

67. Ibid.; Neuberg, *Armed Insurrection*, pp. 11–12.

68. This is the contention of Fischer in *Stalin*, pp. 573–582): David J. Dallin in *The Rise of Russia in Asia* (New Haven: Yale University Press, 1949), pp. 217–223; and Mikhail Heller and Aleksandr Nekrich in *Utopia in Power: The History of the Soviet Union from 1917 to the Present*, trans. by Phyllis B. Carlos (New York: Summit Books, 1986), p. 212. Dmitri Volkogonov almost completely ignores this issue, stressing instead other fundamental differences between Stalin and Trotsky in *Stalin: Triumph and Tragedy*, trans. by Harold Shukman (New York: Grove Weidenfeld, 1991), chap. 10.

The most comprehensive treatments of the subject of Soviet policy in China in the 1920s are Dallin, *Russia in Asia*, and C. Martin Wilbur, *The Nationalist Revolution in China, 1923–1928* (Cambridge: Cambridge University Press, 1983). Two useful studies of Soviet–Chinese relations in this period are F. Gilbert Chan and Thomas H. Etzold, eds., *China in the 1920s* (New York: New Viewpoints, 1976), especially chaps. 1, 2, and 4; and Dallin, *Russia in Asia*, chaps. 7–9.

69. See Edward A. McCord, *The Power of the Gun: The Emergence of Modern Chinese Warlordism* (Berkeley: University of California Press, 1993).

70. See C. Martin Wilbur and Julie Lien-ying How, eds., *Documents on Communism, Nationalism, and Soviet Advisors in China, 1918–1927: Papers Seized in the 1927 Peking Raid* (New York: Columbia University Press, 1956), pp. 138–139.

71. Dallin, *Russia in Asia*, p. 209.

72. In 1922 Lenin asserted that "the revolutionary movements that are on the rise in India and China are already being drawn into the revolutionary struggle." Revolution in China, therefore, would be a more or less logical extension of the theory of colonial revolution developed by Lenin in "Imperialism: The Last Stage of Capitalism." See Dallin, *Russia in Asia*, p. 203.

73. Voitinskii played a leading role in organizing the Chinese Communist Party in 1920; see Arif Dirlik, *The Origins of Chinese Communism* (New York: Oxford University Press, 1989), pp. 191–192.

74. This policy did not preclude the CPSU's support of other warlords for its own purposes. See, for example, the career of the "Christian" warlord, Feng Yu-Xiang, as described in Dallin, *Russia in Asia*, pp. 225–226; Krivitsky, *I Was Stalin's Agent*, p. 77; and N. Mitarevsky, *World Wide Soviet Plots* (Tientsin, China: Tientsin Press, n.d.), pp. 18–21, 34. Mitarevsky's true identity is unknown. Most probably he was a "White" émigré. He was a member of the "Commission for the Translation and Compilation" set up by the Peking Metropolitan Police, and perhaps was in the employ of British security (MI5). Although this monograph has no publication date, Wilbur and How conclude on the basis of internal evidence that it was produced in late 1927, and that it is one of the better collections of this material; Wilbur and How, *Documents on Communism*, p. 566.

75. Nollau, *International Communism*, p. 100; Dallin, *Russia in Asia*, pp. 218–219.

76. For more on Blücher, see Krivitsky, *I Was Stalin's Agent*, pp. 76–77; Neuberg, *Armed Insurrection*, pp. 18–19 fn. 13; Dallin, *Russia in Asia*, pp. 212–216; and Dan N. Jacobs, "Soviet Russia and Chinese Nationalism in the 1920s," in Chan and Etzold, *China in the 1920s*, pp. 38–54.

77. Dallin, *Russia in Asia*, p. 227.

78. See, for example, the amazing career of Hu Hanming, one of Chiang's generals in Canton; ibid., p. 224.

79. Neuberg, *Armed Insurrection*, pp. 105–108.

80. Lih, Naumov, and Khlevniuk, *Stalin's Letters*, Letter 28, p. 130.

81. Ibid., Letter 17, p. 111.

82. Fischer, *Stalin*, p. 576. As Fischer notes, Trotsky singled out this instance for an attack on the hypocrisy of Stalin's policy in China; ibid., fn. 6. It was also at this time, the spring of 1926, that the Kuomintang was made a "sympathizing member" party of the Comintern.

83. Dallin, *Russia in Asia*, pp. 226–227; Neuberg, *Armed Insurrection*, pp. 106–108, 135–150. There is no evidence that either the Comintern or the RU had any role in these "uprisings."

84. Nollau, *International Communism*, p. 103; Dallin, *Russia in Asia*, pp. 227–228.

85. Lih, Naumov, and Khlevniuk, *Stalin's Letters*, Letter 33, 27 June 1926, p. 137.

86. Andrew and Gordievsky, *KGB*, pp. 87–88; Fischer, *Stalin*, pp. 577–582.

87. Lih, Naumov, Khlevniuk, *Stalin's Letters*, Letter 32, 24 June 1927, p. 136; Letter 33, 27 June 1927, pp. 136–137.

88. Ibid., Letter 36, 9 July 1927, p. 140.

89. Nollau, *International Communism*, p. 104; Dallin, *Russia in Asia*, pp. 230–233.

90. Ho was very likely one of the chief writers of the RU's after-action assessment of the Canton and Shanghai uprisings; see Neuberg, *Armed Insurrection*, pp. 18–20, 22.

91. Nollau, *International Communism*, pp. 101–104. Browder, future head of the Communist Party of the United States (CPUSA), was probably used primarily for his U.S. passport, since the Soviets had a low regard for his clandestine abilities; see Krivitsky, *I Was Stalin's Agent*, pp. 74–75. Bukharin, Zinoviev's successor as chief of the Comintern, once observed to Mikhail Trilisser, head of the INO through much of the 1920s, that "in Komintern's view American passports were the best for travel abroad"; see Agabekov, *OGPU*, p. 198.

92. Neuberg, *Armed Insurrection*, pp. 108–113.

93. Ibid., p. 115; Dallin, *Soviet Espionage*, p. 74.

94. Neuberg, *Armed Insurrection*, p. 114.

95. Ibid., pp. 115–117.

96. Ibid., pp. 113–114, 126.

97. Ibid., pp. 117–122. This source gives the number of dead as 4,000 (p. 122). Krivitsky claims the number was 6,000 in his *I Was Stalin's Agent*, p. 78.

98. Dallin, *Russia in Asia*, p. 233.

99. Ibid., p. 232.

100. Dallin explicitly links these changes in policy to the failure of the Chinese revolution in his *Russia in Asia*, p. 232.

101. However, Stalin apparently contemplated having the Fourth Department organize an uprising in Manchuria in 1929, the principal objective of which would be to secure Harbin (see chapter 5).

102. Agabekov, *OGPU*, p. 70.

103. In fairness to the Soviet diplomats, it must also be noted that "nobody at Moscow [*sic*] thought Batcha Sakao could maintain himself in power for long"; ibid., p. 165.

104. Ibid., pp. 167–170.

105. Neuberg, *Armed Insurrection*, p. 9.

106. Ibid., p. 20.

107. Dallin, *Soviet Espionage*, p. 29. Interestingly enough, this was also true for RU operations in the United States, at least as late as the 1930s; see Whittaker Chambers, *Witness* (Washington, D.C.: Regnery Gateway, 1980), p. 287.

108. For background on the early development of Soviet operational art and doctrine, see Jacob W. Kipp, *Mass, Mobility, and the Red Army's Road to Operational Art, 1918–1936* (Ft. Leavenworth, Kans.: Soviet Army Studies Office [hereafter cited as SASO], U.S. Army Combined Arms Center [hereafter cited as U.S. Army CAC], 1987); idem, *Lenin and Clausewitz: The Militarization of Marxism, 1914–1921* (Ft. Leavenworth, Kans.: SASO, U.S. Army CAC, 1988); Harriet Fast Scott and William F. Scott, *Soviet Military Doctrine* (Boulder, Colo.: Westview Press, 1988), pp. 5–15; and Vitaly Rapoport and Yuri Alexeev, *High Treason: Essays on the History of the Red Army, 1918–1938*, trans. by Bruce Adams, ed. by Vladimir G. Treml (Durham: Duke University Press, 1985), pp. 127–138.

109. Starinov's book is based on several of his Russian works, including *Miny zhdut svoevo chasa* (Mines Await their Hour) (Moscow: Voennoe izdatel'stvo Ministerstva Oborony SSSR, 1964). Almost as valuable as Starinov's account is the introductory material provided by Robert Suggs, an authority on Soviet special operations.

110. Starinov, *Abyss*, p. 28; see also Starinov, *Miny zhdut*, pp. 20–21.

111. Starinov, *Abyss*, pp. 51–52. On projected lines of attack, see Leonard, *Kremlin's Secret Soldiers*, pp. 363–366.

112. Starinov, *Abyss*, p. 51.

113. Ibid.

114. Ibid.

115. Ibid., pp. 29, 52–53.

116. Ibid., p. 53.

117. Ibid., p. 55. For a discussion of the effects of collectivization on the partisan cadres, see Leonard, *Kremlin's Secret Soldiers*, pp. 96–98.

118. Starinov provides a partial list of the literature used in partisan training from 1929–1934 in *Abyss* appendix B, pp. 367–368. It is interesting to note that he omits Neuberg, *Armed Insurrection*.

119. Starinov, *Abyss*, pp. 36–37. Unless otherwise noted, all information on the Red Army's partisan warfare schools comes from ibid., pp. 35–42.

120. Pieck, Togliatti, and Thorez subsequently were all prominent in the postwar communist leadership in East Germany, Italy, and France, respectively. Swierczewski later served under Berzin in Spain as "General Walter," and commanded Polish troops raised from POWs during the Great Patriotic War. He was murdered in 1947, perhaps on orders of the NKVD as part of a new purge of Polish officers. Starinov claims that Ernest Hemingway's character "General Golz" in *For Whom the Bell Tolls* was based on Swierczewski; ibid., p. 35 fn. 2, p. 58.

CHAPTER 3

Espionage, 1921–1927

Russia must be saved from war. For this purpose the Soviet Union is compelled to build up her armed forces and protect herself from military assaults. The Soviet Union must also be enabled to fulfill her five-year plans, thus to become economically independent of German industry. . . . It is the task of KPD members to find out in the places where they are working, what kind of machinery and instruments are used, as well as other details.

—Instructions of RU officer "Georg" to his agent
network in Bitterfeld, February 1931[1]

"Georg's" explanation of the objectives of his network at the I. G. Farben plant in Bitterfeld, Germany, also succinctly describes the relationship between Soviet espionage and national policy. The two were inseparably intertwined on every level. The fundamental goal of both was to ensure the survival of the workers' state in what seemed from Moscow's viewpoint to be an increasingly hostile world. This goal in turn could be achieved through two strategies: promotion of world revolution, and building up the material defenses of the Soviet state. Although characterized by some as a conflict between the mutually exclusive policies of "permanent revolution" and "socialism in one state," from the perspective of Stalin and the Fourth Department, these two strategies were in fact quite complementary.

For the Fourth Department and the Comintern, which became increasingly subordinate to the RU throughout the 1920s, the conceptual difference between espionage and partisan warfare was not at first entirely distinct. In the early years, operatives like John LeCarré's "George Smiley" were rare in Soviet service, if they existed at all. Instead, the exuberance of revolutionary fervor determined the Soviet approach to intelligence work. This tended to exacerbate an inherent amateurism resulting in part from the belief that class origins and ideological commitment were more important than "bourgeois" professionalism.

By the mid-1920s, however, the shortcomings of this view, exemplified by scandals like the "Zinoviev Letter" affair, became apparent to many in the Fourth Department. Not coincidentally, efforts to regularize, centralize, and professionalize intelligence work gathered momentum as Zinoviev and the Comintern lost status and power and as "permanent revolution" gave way to "socialism in one state." Nevertheless, the Soviet perspective on historical development, the international environment in which Moscow's intelligence services had to function, and the traditions of conspiracy and revolution shared by the leading figures of the Fourth Department and the Comintern ensured that Soviet espionage would continue to bear the stamp of revolution.

This proved simultaneously to be both the RU's greatest strength and its most serious weakness. The cause of the workers' state inspired a large constituency of workers, intellectuals, journalists, leftists, and the dispossessed. As we have seen, the most important sources of recruits for espionage were the various indigenous communist parties. No matter where they came from, however, they came. With rare exceptions, like in Poland, Japan, and perhaps Great Britain, the RU never had a shortage of potential agents. Their very numbers made up for their lack of training. It might take the hard work of ten such operatives to equal the value of one well trained professional, but there would always be another ten.

At the same time, the emphasis on quantity over quality led to frequent clashes with police. Overall security was very poor, and through the mid-1920s networks were lucky if they functioned effectively for one or two years. Only the naiveté of western governments, which could neither conceive of peacetime espionage on such a scale nor see any real threat in the scores of seemingly small-scale intelligence networks constantly being exposed, made this strategy so profitable for so long, although it also occasionally led to disaster, like the destruction of RU networks in the Baltic states in 1920.[2] On balance, recruiting sources en masse proved both expedient and profitable during the early 1920s, even though "gradually quality began to creep into the work of the GRU."[3] Nonetheless, eventually the carelessness of Soviet agents began to cross the thresholds of national patience, and in the spring of 1927 governments around the world began cracking down on Soviet intelligence. A series of police raids on major espionage centers in Peking, London, Paris, and Berlin led to a serious diplomatic crisis, the "war scare."

EARLY AGENT OPERATIONS

One of the Fourth Department's fundamental important tasks was to acquire information about foreign military, industrial, and scientific developments. This, of course, has always been a major priority of military intelligence. In the case of the Soviet Union in the mid-1920s, however, there were three unique imperatives behind this mission. First, the conspiratorial worldview held by the Bolsheviks led them to prefer espionage to the more "legitimate" study of open sources.[4] Second, Moscow's early diplomatic isolation precluded the possibility of gathering information through more conventional diplomatic channels. And third, as we have seen, the Russian army historically favored espionage as the primary means of obtaining intelligence.

In the early 1920s, the Soviet Union had three major organizations responsible for foreign espionage: the Cheka's INO, the Comintern's OMS, and the Red Army's Fourth Department. Intending to establish operational boundaries, the Politburo laid down a jurisdictional line between the INO and the Fourth Department by assigning the RU responsiblity for gathering technical and scientific intelligence. It was directed to recruit "engineers, specialists, and others who had unique or technical information."[5] The chekists were supposed to concentrate on political intelligence, focusing on emigré and "counter-revolutionary" organizations abroad. In practice, these restrictions were frequently ignored, although technical espionage by the Cheka and its successors never remotely approached the efforts of the *Razvedupr* in scope or success. Until it underwent the bloody purge of the late 1930s, the RU continued to provide superior political intelligence, as well, even though it played no part in Soviet penetration operations targeted against the large Russian community abroad.

In the first few years after the Bolshevik Revolution, the major obstacle to Soviet espionage was the diplomatic isolation of the USSR. The intelligence organs as a result were forced to rely upon elaborate underground organizations known as "fronts." The Comintern established many of the first communist networks and fronts around the world, and many *Razvedupr* and INO residencies built upon these foundations. The RU, however, pioneered the use of commercial fronts (i.e., businesses) for the purposes of espionage, and this strategy was almost certainly the brainchild of Yan Berzin.[6]

Agent networks were directed by RU and Comintern officers using aliases derived from forged or stolen identity papers. This kind of intelligence organization came to be known in Soviet parlance as an "illegal residency." Communications between illegal residencies and Fourth Department headquarters ("Moscow Center") were frequently problematic, since, for security reasons, Soviet intelligence at the time did not use short wave radio.[7] The most secure form of communication was by courier, even though this too was always vulnerable to detection by the authorities, especially in the absence of diplomatic status.

Fronts often were initially set up with funds obtained through the sale of property confiscated from the Russian aristocracy, including some of the imperial crown jewels. A number of well-informed sources support this assertion, including Andrew and Gordievsky as well as Suvorov.[8] Suvorov also claimed that Nicholas II's stamp collection was sold to raise funds for espionage. Elisabeth Poretsky, however, insisted that the crown jewels were never sold, and maintained that the jewels the Soviets actually sold "were much less valuable and in their inexperienced hands brought in very little."[9]

Among the earliest RU fronts were a series of small shops opened up in the early 1920s, first in Germany and then in France, Great Britain, Canada, the United States, and China, and known as the "Mrachkovski Enterprises."[10] In Germany in 1921, some of these were united to form *Wostwag* (West-Osteuropaeische Warenaustausch Aktiengesellschaft). Its ostensible purpose was to coordinate the trade of Soviet imports and exports. In practice, of course, other than some important raw materials the Soviets had few products marketable in the West in the 1920s, and consequently most of the "trade" ended up flowing back to Moscow.[11] By 1925, *Wostwag* was doing well enough to open several other branches throughout Germany and other countries in Western Europe. The next year, one of the brothers responsible for organizing *Wostwag* was assigned by Moscow Center to set up an affiliated firm in China; this became the Far Eastern Fur Trading Company in Tientsin. At about the same time, another *Wostwag* office opened in Urga, Mongolia, where an RU residency had been established following the Red Army conquest of the region in 1921.[12]

Another important front for Red Army Intelligence was commercial shipping. The Soviets had access to shipping companies around the world through two channels: a clandestine one through the Comintern, and another one through the "legitimate" Soviet merchant fleet, which was composed almost entirely of vessels purchased overseas and re-registered under the Soviet flag. In 1930, Amtorg, the Soviet trade concession in the United States, bought thirty ships from the U.S. War Shipping Board.[13]

The Fourth Department found penetration of international shipping to be surprisingly easy. Some of the most radical workers in the world were sailors and merchant seamen, and many of them had been at the forefront of organized revolutionary activity since before the October Revolution. The Comintern relied heavily upon these men, and many of its most dedicated members were the sailors it recruited in the seedy, violent ports of northwest Europe, like the insurrectionists in Hamburg. By 1923, the Comintern also operated a series of "sailors' homes" in Russian ports like Odessa and Murmansk that were used to recruit agents, couriers, and sympathizers among the foreign sailors residing there.[14] These were probably all absorbed by the RU's Naval Section by the mid-1920s. After 1926, the Fourth

Department organized an elaborate courier system out of Hamburg based upon the extensive Comintern networks of merchant sailors.[15]

The chief clandestine functions of the Soviet merchant fleet were to facilitate transportation and communications for the Comintern, RU, and INO; to provide cover for establishing illegal residencies and recruiting networks in ports and shipping centers; and to ship illegal cargo. The latter proved especially important for Soviet operations in China and the Far East, and for the covert cooperation between the Red Army and the *Reichswehr* between 1924 and 1930. By the mid-1920s, some ports, including Hamburg, Bremen, Antwerp, and Rotterdam, were so thoroughly infiltrated by RU networks that Moscow Center classified them as "controlled" and used them as major staging areas for a variety of covert operations.[16] These networks were usually ultimately under the direction of the Naval Department of the RU.

Red Army Intelligence also derived several other advantages from its maritime networks. For one thing, they ensured a ready supply of legal documents, including passports and other identity papers, for officers and agents traveling under false identities. This in turn meant that infiltrating countries with busy ports was relatively safe, at least until 1927. It also meant that major ports, like Danzig, Amsterdam, Marseilles, Hamburg, Shanghai, and New York, would be especially lucrative sites for intelligence operations.[17]

One important consequence of the police raids in 1927 was the exposure of some of the Comintern and Fourth Department commercial shipping networks. Nevertheless, although many counterintelligence services thereafter stepped up surveillance and security measures at ports of entry, until its demise in 1991 the USSR successfully continued to use merchant shipping for clandestine operations.[18]

One of the more cynical fronts used by the Fourth Department and the OGPU was the Soviet Red Cross. The Soviet Red Cross was organized hastily in 1918 to replace the Russian Red Cross in order to collect the funds promised to the latter by various international organizations (including $3.5 million from the American Red Cross). From its inception, Moscow used it to provide cover for intelligence activities. The Soviet Russian Red Cross office in New York served as a base for both chekist investigation of Russian emigrés and RU "talent scouting" (i.e., spotting likely recruits for clandestine work) and was eventually closely affiliated with Amtorg.[19] In an affidavit prepared for a U.S. congressional committee in 1930, OGPU defector Mikhail Hendler claimed that the Soviet Red Cross Mission in Bulgaria in 1922 was really composed entirely of RU and INO officers. He identified the chief of the *Razvedupr* contingent, "Boris," as the man in charge of "operative work . . . [which meant] organization of terroristic acts, destruction of munition supplies, assassination of officials, and so forth."[20]

Early Fourth Department success with these front organizations paved the way for the large-scale, elaborate international operations based out of Soviet trade missions in Berlin (the *Handelsvertretung*), London (Arcos), New York

(Amtorg), and several other countries. And after the "Botzenhard Affair" in Germany in 1924 (see chapter 6), Soviet intelligence officers operated from these bases with a large measure of diplomatic immunity. Soviet espionage organs also used the cover of official and semi-official Soviet organizations like the news agency *TASS*.

The most important objective of the RU residencies based at these fronts was to acquire foreign technology and hardware. Moscow may have spent as much as 26 million rubles in gold during 1924–25 alone for this purpose.[21] Soviet trade concessions and legations also facilitated efforts to infiltrate scientific and academic institutions, and in some cases (particularly in Great Britain and Germany) supported broader programs of subversion. Comintern staffs attached to the legations frequently supervised and financed local communist parties.

Beginning with Poland in 1920, Soviet Russia gradually established diplomatic relations at some level with most of the international community throughout the 1920s. Instead of taking advantage of diplomatic immunity as it became available to prudently redirect their energies away from the politically risky illegal residencies that had been established earlier out of necessity, Soviet intelligence now exploited embassies, consulates, and trade missions to facilitate the rapid expansion of both their covert and diplomatic presence abroad. Intelligence networks directed from diplomatic bases were called "legal residencies." The organization and operation of individual residencies throughout the 1920s and 1930s was in practice often a haphazard ad hoc affair, more dependent "on local circumstances, often on luck, and, perhaps most important, on the personality of the resident" than on any established procedures.[22] This caused ongoing headaches for Moscow Center, which, with limited success, continued struggling to promote professionalism. Nevertheless, by the late 1920s, the basic operating principles of both illegal and legal residencies were firmly established.[23]

With diplomatic representation, international travel became easier for Soviet officials, which in turn simplified the transportation of secret material, both documents and hardware, by diplomatic pouch and courier. This remained Moscow Center's preferred means of communications, for it was highly suspicious of radio communications, and was aware by at least 1923 that the British were breaking into Soviet diplomatic radio traffic. As a result, the RU continued to rely heavily on couriers throughout the interwar period.

During most of the 1920s, legal and illegal residencies frequently remained in close contact with each other, largely because of their mutual Comintern connections. By the late 1930s, however, Moscow Center finally enforced the complete separation of these organizations for security reasons, a step that proved most providential, for when the Nazi occupation of Europe completely disrupted RU legal residencies, most of the underground apparatus managed to survive, and eventually provided information decisive for the defeat of the Third Reich.

Enough information exists about two specific Fourth Department residencies for us to get some sense of what these were like during the 1920s. These two examples are from opposite sides of the globe, but taken together are probably illustrative of *Razvedupr* operations in general. Study of the Vienna residency sheds light on the social and administrative context of RU diplomatic posts, while the Peking residency provides insight into the complexity and scale of RU operations in Asia.

THE VIENNA RESIDENCY, 1924–1927

Elisabeth Poretsky, wife of RU officer Ignace Poretsky, provides a glimpse of life inside a Soviet legal intelligence residency in her memoirs. Ignace was one of several intelligence officers transferred to Vienna after the Hamburg Uprising.[24] This residency, based out of the Soviet Embassy, soon became the major staging area for RU espionage in the Balkans and Turkey.[25] At the time, the chief of the Fourth Department residency (the "resident") was probably Nikolai Krebs, a.k.a. Felix Wolf, Nikolai Rakov, and "Inkov."[26]

At the Soviet Embassy, diplomatic personnel associated frequently and intimately with the OGPU and RU. The Poretskys socialized with all of the Soviet employees at the embassy, apparently without any of the official restrictions later placed on Soviet Embassy staff during the Cold War. Most of the staff lived on the diplomatic compound. They organized social events and cultivated that peculiar variety of "palace intrigue" common to such posts. Elisabeth Poretsky observed that in Vienna the chief sources for such mischief were "the petty jealousies and frictions among the wives," who lived immensely boring lives and had little contact with anyone outside the embassy.[27] Exacerbating this insularity was the fact that it was not uncommon for Soviet citizens stationed there to marry from within their own community.

The staff represented a surprisingly politically diverse group. Throughout the 1920s, it was not uncommon for Red Army Intelligence to employ people with views regarded by the Soviet leadership as unorthodox or even heretical. For their own protection, and, we may suspect, the good of the *Razvedupr* as a whole, such individuals were usually posted far from Moscow. Several of these free thinkers, including even some noncommunists, ended up in Vienna. Although these officers were usually particularly good at their work, such ideological tolerance eventually provided Stalin further "evidence" of Red Army treachery and an additional pretext for purging the RU in the late 1930s.

There seem to have been fairly good relations between the INO and the RU in Vienna, in spite of the fact that to a certain extent their missions overlapped and thus aggravated the competition between them. That a relatively cordial atmosphere existed at all is somewhat surprising, not only because of the traditional enmity between the two organizations, but also because the

INO and the RU frequently "used the same approaches and networks and were interested in the same political groups, primarily Balkan refugee organizations in Vienna."[28]

RU personnel in Vienna consisted of intelligence officers, like Poretsky and Felix Gorski—another Pole—and the military attachés and their staffs. According to Elisabeth Poretsky, however, the attachés, who technically commanded the RU contingent, were frequently Red Army veterans with little or no training in intelligence work. Furthermore, she recalled, "many of them were completely unable to evaluate or understand the reports the men submitted and a surprising number showed signs of mental instability." Several of these attachés "manifested forms of exhibitionism" and were eventually transferred.[29] One beneficial consequence of this state of affairs was that intelligence officers posted to Vienna like Ignace had greater freedom to plan and carry out their work.

At that time, Moscow Center followed the standard practice in the world of professional espionage of transferring any officer who was identified by the local police. The Poretskys found themselves in this situation in 1927 when the Austrian police arrested Ignace. He was not held long, and upon his release returned briefly to Moscow. Later that year, he was awarded the Order of the Red Banner, and early in 1928 Moscow Center assigned Poretsky to Prague, where he was supposed to organize a network to operate against Poland. Before Poretsky could make any real progress, however, he was re-ordered to Amsterdam, where, as we shall see in the next chapter, he was put in charge of the illegal residency operating against Great Britain. The reasons for this abrupt transfer remain unclear. It may be that Polish counterintelligence simply proved too formidable. Another possibility is that the RU managed to establish an alternative penetration of Poland, either with another network or through German or French sources. Another consideration is that after the collapse of Soviet intelligence networks in the wake of the Arcos raid, the Fourth Department needed its best men to re-organize penetration of Great Britain.

From Elisabeth Poretsky's account, we can tentatively conclude that during the period she and her husband were stationed there, the intelligence gathered by the Vienna residency was probably of limited value. The shortage of qualified intelligence officers was aggravated by the mountains of material gathered, and the fact that Vienna proved to be a veritable minefield of forged documents. This situation was made worse by the lack of officers skilled in foreign languages and a perpetual shortage of competent translators, a problem that bedeviled the RU throughout the 1920s.[30]

THE PEKING RESIDENCY

As we observed in the previous chapter, Soviet objectives in Asia reflected both revolutionary ideology and Russian imperialism. In the 1920s the former was reflected in Moscow's commitment to the goal of revolution in China, as described in the previous chapter. The latter focused on the Soviet relationship with its main rival in the region, Japan. Tension between these two states traditionally centered on the Korean peninsula and Manchuria. The operations of the Fourth Department's residency in Peking took place within this context.

In 1920–21, the Red Army occupied Outer Mongolia, enabling the *Razvedupr* to establish an outpost in Urga.[31] By the middle of the decade, a series of residencies had been organized throughout much of the rest of Asia. The most important of these was the large post in Peking called "Residency No. 4," which served as the administrative center for intelligence operations in the entire region. In addition, there were twelve numbered residencies and four named individually—Gloubokovsky, Alfa, Ossip, and Svetlanin. The numbered residencies were, in ascending numerical order, Mukden (No. 1), Seoul, Harbin, Peking, Kalgan, Canton, Tsitsihar, Kaifeng, Shanghai, Dairen, Chungsha, and Shantung.[32] All of these were supervised from Peking, which by the mid-1920s was called "Peking Center," thereby achieving a status rivaled only by Berlin and exceeded only by Moscow.

Among the residents in 1925 was Wilhelm Zaisser, a German communist who had participated in the Hamburg Uprising. In 1924, he left the KPD for Red Army Intelligence.[33] After attending the Moscow Military Academy, Moscow Center sent him to China. Throughout much of the period between 1925 and 1927 the RU resident in Peking was probably "Yanofsky."[34] Other prominent RU officers who worked in China at one time or another included Ho Chi Minh and the mysterious Frenchman known as "Muraille."[35]

Together, the complex of Asian residencies probably made Peking Center one of the largest Fourth Department operations in the world. By 1925 the demands of espionage and the rapidly increasing numbers of Soviet advisors assigned to Chiang Kai-shek's armies combined to overwhelm Soviet administrative capacity in Peking. The Red Army decided therefore to reorganize these operations. The result was a unified command structure for coordinating all political-military work in China, the "Peking Military Center" (PMC).

The PMC was composed of three main branches, each with its own chain of command: the Military Attaché, the Military Section of the Chinese Communist party, and the RU residency. In addition, the OGPU had both a counterintelligence section and an INO section. The military attaché was in overall command of the PMC, although his primary responsibility was to support the activities of Red Army advisors in China. The relationship between the Red Army advisors and the Fourth Department was complicated and not always harmonious. The major problems were organization and jurisdiction. The advisors and the RU apparatus had their own distinct chains of command. Both were also technically under the authority of the Soviet ambassador, and by 1926, the military attaché in Peking (see next chapter).[36] Further confusing this arrangement was the fact that the duties and assignments of each organization frequently overlapped, for instance, intelligence gathering and weapons smuggling. This situation was exacerbated by the presence of a small but politically powerful GPU contingent (including an INO section) at the Peking Embassy. These chekists, although primarily charged with counterintelligence and security, nevertheless frequently interfered with the advisors and the Fourth Department residency.[37]

The authority of the military attaché extended to the RU residency in Peking, although residencies in Manchuria, Korea, and Mongolia were directed by Moscow Center.[38] This arrangement reflected the standard Red Army chain of command.[39] In practice, however, the Peking resident actually supervised the activities of the other affiliated residencies, and the *Razvedupr* station chief preferred to go straight to Moscow for direction, even when given orders by the attaché. This caused serious friction between the RU and the military attaché.[40]

Interdepartmental disputes also predictably arose. The residency staff, much to the consternation of the attaché, remained steadfastly dedicated to their mission of intelligence gathering. Korff, the first military attaché at the PMC, sent the following message to the chief of the RU residency in Peking in 1926: "The Intelligence work in China is not being done in order to study this country in general, 'in all respects', as a 'probable' (I should rather say 'improbable') or possible adversary, but for the sake of an immediately practical and properly established activity which is being carried out according to instructions from the same source—Moscow." Korff went on to remind the residency that it was to carry out its missions "from the operative [operational] point of view."[41] Moscow Center had other concerns with the PMC, as well. The performance of its agents was so poor that in October 1926 it sent a message to all residencies in China calling attention to consistent "defects" in their reporting.[42]

Communications between Moscow Center and the residents in Asia seem to have been primarily conducted through couriers and diplomatic pouch. Directions to all of the RU residencies in the region were generally routed through the PMC. The reverse seems to have frequently been the case, as well. The sheer volume of secret material found by the police in their April 1927 raid on the PMC suggests that it served as a clearinghouse not only for material sent to the Peking RU residency, but also for all Fourth Department operations in Asia. Diplomatic posts provided Fourth Department residencies with secure bases of operations, and the *Narkomindel* was also responsible for ensuring that "the workers of the Intelligence Department [have] proper dwellings which may guarantee the safety of their work and the safekeeping of their secrets."[43] As a consequence, huge reinforced concrete vaults deep within the actual residency headquarters were constructed at the PMC.

Fourth Department officers carried out operations based on the following directive:

The direction and the scope of the [intelligence] work are governed by two factors: the possibility of wars between the U.S.S.R., Japan and China and the possibility of the development of the nationalist-revolutionary movement in China. . . . The first factor dictates the necessity of minutely studying North China and Korea, as the future seat of war, their resources and armed forces, and their connection with the nationalistic movement. The second factor dictates a similar study of the rest of China as a source . . . of strength in the fight against local and foreign imperialists and consequently as a possible ally of the U.S.S.R. . . . against . . . Japan, England, America and others.[44]

The residencies directed by Peking Center monitored and studied the various military establishments in China; "the circumstances which have an influence on the development and strengthening of the [Chinese] armies"; and overall Chinese war-making capability. They also carried out geographical studies of the region and gathered intelligence about the activities of other foreign governments in China, especially in connection with China's military capabilities and intentions. Moscow Center instructed "Michael" (the code-name for the RU resident at the PMC) to provide "timely information" about all of these questions to Moscow, Peking Center, and the Siberian RU residency at Vladivostok."[45]

In addition to gathering intelligence, smuggling weapons, and participating in the advisor program, Fourth Department agents and officers in China probably carried out "terroristic acts," including assassinations and bombings. Korff felt it necessary sometime in 1926–27 to try and clarify this aspect of Soviet operations in China. His proposal reflected well-established policy that responsibility for pure intelligence gathering be reserved exclusively to the RU residency ("Michael"), leaving the GPU section, composed of departments for counterespionage (headed by "Liharin") and political operations ("Vedernikoff") to carry out "external and internal counter-espionage, the functions of censure and punishment and of observation [surveillance], the promotion of terroristic acts, as well as the measures to be taken in connection with the corruption of the 'Whites' [i.e., expatriot opponents of the Bolshevik regime], on condition that they work in contact with 'Michael.'"[46]

In Asia, as elsewhere, Red Army intelligence officers operated under a variety of covers. In addition to serving on the staffs of Red Army advisors to the Kuomintang, these included positions in commercial enterprises and diplomatic posts. The relatively few legitimate Soviet diplomats were required to use their authority and positions to fully support RU operations, including supplying their own passports when necessary.[47] On occasion the RU was also required to assist the OGPU in placing its operatives.[48]

RU personnel also held positions as consuls, consul generals, and staff members. When necessary, new diplomatic positions were created, sometimes out of thin air, and somehow justified to the Chinese or Japanese authorities. On one occasion, the consul general in Seoul, who was also a military intelligence officer, noted in a report to "Michael" on the progress of his efforts to recruit agents in Korea that he had two vacant positions available on his staff for "'officials with special commissions.'"[49] On another occasion, the *Narkomindel*, apparently at the request of the Fourth Department, manufactured an entirely new diplomatic position in order to provide cover for an intelligence officer.

The inexperience of many RU officers exacerbated problems with security. Many with diplomatic cover were so obviously unqualified that they immediately attracted the suspicions of the local police. On at least one occasion, the resident himself suffered from such limitations. "Souhoroukoff," the resident in Mukden, reported Japanese and Chinese investigations of his cover to Moscow Center and asked for advice. He observed that "my two-years' stay here [in Mukden] . . . has contributed to the revealing of my real character." Perhaps short of potential replacements, Moscow dangerously suggested that he try and rebuild his cover by devoting himself exclusively to diplomatic work "in order to rehabilitate [himself] a little in the eyes of the Chinese and Japanese." In his acknowledgment of this order, Souhoroukoff offered the advice that his successor should be well versed in "at least one European language, otherwise he would only be harmful in playing this part [vice-consul], unless he really performs functions corresponding to the post he is supposed to occupy."[50]

Moscow Center encouraged its residents to establish fronts "'on the street' under the flag of a commercial firm," such as a restaurant.[51] One of the more ambitious and profitable of these fronts operated through the legitimate offices of the famous Chinese Eastern Railroad (CER), the main east-west communications link running through Manchuria.

The *Razvedupr* penetration of the CER provided access to a large amount of significant intelligence, including all the information flowing through the company's headquarters, such as technical plans, blueprints, geographical and geological reports, data about Chinese armies in eastern China, and general details about China's railway network. It also facilitated contact with civilian, military, and foreign officials involved in the transportation industry, many of whom were in turn either recruited themselves or used to develop further contacts for recruitment. The CER also proved to be a useful conduit for the anti-imperialist propaganda work of the Harbin residency.

Last but certainly not least, the RU was able to pilfer the CER's accounts to support intelligence operations and to pay for salaries, free rail passes for the residency's officers and agents (many of whom were not employed by the CER), and "some of the Chinese Eastern railway publications as well as foreign papers and literature."[52]

RU operations in Asia also shed light on its financing of agent operations. The Chinese residencies were provided with funds in a variety of currencies, no doubt both for security reasons and to facilitate payment of agents in appropriate funds. For one month, May 1926, the four residencies in Mukden (No. 1), Harbin (No. 3), Peking (No. 4), and Shantung (No. 12) received 11,200 gold dollars; 6,842.67 Chinese dollars; 7,696.29 yen; 2,972 gold rubles; and 90.80 fengpiaos, a total equivalent to 40,000 Chinese dollars. The average total monthly expenditure of all the residencies combined was about 50,000 Chinese dollars, so clearly these four residencies received the lion's share of this funding.[53] Other sources of cash, however, were also available, including salaries and payments from the Commissariat of Foreign Affairs and money embezzled from the CER.

A major objective of Soviet policy in China was to monitor and sabotage the activities of the "foreign imperialists," especially Great Britain.[54] In late 1926, a memo circulated by Moscow Center discussed at length the responsibilities of the RU residencies in Asia. Similar in outline to the 1925 document described above, this specified nine general objectives of the residencies' work, seven of which concerned the foreign presence in China. One of these, for example, was to gather intelligence on "the activities of the British in Tibet and Western China." Others included monitoring the views of the "imperialist" powers on a broad range of regional issues, ranging from Japan's aggressive policy in Manchuria and Mongolia to proposed changes in Chinese customs policy. In another reference to ongoing problems with intelligence gathering, the memo concluded that "we [Moscow Center] emphasize once more that . . . agents should display the greatest energy," and specified that more "documents should be procured."[55]

The British were predictably the chief foreign target of RU operations in China. The Fourth Department used a variety of strategies to twist the lion's tail. It promoted propaganda among the Chinese and the foreign news media that emphasized such "issues" as the usurpation of Chinese sovereignty by British imperialists, and the scheming of Britain's ruling classes against the international working class. There were also ongoing attempts to foster subversion among British colonial troops stationed in China.[56]

Red Army Intelligence also succeeded in infiltrating some foreign legations, including those of Britain, France, the United States, Japan, Italy, and probably Germany as well. "Russian" officers and agents recruited "foreigners" (i.e., Europeans), and Chinese recruited Chinese.[57] Indeed, Peking was the one "non-European capital in which European missions were most vulnerable to Soviet penetration in the pre-Stalin era."[58] At the end of 1926 "Michael" reported to Moscow that his officers had recruited some "boys" (i.e., Chinese manservants) on the staffs of the Japanese military attaché, the British legation, and the American commercial attaché. Before the police raid in April, the Fourth Department also recruited at least one other Chinese national on the staff of the British legation.

The Soviets had access to information not only from the British, Japanese, and American embassies, but also from the French and Germans.[59] Whether this was provided by agents in the French or German diplomatic communities, or from the RU agents in the other embassies, is unclear. In either case, the immense bulk of information obtained by the Fourth Department demonstrates the poor level of security among the diplomatic community in Peking. It also suggests the latter's fundamental misunderstanding of Chinese sensibilites, as well as their underestimation of the threat posed by Soviet espionage.[60]

More than any other factor besides Chiang Kai-shek's decision to turn against the CCP and Moscow, Soviet covert operations against European interests in China, and in particular those of Great Britain, were what probably finally provoked the Chinese authorities into launching a full-scale police raid on the PMC on 16 April 1927. Marshal Chang Tso-lin authorized this action, which resulted in the destruction of a good portion of the Soviet diplomatic compound, dozens of arrests, and the discovery of thousands of incriminating documents. Moscow complained loudly and denounced the documents as forgeries; subsequent analysis by western experts established that although a few of the papers might have been forged, most likely by White Russian émigré groups, the vast bulk of the material was indeed authentic.[61]

This raid was the first in a long spring and summer filled with intelligence-related fiascos that culminated with the "war scare" described in the next chapter. In China, subsequent police raids on Soviet diplomatic posts took place in Shanghai on 25 October and in Canton in December, the result of both the Peking raid and the collapse of Stalin's pro-Kuomintang strategy.[62] There is no clear indication of the objective damage done to Soviet intelligence operations. However, by the late 1920s, Shanghai, not Peking, had become the major center for covert Soviet operations in Asia, and continued to remain so until World War II.

FRANCE, 1921–1927

France was a major target of Soviet intelligence for three reasons. First, in the 1920s Moscow regarded France as second only to Great Britain as the most dangerous enemy of world socialism. Its policies in Eastern Europe, most particularly its alliance with Poland and support for the Little Entente, were seen as proof of French hostility toward the USSR.[63] Although Moscow regarded Poland as the greatest military threat, it believed that the Poles could only seriously menace the USSR with generous French military and economic support. Moscow Center also assumed that France regularly supplied arms and ammunition to hostile states in the Baltic and Balkans. As we will see in chapter 7, the central role the Soviets expected France to play in supporting any likely attack on the Soviet Union was clearly and consistently described in Red Army threat analysis from 1926 to 1933.

Second, in the 1920s most observers, including those in Moscow, considered the French army to be the world's largest, most experienced, and most technologically sophisticated. France therefore was a natural target of espionage. In Moscow's view, France, together with Germany, represented the best source for modern military technology and hardware; as late as 1931, for example, the Red Army concluded that "France leads the world in the technique of aviation."[64]

Third, sources in France probably represented the best possible access to information from countries difficult to penetrate directly, like Poland, the Baltic states, and even Great Britain. The proximity of the massive RU presence in Germany, and the close ties between French and American Fourth Department networks, no doubt enhanced France's value as a target for penetration. It should also be noted that France was an equally important target of the OGPU, for the large Russian émigré community there harbored many anti-Soviet organizations.

The *Razvedupr* first set about trying to establish intelligence networks in France in 1919–1920.[65] Reflecting the general makeup of its personnel in the early years, its agents in France came from a diverse ethnic background that included both émigrés and French citizens with Eastern European ancestry. One problem confronting the Soviets, however, was that far more so than the communist parties in Germany, the Baltic states, China, or even Great Britain, the French consistently displayed an exasperatingly independent streak.

The French Communist Party, or *Parti Communiste Français* (PCF), therefore posed a special challenge for Soviet intelligence. The PCF was born in 1920 in an atmosphere of acrimony at a meeting of the well-established French Socialist Party (the SFIO, *Section Française de l'Internationale Ouvrière*) at Tours. In a sequence of events ironically similar to those that led to the creation of the Bolshevik Party, a majority of the members at this conference decided to follow a directive issued by the Comintern, and form a revolutionary communist organization based on the principles espoused by Lenin.[66]

The membership of the PCF nevertheless behaved most independently for the next several years, frequently frustrating Moscow's attempts to turn it into a disciplined and useful part of the Comintern. It remained resolutely nationalist, and preferred submission to the French authorities over confrontation.[67] Moscow finally embarked upon a full-scale program of "bolshevization" beginning in 1924, with the intent of creating a revolutionary party in the mold of the other members of the Comintern. Over the next three years, Moscow directed a purge of the PCF leadership, the construction of a new party structure, and enforcement of "democratic centralism," and encouraged efforts to recruit genuine workers for key leadership positions, all the while struggling to curb the nationalist tendencies of the French comrades.[68]

In terms of the needs of Soviet intelligence, the effect of these changes was mixed. It may not have been until this re-organization that the PCF even incorporated the section for liaison with the OMS and Red Army Intelligence required of all Comintern parties. This change may have significantly enhanced the value of the PCF as a base for intelligence work; certainly the years after 1924 saw a significant increase in the intensity of RU operations in France.

Yet the membership of the PCF remained a problematical source for agents. Unlike virtually every other communist party in the world, French

communists had no underground tradition, and were hopelessly inexperienced in conspiratorial work. Their numbers, although relatively large compared to most countries except Italy and Germany, continued to decline
throughout the decade. Even the PCF's occasionally strong showings in elections were due more to the unpopularity of current office holders than to
increased support.[69] And no degree of "democratic centralism" could completely suppress the average party member's independence. This, combined
with the strong nationalism of many in the party, created an unpredictable situation every time a Soviet intelligence officer attempted to recruit a French
comrade.

Nevertheless, lacking any diplomatic outposts in France until 1924,
Moscow Center was forced to rely on French communists. From the point of
view of security, this was a form of "Russian Roulette" that led in 1927 to the
temporary collapse of most of the Fourth Department *apparat* in France. The
one bright spot in this situation was that the French authorities were (possibly
for good reason) far more concerned about the anticolonial and subversive efforts of the PCF than any threat it posed as an agency of foreign espionage.

Early attempts by the Soviet clandestine services to use the PCF led the
French Politburo to seek Trotsky's support for an end to Moscow's use of
their members for such unseemly adventures. The PCF adamantly argued
against mixing "revolutionary politics" with espionage. According to Boris
Souvarine, one of the French communists who made the case in Moscow,
Trotsky assured them that he shared their concerns, and promised that he
would take appropriate action. Whether or not he actually did so is unknown. Subsequent RU activities in France, however, indicate that any such
restraint was purely tactical and temporary.[70]

In 1924, intelligence officers were specially assigned to France to coordinate the RU's increasing technological and industrial espionage effort. A primary target was French military aviation. An important step forward in
bringing some sense of administrative coherence to these operations came
that year when Moscow Center assigned Jean Cremet to head the illegal residency. Cremet was a prominent French communist personally selected for
this post by Stalin, who sought to manipulate his rise in the PCF in order to
make Cremet his creature, thereby increasing his control over the French
party. No one in the PCF leadership apparently knew of Cremet's clandestine
work; he was even elected to the French Politburo in June 1926.[71]

In a remarkable violation of the major tenets of conspiracy, Cremet, already a prominent and well-known communist, ran for and won a seat on the
Paris City Council shortly after his appointment to head the illegal residency.
Attending to his other duties, including running an espionage *apparat* that,
at its peak, may have had hundreds of agents, absorbed so much of his energy
that he ended up spending little time either in the City Council or with the
PCF Central Committee. He answered inquiries about his frequent absences
by claiming to be "gravely ill."

Together with his wife, Louise Clarac, Cremet proved remarkably successful in recruiting agents and gathering intelligence. Under his supervision, and frequently through his contacts in the PCF, networks were established in French dockyards and ports, arsenals, military schools, and armaments factories. Their agents gathered intelligence on and examples of new types of ammunition, gas masks, naval and tank armament, aircraft navigation systems, hydrophones, naval armor plate, and blueprints for submarines and munitions factories. Cremet often transmitted his agents' findings personally, making numerous trips to Berlin and Moscow. These efforts were characterized more by their enthusiasm than their professionalism, and such poor security was bound to lead to grief. By 1926 at the latest Cremet's brazen behavior began to attract the attention of the *Sûreté Général*. Such a situation was an inevitable consequence of the Fourth Department's preference for revolutionary zeal over professionalism. Even so, the recklessness of Cremet and the carelessness of Moscow Center seem inexplicable. In part, perhaps, the RU saw in Cremet's results justification for his methods. Another, and not necessarily exclusive, possibility was that Stalin's patronage of him discouraged closer supervision by Moscow Center.

In October 1924, France extended diplomatic recognition to the USSR.[72] Soviet intelligence officers affiliated with the new diplomatic posts poured into France. They worked from the embassy, the consulates, the Soviet trade legation, and the affiliated Franco-Russian trading consortium based in Paris, *Torgpredstvo*. By 1925 the chief of the RU Paris legal residency was a Polish veteran of the Fourth Department, "Uzdanski-Yelenski," a.k.a. "Abraham Bernstein." Uzdanski had been stationed in Warsaw until 1924, when he was expelled and then subsequently re-assigned to Vienna the following year, where he ran operations in the Balkans (and probably worked with Ignace Poretsky).

Uzdanski's liaison to Cremet's network was a Lithuanian student named "Stephan Grodnicki," described later by a French court as "young and elegant and one to whom delicate assignments were given."[73] Using the diplomatic pouch, through Grodnicki, Uzdanski was able to transmit to Cremet a list of precise information desired by the Red Army as well as Soviet scientists and engineers. Known as the "questionnaire," this method of gathering information seems in hindsight to have been extraordinarily risky. In addition to the revealing nature of their questions, these documents, used by Fourth Department residencies all over the world, were often accompanied by "book-length lists of foreign military technology" that the RU residents were ordered to steal as soon as possible. The questionnaires were compiled in the USSR by engineers and technicians, and forwarded to military attachés and Fourth Department residents. After arranging for the translation of these lists into the local language, military attachés would then usually hand them over to the illegal liaison officer for distribution to the networks.[74]

Moscow Center had ongoing problems with agents failing to adequately fill out the questionnaires. This led to a memo issued sometime before the spring of 1927 called "Circular N 5/P," which demanded that the residencies do a better job. The circular noted that "in some countries up to 60% of the questions remained unanswered, and in most of the countries which we have to throw light upon this defection [sic] reached 35–40%."[75] Clumsy handling of the questionnaires also provided police with further evidence of Red Army Intelligence activities. In 1925, Cremet's wife and fellow agent, Louise Clarac, tried to persuade an old communist associate of hers, M. Rousset, who had connections with the arsenal at Toulon, to fill out a questionnaire. Clarac offered the standard justification that such information was necessary "to protect the Red Army" and "defend the working class." Rousset, however, concluded that this was nothing more than blatant espionage, and reported Clarac to the police. The Sûreté had Rousset play along, using Clarac to pass misleading information to the Soviets.

However, given Moscow Center's other resources in Germany and elsewhere, and the fact that until 1927 the vast bulk of its *apparat* in France remained undetected by the authorities, it probably had a good idea of which information was genuine and which was not. Nevertheless, although the network had been compromised, and police surveillance of known and suspected Red Army agents increased, the French authorities may have later had cause to regret their patience, for Cremet's agents managed to achieve some notable successes before the *apparat*'s destruction.

Some of them, posing as designers, were able to infiltrate the tank research bureau in Versailles, and two municipal officials in St. Cyr, a town known for its communist sympathies but also, ironically, the site of the French military academy, were also recruited.[76] The most important results, however, were achieved in Versailles, at the *Centre d'Etudes Militaires*. A mysterious RU officer, known variously as "Paul," "Boissonas," "Henri," "Albert," and, most frequently, "Muraille," had by 1925 established a network of PCF members who worked in the print shop. For almost three years, this group of about ten men, who had access to "hundreds of confidential and secret papers," collected and made copies of sensitive documents that they passed on to one of Louise Clarac's contacts, Jean Rougeayres.

Another Fourth Department operation was run out of a small office in Paris that ostensibly housed a firm manufacturing fire extinguishers. An RU officer named "Boris Ogareff," who lived with his Australian wife in Boulogne, had used this firm as a cover for his espionage activities since 1924. One of Ogareff's primary objectives was "to recruit ex-British officers in France."[77]

Ogareff's network may have been subordinate to Uzdanski; on the other hand, given its unusual focus, which may have been a preliminary to later Soviet deep penetration operations in Britain, this *apparat* might have been a separate residency answering directly to Berlin or Moscow Center. In any case, by 1926, his activities had become known to the authorities in France (and possibly Great Britain), and by December 1926 his network seems to have been completely disbanded.[78]

By the end of 1926, Cremet's reliance on PCF members to carry out espionage had put his network in a precarious position. Always a special target for police surveillance, the communists' close connection to Red Army Intelligence became more and more clear to the *Sûreté*. Furthermore, in an incomprehensible display of bad judgment, on at least two occasions Cremet tried to use his Party authority to pressure reluctant communists into committing espionage. In October 1925, one of Cremet's "assistants," Pierre Provost, attempted to get a man named "Singré" to fill out a questionnaire about French mechanized warfare capabilities. Singré informed the authorities. At about the same time, another party member named "Cochelin" also, was approached by another of Cremet's agents, "Sergent," with a similar questionnaire.[79] Cochelin also reported the approach to the police. In both these cases, the *Sûreté* once again decided to leave the men in place, playing them back against the RU; the French were probably unaware at first of the connection between these two cases and the Cremets.

Early in 1927, however, the French police had amassed enough evidence to break up Cremet's network. They told Cochelin to arrange to receive a new questionnaire, and to set up a meeting with Grodnicki in order to return it. This meeting took place on 9 April 1927. The police followed Grodnicki from there back to his rendezvous with Uzdanski, at which point both were arrested.

Within the next few days most of Cremet's network unraveled—except for Muraille's ring of typesetters at Versailles—and over a hundred people were arrested and charged with espionage. French authorities characterized the spy ring as "the largest espionage affair to be uncovered since the war."[80] French officials feared that not only espionage was involved; there were allegations that "preparation was being made for large scale sabotage of war material."[81] The French also suspected that the intelligence gained from the Uzdanski spy ring was being distributed to a third unidentified country, although none of the later sources mention this.

The wave of arrests created a major breach in Franco-Soviet relations. A series of further Soviet provocations, mostly the result of Comintern machinations, only served to aggravate the situation. In the following months, Jacques Doriot, who was a member of the French Politburo in the mid-1920s and was later briefly associated with Muraille's network in France, was arrested together with nine of his associates. They were imprisoned for "subversive activities" in French colonies overseas.[82] The French government demanded that Moscow recall its ambassador, Cristian Rakovsky, after they obtained a letter by him describing his intentions to encourage desertion in the French army in the event of war.[83] In June, the head of the French railwaymen's union, Pierre Semard, was imprisoned for inciting mutiny in the French army.[84] Paris issued a warning to Moscow and threatened to break off diplomatic relations. It was the worst crisis in Franco-Soviet relations prior to the advent of the Third Reich, and was another major factor in the 1927 "war scare."

Thereafter, it took Soviet military intelligence considerable effort to rebuild a useful organization in France, but the lessons learned before 1927 were eventually put to good use.

GREAT BRITAIN, 1921–1927

The Bolsheviks always reserved a special paranoid hatred, tinged with respect, for the British "ruling circles." Throughout the interwar era, the Soviets regarded Great Britain as the evil genius behind world counter-revolution. Even Red Army threat assessments, focused as they were on the immediate military threat of the "western neighboring coalition" (Poland, Romania, Finland, and the Baltic states), consistently saw the might of the British Empire looming in the background of any potential conflict.

Great Britain was therefore a top priority for espionage. Unfortunately for Moscow, several factors combined to make penetration of this target very difficult. The Communist Party of Great Britain (CPGB) was minuscule in size and even smaller in influence. Although there was a large, highly organized, pacifist and politically powerful working class, no matter how much spleen it vented at the Conservative party, it remained to its very core patriotically devoted to the empire. Recruiting agents from the "lower classes" was extraordinarily difficult; ironically, it was the British aristocracy that eventually proved most amenable to treason.

Furthermore, the Soviets regarded the British security forces (MI5 and Scotland Yard) as most formidable. The police raid on Arcos in 1927 even forced Moscow Center to go so far as to declare Great Britain a "denied area," meaning that espionage against it had to be carried out exclusively from adjacent countries, since direct penetration was now far too dangerous. Like the French, the British saw Soviet espionage as a distinctly secondary threat to Comintern-sponsored subversion in the empire, and targeted their counterintelligence efforts accordingly.

Between 1921 and 1927, the primary center for Soviet clandestine operations in Great Britain was the London headquarters of the All-Russian Cooperative Society, Ltd., better known as "Arcos." Arcos soon had a number of branches scattered throughout the British Empire, including India and Hong Kong. Its subsidiary and branch offices included both Amtorg in the United States and the Mrachkovskiis' *Wostwag* in Germany.[85] The main headquarters, which was called the "Soviet" or "Russian House," was set up in 1921 in the financial district of London ("the City") at 49 Moorgate. This building housed both the Arcos staff and, in the absence of formal diplomatic relations, the Soviet Trade Delegation. The *Razvedupr*, INO, and Comintern all took full advantage of the friendly disposition of Ramsey MacDonald's Labour government in order to exploit Arcos's potential for espionage and subversion.[86]

British counterintelligence naturally kept the Russian House under close surveillance from the moment it opened for business. Of even greater value, however, was the information supplied by the British Government Code and Cypher School (GC & CS), established shortly after World War I. The GC & CS broke Soviet diplomatic and intelligence codes as early as 1920, during the Soviet-Polish War. By 1927 at the latest, British counterintelligence was well informed about those Soviet diplomatic operations throughout the empire that were coordinated from 49 Moorgate.[87]

In the early 1920s, as noted above, the primary concern of the British authorities was not Soviet espionage but rather Soviet and Comintern efforts to promote subversion in the far reaches of the empire, particularly in India, as well as Comintern meddling in the Labour Party and British trade unions.[88] British fears seemed confirmed in 1924 by a letter purportedly sent by Zinoviev to the CPGB. Scotland Yard and MI5 told the Foreign Office that the letter was genuine, whereupon the Foreign Office released the text to the British press. The contents of the document, which, among other things, suggested that Comintern agents were organizing cells within the British army and near military installations, created a political firestorm. The public outcry in Britain proved to be an important factor in the subsequent defeat of MacDonald in the 1924 general elections.[89]

Publicly, Moscow claimed that the letter was a forgery, the work of "White émigrés." Privately, the executive director of the Comintern, Otto Kuusinen, observed that although the letter was not genuine, its portrayal of Comintern policy was accurate.[90] The Politburo apparently suspected that the letter was real, for it sternly reprimanded Zinoviev, perhaps on Stalin's prodding, and the Executive Committee of the Comintern did the same to the British communists. The incident provided Zinoviev's enemies in Moscow with even more ammunition.

Although the letter was almost certainly forged—probably by Polish Military Intelligence—Moscow nevertheless took steps to drastically curtail the Comintern's clandestine operations, turning all military-related responsibilities over to the RU, and assigning the INO all other intelligence and security operations. Thereafter, until the Spanish Civil War, the Comintern was supposedly restricted primarily to agitation-propaganda work, as well as providing support, when needed, for the intelligence services; the major exception was in China.[91] In practice, however, the Comintern and its OMS continued to recruit for covert work and conduct espionage, especially in Asia, under the direction of the Fourth Department. The Comintern also remained active throughout the British Empire, and in particular India, and there were public accusations in Britain that Arcos provided funds for the general strike of 1926.[92]

Another consequence of the Zinoviev Letter affair was that Arcos became even more dedicated to espionage. Indeed, according to Peter Costello, from the start, most Arcos managers were "handpicked officers of Soviet Military Intelligence," and their primary task was industrial espionage. Although most sources discuss Arcos almost exclusively in terms of INO, or, at most, both

INO and RU operations, the targets for espionage sponsored by Arcos were mostly military. More importantly, the authoritative sources used by Costello, many of which are copies or summaries of documents captured in the police raid, also suggest that the agency directing most of this activity was the RU.[93] Little information has publicly surfaced so far about specific cases of Fourth Department espionage in Great Britain in the 1920s. We do know that particularly attractive targets were aircraft, submarine, naval gunnery, and torpedo technology, armored and motorized vehicle engines, and new industrial chemical processes.

By 1927, echoing the course of events in France and China, Soviet espionage based out of Arcos became blatant enough to convince the British that it was time to act. The connection between Red Army Intelligence and Arcos was clear to MI5 from GC & CS decryptions. Before MI5 took action, however, it needed to devise a pretext for raiding the compound that would not tip off the Soviets that their radio signals were being decoded.

Such an opportunity presented itself in March 1927 when a Lloyds of London employee, George Monckland, told Special Branch that a man named Wilfred McCartney (an RU agent) had offered to pay him for information about arms shipments insured by Lloyds.[94] MI5 decided to use Monckland to set up Arcos. They provided Monckland with a copy of a supposedly "Secret," though in actuality obsolete, RAF manual entitled "Regulations for Training Flying Personnel of the Royal Air Force."[95] Monckland passed the document to McCartney, who shortly thereafter turned it over to a member of the trade delegation from the Russian House.

The Special Branch of the London Metropolitan Police raided the Arcos headquarters in the early hours of 12 May 1927. Like the raid on the PMC less than a month before, the Russian and British members of the Arcos staff were taken completely by surprise, and watched in stunned amazement as the police discovered piles of sensitive and incriminating documents, most of which pertained to Comintern activities. The police also found the specially constructed concrete and steel vault, similar to that at the PMC, used for storing intelligence material. They stopped the frantic efforts of two Soviets to burn the papers, and most of them were recovered intact. Despite the claims of Moscow and its supporters to the contrary, the documents seized at the Russian House clearly demonstrated that Arcos had been supporting a massive Soviet intelligence and subversion effort that, although aimed primarily at Great Britain, had connections to Soviet operations around the world, from China to the United States.[96]

The British Government protested to Moscow, and despite opposition from some elements of the Labour Party and the trade unions moved to expel the Soviet trade delegation and abrogated all the trade agreements between the two countries. On 26 May, accompanied by a two-part White Paper detailing extensive examples of "hostile action" by Soviet agents against Great Britain, the British government officially severed diplomatic relations with the USSR. Several Soviet nationals, "ordinary employees" who worked at the Arcos building but were uninvolved in the covert operations there, defected in June. Called *nevozvrashchentsy* ("non-returners") in Moscow, these people provided Scotland Yard with an even more complete picture of the intrigues organized and directed from the Russian House.[97]

Another consequence of this diplomatic crisis was that in the course of the public furor over the Arcos raid, the Soviets were alerted, for the second time in five years, that their diplomatic ciphers had been broken. Some historians have concluded that "the high priority given [by the British] to wartime sigint [i.e., ULTRA in World War II] security reflected awareness of the damage done by poor interwar security—in particular the loss of the Soviet codes in 1927."[98]

MI5 and Special Branch continued to watch McCartney, who proved difficult to keep under surveillance because for some unknown reason he had access to several legitimate passports issued him by the British Passport Office. In November 1927, however, he and a fellow RU agent, a young German student named Georg Hansen, were arrested. A search of McCartney's residence netted a "formidable quantity of documents," including a codebook and a notebook filled with extensive observations of Royal Army exercises at Tidworth in September.[99] His subsequent trial marked the "first instance of Soviet military espionage to reach the British courts."[100]

Following the raid on Arcos, and the substantially increased scrutiny of MI5, which led Moscow Center to declare Great Britain a "denied area," the base for *Razvedupr* operations against Britain was moved to the Continent—first to Paris and then to Amsterdam. The Fourth Department maintained a presence in Great Britain, however, in the form of a few deep-cover illegal networks established earlier that had no connection to Arcos. Some of these were in British schools and universities, for, like the OGPU, the RU saw in the British educational and scientific elite opportunities to acquire both information and new converts to the cause of the revolution.

The major focus of RU interest in British academia was Cambridge University, where, since 1920, the brilliant young Soviet scientist Peter Kapitza had worked with Sir Ernest Rutherford's research team at the Cavendish Laboratory in an effort to discover a means to split the atom. Regardless of whether or not Kapitza was a willing agent of the RU or any other Soviet intelligence organization, or merely a scientist engaged in legitimate international cooperation, Moscow closely monitored his work, and was from an early date aware of at least some of its potential.

Indeed, the *Razvedupr* apparently considered this research to be so promising that by 1926 it organized an entire illegal residency at Cambridge University, insulated from all its other operations in Great Britain. As a result, "the Soviet intelligence apparatus was already in place at Cambridge when Anthony Blunt [senior member of the 'Cambridge Spy Ring'] entered Trinity College as a first-year Scholar in October 1926."[101] This residency also enabled Red Army Intelligence to follow the development of atomic weapons in the West almost twenty years before anyone outside of New Mexico had ever heard of Los Alamos.

CONCLUSION

In retrospect, we can see some important trends in Red Army espionage from 1921 to 1927. First, as intelligence operations increased in number and complexity, Moscow Center sought to compensate for its generally poorly trained personnel by increasing centralization. This eventually led to huge centers for coordinating diplomatic, espionage, and subversive activities based out of commercial fronts, like Arcos and the PMC, at which intelligence assets and communications facilities could be concentrated. Similar organizations were established in Germany, the United States, and elsewhere throughout the 1920s.

Second, the Fourth Department almost from the very day the Comintern was founded in 1919 began to absorb the latter's intelligence assets, including individual agents and entire networks. This process greatly accelerated after the Zinoviev Letter affair. One important implication of this is that much of the history of the Comintern needs to be rewritten.

Third, because of its very nature and the circumstances it faced in the early 1920s, the RU relied on large numbers of ideologically enthusiastic but usually unskilled and amateurish agents. This combined with poor security in general to make Red Army Intelligence networks both numerous and short lived, and tended to lead to mass and highly publicized arrests that did little to promote abroad an image of the USSR as a "normal" state. The average duration of the networks described in this chapter was two or three years. As we shall see, however, this longevity gradually increased as the RU gained experience and built up a cadre of highly skilled, professional intelligence officers.

NOTES

1. Dallin, *Soviet Espionage*, pp. 110–111.

2. Suvorov asserts that the RU networks in the Baltics were exposed because the Red Army agents there could not tie a necktie properly; Suvorov, *Soviet Military Intelligence*, p. 13.

3. Ibid., p. 14.

4. In May 1927, Yan Berzin rejected such a study of open source material on German economic planning during the world war; see Samuelson, *Soviet Defence*, p. 38.

5. The INO nevertheless continued to try to poach on this territory; see Corson and Crowley, *New KGB*, p. 280.

6. Andrew and Gordievsky state that this was one of the main reasons, in addition to his pioneering work in sigint and his recruitment of Sorge, why Berzin was the only RU officer whose portrait was hung in the Memory Room of the KGB's First

Chief Directorate (the successor to the INO); see Andrew and Gordievsky, *KGB*, pp. 173–174. Also, see Corson and Crowley, *New KGB*, p. 278.

7. Dallin, *Soviet Espionage*, p. 32.

8. Andrew and Gordievsky, *KGB*, pp. 69–70; Suvorov, *Soviet Military Intelligence*, p. 13.

9. Poretsky, *Our Own People*, p. 53.

10. Corson and Crowley asserted that the founders of these firms were two Polish brothers, Aaron and Abraham Ehrenlieb; see Corson and Crowley, *New KGB*, pp. 279–280. Jacob Mrachkovskii was identified by Suvorov as the brother of Sergei Mrachkovskii, in Suvorov, *Soviet Military Intelligence*, p. 14. Sergei, a Central Committee member, was later charged by the OGPU with running a "Trotskyite printing press" and participating in the "plot" to kill Sergei Kirov; he was consequently a defendant in the first "Show Trial" of August 1936; see Robert Conquest, *The Great Terror: Reassessment* (New York: Oxford University Press, 1990), pp. 83–94, *passim*. Whether or not Sergei Mrachkovskii was in fact the other "Ehrenlieb" brother is unknown.

11. For information about Soviet-German trade, see R. H. Haigh, D. S. Morris, and A. R. Peters, *German-Soviet Relations in the Weimar Era: Friendship from Necessity* (Aldershot, Engl.: Gower Publishing Company, 1985), p. 135.

12. In 1935 Aaron tried to open a branch of *Wostwag* in New York, but was denied a visa by the State Department. Corson and Crowley, *New KGB*, pp. 280–281; Suvorov, *Soviet Military Intelligence*, p. 14.

13. Ironically, many of these ships, including several obtained by the Soviets from the United States before and during World War II, were used as prison ships by the OGPU and for transporting prisoners to the gulags; Corson and Crowley, *New KGB*, p. 295.

14. Hilger and Meyer, *Incompatible Allies*, p. 108.

15. The RU's efforts in this regard were greatly facilitated by the assistance of Edo Fimmen, the chief of the Hamburg Seamen and Transport Workers' Union. Andrew and Gordievsky, *KGB*, p. 93.

16. Corson and Crowley, *New KGB*, p. 292.

17. The only major concern J. Edgar Hoover had about clandestine Soviet activity in the United States before World War II seems to have been Comintern and CPUSA (Communist Party of the United States) efforts to organize networks, infiltrate unions, and control shipping "on the Pacific Coast, the Gulf Coast and . . . the Atlantic Coast"; see "Confidential Memo, FBI Director J. Edgar Hoover, August 24, 1936," in Athan Theoharis, ed., *From the Secret Files of J. Edgar Hoover* (Chicago: Ivan R. Dee, 1991), pp. 180–182.

18. Corson and Crowley also note that RU access to merchant shipping facilitated the kidnapping and return to Moscow of defectors and other "traitors"; see their *New KGB*, pp. 293–294.

19. Ibid., pp. 305, 436, 446, 448–449.

20. Ibid., pp. 296–297.

21. Yu. D. Dyakov and T. S. Busheyeva, *The Red Army and the Wehrmacht: How the Soviets Militarized Germany, 1922–33, and Paved the Way for Fascism* (New York: Prometheus Books, 1995), p. 132; TsGASA, f. 33987, op. 3, d. 151, l. 77–9.

A few comments on this source are necessary. This is the English translation of a Russian collection of documents, Yu. L. D'yakov and T. S. Bushueva, *Fashistskii mech kovalsya v SSSR* [The Fascist knife forged in the USSR] (Moscow: "Sovetskaya Rossiya," 1992). The translation, although adequate, was obviously done in haste and suffers from numerous errors. For example, the transliteration of D'yakov's name is incorrect (indeed, the English edition uses two different spellings for it, neither of which are D'yakov). Furthermore, for some inexplicable reason, although all the documents in the Russian version are clearly from TsGASA (Central State Archives of the Soviet Army), a variety of puzzling abbreviations are used in the English translation. Most of the citations used here are, for the sake of convenience, taken from the English edition. In the case of egregiously bad translation, I double-checked the original for improvement. I have also used the archival identification of TsGASA throughout. Citations from the English edition will be given as Dyakov and Bushuyeva, *Red Army*; for the Russian, it will be thus: D'yakov and Bushueva, *Fashistskii mech*. Documents contained in these works will be cited as follows: authors, title, p. (in book); TsGASA, f., op. (if given), d. (if given), l. (pages of document, if given).

22. Poretsky, *Our Own People*, p. 81.

23. Suvorov, *Soviet Military Intelligence*, p. 18.

24. All information about the Vienna RU residency is from Poretsky, *Our Own People*, pp. 58–71.

25. The Fourth Department residency in Turkey was responsible for operations in Arabia and the Balkans; see Agabekov, *OGPU*, p. 209. RU residencies in the Near and Middle East were mainly concerned with the Caucasus, Central Asia, and Afghanistan; their primary objective, as always, was to monitor and sabotage British activities in the region. As of 1931, the Fourth Department *rezident* in Ahwaz, Persia, was "Hippolitov." He officially held the post of Soviet consul; earlier he had served in a similar capacity in Tashkent. Ibid., p. 23.

26. Poretsky, *Our Own People*, p. 59.

27. Ibid., pp. 62–63.

28. Ibid., p. 66.

29. Ibid., p. 69.

30. Apparently the Fourth Department did not even employ anyone who knew French, a language central to both intelligence operations and diplomacy, at the Vienna residency. Ibid., p. 71.

31. Dallin, *Rise of Russia in Asia*, pp. 188–191.

32. Mitarevsky, *World Wide*, p. 79, also see ibid., p. 193.

33. Zaisser went on to command an International Brigade under Yan Berzin in Spain as "General Gomez"; he organized pro-Soviet German POWs during World War II and served as the German Democratic Republic's first head of the Ministry for State Security until 1953. See Dallin, *Rise of Russia in Asia*, pp. 89–90; and Neuberg, *Armed Insurrection*, pp. 19 fn. 14.

34. Mitarevsky, *World Wide*, p. 14.

35. Neuberg, *Armed Insurrection*, p. 22. In early 1924 Ho Chi Minh was vice-president of a special bureau of the Comintern responsible for overseeing and organizing peasant movements; see ibid., p. 22. For more on "Muraille," see below and next chapter.

36. Mitarevsky, *World Wide*, pp. 13–15, 71–72.

37. Ibid., chap. 11.

38. Ibid., pp. 14–15.

39. Ibid., p. 14.

40. Ibid.

41. Ibid., p. 72.

42. Ibid., pp. 72–75.

43. Ibid., pp. 61–62.

44. Ibid., p. 60.

45. Ibid. This last instruction is probably a good indication of both the difficulty of communications for the Fourth Department (radio communications were subject to frequent technical problems and vulnerable to the code-breaking efforts of hostile powers), and the problem of relaying information securely over great distances, especially to and from Asia.

46. Ibid., pp. 170–171.

47. Ibid., pp. 61–62.

48. Ibid., pp. 64–65.

49. Ibid., p. 62.

50. Ibid., pp. 63–64.

51. Ibid., p. 61.

52. Ibid., pp. 65–68. RU domination of the CER also allowed the GPU to infiltrate its people into the railroad; the chekists even managed to get the CER to partially pay for their operations. The Harbin RU resident, Seversky, complained to Moscow about this in May 1926; see ibid., pp. 70–71.

53. Ibid., p. 79. Mitarevsky does not give a breakdown on how much of this total was spent by each residency. Residency No. 11 (Changsha) requested from Moscow 29,000 gold dollars, more than Beijing, Mukden, Harbin, and Shantung combined.

54. See, for example, Berzin's remarks in the 1926 threat assessment discussed in chapter 7.

55. Mitarevsky, *World Wide*, pp. 76–77.

56. For some examples, see ibid., pp. 157–162.

57. Ibid., pp. 168–169.

58. Andrew and Gordievsky, *KGB*, p. 87.

59. See, for example, the documents cited by Mitarevsky in *World Wide*, chap. 10.

60. Western diplomats in general failed to take Soviet espionage seriously; Corson and Crowley, *New KGB*, p. 46.

61. Dallin, *Russia in Asia*, pp. 231–232.

62. Ibid., p. 232.

63. For more on Soviet perceptions of French foreign policy, see chapter 7.

64. Agabekov, *OGPU*, p. 195; Dallin, *Soviet Espionage*, pp. 25–26.

65. Unless otherwise noted, information about Fourth Department operations in France comes from Dallin, *Soviet Espionage*, chap. 2.

66. For the early history of the PCF, see the following sources: Edward Mortimer, *The Rise of the French Communist Party, 1920–1947* (London: Faber and Faber, 1984), Part 1; M. Aderath, *The French Communist Party, a Critical History (1920–84): From Comintern to 'the Colours of France'* (Manchester: Manchester University Press, 1984), pp. 15–58; Ronald Tiersky, *French Communism, 1920–1972* (New York: Columbia University Press, 1974), pp. 13–53; and Robert Wohl, *French Communism in the Making, 1914–1924* (Stanford: Stanford University Press), 1966.

67. Tiersky, *French Communism*, p. 45.

68. Mortimer, *Rise of the French*, chap. 3.

69. Adereth, *French Communist Party*, pp. 45–50.

70. Dallin, *Soviet Espionage*, p. 28.

71. Ibid., p. 32.

72. This followed recognition by several other countries that same year; in addition to Great Britain, these included Italy, Norway, Austria, Greece, Sweden, China, and Denmark; Heller and Nekrich, *Utopia*, p. 209.

73. Dallin, *Soviet Espionage*, p. 37.

74. Suvorov, *Soviet Military Intelligence*, p. 17; Dallin, *Soviet Espionage*, p. 34.

75. Mitarevsky, *World Wide*, p. 199.

76. Ibid.; see also Fischer, *Stalin*, p. 579.

77. Peter Shipley, *Hostile Action: The KGB and Secret Soviet Operations in Britain* (London, Pinter, 1989), p. 37.

78. Shipley, who cites this case from a British Home Office file (PRO: HO 24834), provides no information about any government action by the British or French against Ogareff. The context of his description, however, implies that the French were responsible for shutting his operation down, probably in December 1926. It also remains unclear whether or not the *Sûreté* connected this episode to the activities of Cremet or Uzdanski.

79. Sergent was one of the two St. Cyr Communist city councilmen in Cremet's network referred to above.

80. Dallin, *Soviet Espionage*, p. 36.

81. *New York Times*, 11 April 1927.

82. Fischer, *Stalin*, p. 579; also see Wohl, *French Communism*, pp. 407–411.

83. Heller and Nekrich, *Utopia*, p. 215.

84. Fischer, *Stalin*, p. 579.

85. Ibid.

86. Nigel West, *MI5: British Security Service Operations, 1909–1945* (London: The Bodley Head, 1981), p. 54. On Arcos, see also John Costello, *Mask of Treachery: Spies, Lies and Betrayal* (New York: Warner Books, 1989), chap. 4; and Corson and Crowley, *New KGB*, pp. 283–284.

87. The GC & CS was the successor to the famed "Room 40" of the British Admiralty, which broke German military and diplomatic codes in World War I, and intercepted and decoded the Zimmerman Telegram. The GC & CS was in the 1930s moved to Bletchley Park, and during World War II was responsible for breaking German "Enigma" codes and producing ULTRA intelligence. On the GC & CS and Soviet radio communications in the early 1920s, see West, *MI5*, pp. 49–50, and Costello, *Mask of Treachery*, pp. 85–86.

88. As indicated earlier, this was an important factor in British concerns about Soviet operations in China, and probably a contributing motivation for the Chinese police raid on the Peking Military Center.

On the Comintern in Britain in the early 1920s, see Nollau, *International Communism*, p. 97; Fischer, *Stalin*, pp. 559–560; and Shipley, *Hostile Action*, pp. 23–38. Anthony Cave Brown and Charles B. MacDonald cover similar ground in *On a Field of Red: The Communist International and the Coming of World War II* (New York: G. P. Putnam's Sons, 1981). However, Brown and MacDonald's work is superficial and contains numerous factual errors.

89. The best summary of the Zinoviev Letter affair is Fischer, *Stalin*, pp. 458–463. See also Andrew and Gordievsky, *KGB*, pp. 92–93; West, *MI5*, pp. 50–51; Costello, *Mask of Treachery*, pp. 93–94; and Corson and Crowley, *New KGB*, pp. 86–89.

90. Kuusinen, *Before and after Stalin*, pp. 50–51.

91. Andrew and Gordievsky, *KGB*, p. 93.

On the Zinoviev Letter and Polish Military Intelligence, see Anna M. Cienciala and Titus Komarnicki, *From Versailles to Locarno: Keys to Polish Foreign Policy, 1919–1925* (Lawrence: University Press of Kansas, 1984), p. 229. A Polish military intelligence officer attached to the Berlin legation, Captain Paciorkowski, arranged for Russian émigrés to produce the forgery. The objective of this operation, speculate Cienciala and Komarnicki, was to sabotage ratification of the recently negotiated series of Anglo-Soviet trade agreements (p. 229). According to Richard Gid Powers, who cites as his source the *New York Evening Post*, these "anti-Soviet Russians" were arrested in 1929 and confessed to "wholesale frauds over a five-year period" that included the Zinoviev note; see his *Not without Honor: The History of American Anticommunism* (New York: The Free Press, 1995), p. 84. They also may have tried to pass other similar documents, the ultimate provenance of which remains unknown, to American anticommunist journalists in 1924 and again in 1928, including incriminating material supposedly from Amtorg. Ibid., pp. 83–85; on Amtorg, see chap. 6.

92. Shipley, *Hostile Action*, p. 37.

93. Costello, *Mask of Treachery*, p. 88.

94. Ibid., pp. 97–102; and West, *MI5*, pp. 53–58.

95. Shipley claims that the document passed to McCartney via MI5 was an army manual called "Descriptions of and Instructions for Wireless Telegraphy" (p. 39).

96. Corson and Crowley, *New KGB*, pp. 285–286.

97. Ibid., pp. 286–287.

98. Christopher Andrew, "Introduction: Intelligence and International Relations 1900–1945," in *Intelligence and International Relations 1900–1945*, ed. by Christopher Andrew (Exeter, U.K.: Exeter University Publications, 1987), p. 4; also see Corson and Crowley, *New KGB*, p. 286.

99. West, *MI5*, pp. 59–62.

100. Shipley, *Hostile Action*, p. 41.

101. Costello, *Mask of Treachery*, pp. 106–107. See also Shipley, *Hostile Action*, pp. 29–30; Andrew Sinclair, *The Red and the Blue: Intelligence, Treason and the Universities* (London: Weidenfeld and Nicolson, 1986), pp. 26–29; and Peter Wright, *Spycatcher: The Candid Autobiography of a Senior Intelligence Officer* (New York: Viking Penguin, 1987), pp. 259–260.

CHAPTER 4

Espionage, 1928–1933:
Part 1

The years between 1928 and 1933 were characterized by the consolidation of Stalin's power in the USSR and the continued expansion of the Red Army Intelligence Directorate's capabilities abroad. These developments were closely related. The Red Army had a vested interest in the creation in the Soviet Union of a large and sophisticated industrial base, for this was necessary for the transformation of the Soviet military into a modern force. Threat assessments prepared by the RU emphasized the importance of such a transformation in response to the growing imperialist threat. These views coincided with Stalin's, for he sought to transform the Soviet Union into a modern industrial society by carrying out a "revolution from above." He also hoped to make the USSR into a genuine workers' state by eliminating the independent peasantry. These goals were reflected in the planning and execution of the first Five Year Plan. The Fourth Department played a central role in this process not only by providing in its threat analysis an important justification for such a policy, but also by obtaining through espionage much needed technical information on everything from chemical manufacturing processes to sophisticated machine tools to the application of advanced metallurgical techniques used to rifle tank guns.

The international environment also saw profound changes. By 1932, much of the capitalist world had tumbled into a deep economic depression that created new opportunities and new dangers for Moscow. The depression brought an upsurge in admiration for the USSR by many in the West who regarded with amazement and awe the one state that seemed to have avoided the disaster. Soviet intelligence took advantage of this sympathy to recruit agents in the highest political, social, and cultural circles. Meanwhile, Japan's polices in the Far East became more aggressive. A brief but bloody Japanese occupation of Shanghai in 1932 followed hard on the heels of the conquest of Manchuria, which began in late 1931 in the wake of the "Mukden Incident." At the same time in Germany, the virulently anti-Soviet National Socialists steadily gained political support, leading President Paul von Hindenburg in January 1933 to appoint Adolf Hitler chancellor. The emergence of these two powerful threats led Moscow to fundamentally reassess its strategic position.

THE "WAR SCARE"

The 1927 "war scare" has until quite recently remained controversial. In retrospect, its chief significance now appears to be the role it played in consolidating Stalin's triumph over his political opposition. This "war scare" resulted from a combination of real crises, Soviet paranoia, and Stalin's opportunism. Few in the senior Soviet leadership seem to have really believed that war was imminent.

In May 1926, Joseph Pilsudski, the Polish general who had defeated Tukhachevsky near Warsaw in 1920 and who was regarded by Moscow as one of its most "implacable enemies," came to power in Poland following a military coup.[1] The Soviets viewed this development with alarm. Shortly thereafter, within the first six months of 1927, there occurred a series of international crises, most of which were the result of provocative Soviet clandestine operations.

During this time, Soviet spies were exposed and arrested in Czechoslovakia, Poland, Turkey, Switzerland, and Lithuania.[2] Early that same April the Cremet scandal began in France. Later that month came the raid on the Peking Military Center, soon followed by Chiang Kai-shek's attack on the Chinese communists. Meanwhile, by May increasing tension between Great Britain and the USSR, spurred by the police raid on Arcos headquarters, resulted in the severance of diplomatic relations. That same month an RU lieutenant colonel named Yevgenni Kozhevinko (a.k.a. "Eugene Pick") defected to the Nationalists in China.[3] In Warsaw in early June a "Russian monarchist" assassinated the Soviet ambassador to Poland, Pyotr Voikov, who allegedly had participated in the executions of Tsar Nicholas II and his family.[4] In July, police arrested 700 communists in Berlin. And throughout that year, there were numerous smaller crises, including the defections of three OGPU officers and the expulsion of the Fourth Department naval attaché in Sweden.[5]

By the end of June 1927, tensions between the USSR and many of its European neighbors led some people in Moscow to begin to seriously worry about war.[6] Following the Arcos raid, the OGPU had arrested several "former noblemen" who held positions in the Soviet government; twenty of them were shot the day after Voikov's murder. Throughout the summer and fall, the Soviet leadership organized numerous mobilization drills and "militarized activities" designed to prepare the public for hostilities.[7] By the end of the year, the collapse of Soviet policy in China contributed to the sense of crisis.

For many years, scholars have debated whether or not this "war scare" was genuine from the Soviet perspective. Recently released documents, however, clearly indicate that the Soviet leadership did not, in fact, believe that war was imminent. The Fourth Department, the agency most responsible for making such a determination, concluded in threat assessments prepared in 1926 and 1927 that, although the likelihood of a conflict with the capitalist world was objectively increasing, an outbreak of hostilities in the near to intermediate future was highly unlikely. In early 1927, after Pilsudski's coup but presumably before the police raid on the PMC, Yan Berzin estimated that "in what was undertaken during 1926 and is anticipated for 1927, we do not see any immediate war preparations during 1927."[8] And in July, even after the major crises in Peking, London, and France, Tukhachevsky, reflecting the views of the RU, asserted that "the Red Army proceeds precisely from the assumption that war would be unlikely during the next five years." He went on to observe that "otherwise, if we assume war as probable before that date, it would not make sense to work on a 5-year plan, which in any case would be interrupted by the war."[9] Both of these statements were in documents widely circulated among the Soviet leadership. The fact that planning and execution of the Five Year Plan proceeded undisturbed (at least by the prospects of imminent foreign conflict) demonstrates the validity of Tukhachevsky's conclusions.

In fact, the "war scare" proved immensely opportune for Stalin, who used it to foster an air of crisis, both in the Soviet Union and among communist sympathizers abroad, which would facilitate his bid for supremacy in the CPSU leadership and build support for his foreign and domestic policies. Commissar for Foreign Affairs G. Chicherin told American journalist Louis Fischer in 1929 that "in June 1927 I returned from Western Europe. Everyone in Moscow was talking about war. I did my best to dissuade them: 'No one is planning to attack us,' I insisted. Then I was enlightened by a colleague. He told me: 'Hush, we know that. But we need this for the struggle against Trotsky.'"[10] By October 1927, as we have seen, Stalin had indeed managed to engineer the expulsion of Trotsky and Zinoviev from the Central Committee, and in the following month they and their supporters were expelled from the Party. In January 1928 the Politburo banished Trotsky and his family to Alma-Alta; a year later he was deported.[11]

Despite the fact that the "war scare" was almost certainly a deliberate fabrication fully supported by Stalin, he may have nevertheless believed the essential elements of it. There is good reason to suppose that Stalin did, in fact, think the British were behind the Soviet diplomatic setbacks of 1927, and that he saw the arrests, raids on Soviet diplomatic posts, assassinations, and defections as part of an elaborate plan orchestrated by the British Conservative Party to sabotage Soviet interests. Like all good conspiracy theories, this one had the advantage of being able to explain everything, from the setbacks in China, to the Arcos raid, and the murder of Voikov, which Stalin argued had been "organized by the agents of the Conservative Party in imitation of the assassination of the Archduke Franz Ferdinand."[12] This conspiratorial view of the world was not unique to Stalin, however; and, as we shall see, it largely determined the course of Red Army Intelligence threat assessment.

REFORM OF OPERATIONS

The failures of 1927 led the Fourth Department to reassess its foreign intelligence operations. This in part reflected the increasingly sophisticated debate going on in the Red Army, which relied heavily, like many before it in the Russian army, on historical analysis. It is no coincidence that the RU adopted a similar approach. *Armed Insurrection*, compiled in 1928, was an effort to understand the lessons of five years of failed attempts at promoting revolution (see chapter 2). The following year saw the publication of a textbook on *razvedka* called *Operativnaya razvedka* (Operational Intelligence) under the auspices of the Frunze Military Academy.[13] This work sought to define the elements of *razvedka*, and analyzed intelligence operations through historical examples and recent experience.

These monographs demonstrate both the increasing sophistication of Red Army thinking and the RU's growing emphasis on professionalism. Indeed, *Armed Insurrection* and *Operational Intelligence* were used in classes taught at high-level Red Army schools, including the Frunze Academy. This suggests that by the early 1930s, if not earlier, instruction in intelligence methods and operations was incorporated into the curriculum for training senior staff officers. The objective may have been to improve the overall skills and performance of Red Army command staffs, to increase the pool of potential recruits for RU foreign operations, or, most probably, both.

The embarrassments of 1927 also led to major changes in how the Fourth Department and the INO functioned abroad. The separation between legal and illegal residencies became more rigorous, and Moscow Center promulgated standardized procedures for handling and disposing of sensitive material. Former INO officer G. S. Agabekov reported that after receiving this directive, which no doubt reflected the bitter experience of the PMC and Arcos raids, the RU and INO residencies in Teheran sorted "huge piles of paper for destruction. For a whole week these papers burned in the yard of the embassy."[14]

As noted previously, several sources, including David Dallin, and Christopher Andrew and Oleg Gordievsky, have asserted that Moscow Center ordered that intelligence operations and personnel be henceforth "strictly forbidden" from having any association with the local communist parties.[15] The Comintern, whose status dropped precipitously after the Chinese disaster, was supposedly also severed from virtually all connections with intelligence. The evidence clearly demonstrates, however, that the responsibilities of the underground organization of the Comintern, the OMS, for espionage and clandestine recruitment actually increased, especially in Germany, the United States, and China (see next two chapters). Before the reforms, OMS networks were usually run directly by a Soviet intelligence officer, or a local party member co-opted by the RU. After 1927, agents of the OMS usually acted as liaisons between the Comintern and Red Army Intelligence, relaying Moscow Center's instructions to the local communist underground but otherwise remaining aloof from actual espionage.

This arrangement obviously meant that for all practical purposes liaison between the Comintern and the Soviet intelligence services continued. The main effect of the changes was not to sever this relationship but to add to it an extra layer of security. If Moscow Center decided to directly recruit a foreign communist, he or she was required to resign immediately from the Party. From 1927 on, this remained standard procedure.[16]

THE *SPETS OTDEL*

The public revelations in the Arcos trial confirmed earlier Soviet suspicions that their wireless communications, including diplomatic radio traffic, had been compromised. The British code breakers were dismayed to see all their hard work ruined by these disclosures. The operational head of GC & CS, A. G. Denniston, commented that the chief result of this publicity was to "compromise our work beyond question."[17] As it turned out, Great Britain was not the only foreign power reading Soviet radio messages. The Poles, French, Italians, Japanese, and probably others as well had regularly managed to break into Soviet wireless traffic since the early 1920s.[18]

The Fourth Department and the INO responded to this problem in two ways. First, they adopted the unbreakable "one-time pad" cipher system for most agent communications; this managed to foil even the British GC & CS until World War II.[19] Second, Yan Berzin proposed that a special department be created solely for the purposes of decrypting foreign radio traffic. This was hardly a unique idea, for, as noted above, several nations were already committed to similar operations. Indeed, Imperial Russia had been notably adept at code breaking, and Christopher Andrew notes that before 1914 Russian cryptanalysts "succeeded . . . in decrypting, at least intermittently, the diplomatic traffic of all the great powers."[20] The decision taken sometime around 1930 to build up a sizeable "sigint" operation probably resulted from a combination of factors. These included the need to improve Soviet radio security; the availability of technical and personnel resources that simply did not exist before; and recent espionage coups, like the recruitment of a cipher clerk in the British Foreign Ministry, who provided materials facilitating code-breaking efforts.

Consequently, a joint RU/OGPU unit called the *Spets otdel* (Special Department) was established under the direct command of the OGPU. This unit traced its roots to a Cheka department created in 1920 or 1921. Although

Andrew and Gordievsky assert that the purposes of the early sigint unit "at this stage seem to have been rather assorted and largely concerned with labor camps," by the mid-1920s it was routinely deciphering the diplomatic traffic of most of the European powers, including Great Britain.[21] By 1929 or 1930, it was breaking into coded foreign traffic frequently enough to issue a weekly summary of its encryption solutions to the OGPU command and the Central Committee.[22]

The new sigint unit was housed originally in an office of the *Narkomindel* on Kuznetsky Bridge. As the OGPU's ascendancy over the Fourth Department began in the mid-1930s, the chekists gained more control over the sigint unit, and by 1935 it was relocated to OGPU headquarters at Lubianka. The man in charge was an OGPU officer named Gleb Boky; his second-in-command was a Fourth Department colonel named P. Kharkevika.[23]

Andrew and Gordievsky maintain that the *Spets otdel* became "the world's largest and best-resourced sigint agency" in the 1930s. Its efforts were deliberately supported by espionage. Although most of the specific accomplishments of Soviet sigint remain unknown, there is good reason to believe that it achieved important successes, most notably against the Japanese in the 1930s. Indeed, Andrew and Gordievsky have suggested that much of the information later attributed to the activities of Richard Sorge was actually derived from the penetration of Japanese military and diplomatic radio traffic.[24]

A special school for training Fourth Department officers in radio intelligence work was also established at about the same time. The Radio School of the Intelligence Directorate was created probably sometime in 1930 or 1931 on the outskirts of Moscow in the Lenin Hills district. Like the *Spets otdel*, this was a joint OGPU–Red Army operation. Originally mostly a collection of antennae, the school grew rapidly as new administrative buildings and laboratories were added.[25] The school's first director was probably a former Austrian officer and signals expert named "Lyamberg." Most of the students were "foreign," so German, French, English, and Italian were more common than Russian. Most of them were "the Red Army's most valuable illegal agents, foreign Communists, or Comintern operatives."[26] Coursework consisted of technical training and political indoctrination by the Fourth Department's Political Division. Students were taught theoretical information, like the physics of radio communications, as well as how to operate a wide variety of radio equipment, ranging from the ordinary to the exotic.[27] The school's illustrious graduates included RU star Ruth Werner and several of Richard Sorge's radio operators.

FRANCE

France remained a lucrative target for Berzin's Fourth Department. Soviet penetration of the French chemical and armaments industries continued, and intelligence on French developments also proved valuable in judging the credibility and intentions of Moscow's German partners.[28] Not only was intelligence available on French military intentions and capabilities, but through French sources the RU could also assess the military potential of a variety of other nations, including Poland, with which Paris maintained especially close military and intelligence ties, and Romania. France also made a good base of operations against other intelligence targets, such as Great Britain and Germany.

The precise organization of Fourth Department operations in France after 1927 remains hazy. David Dallin's description suggests that one major residency in France was responsible for supervising several smaller networks. If so, this would have been analogous to Berlin Center and the PMC. Such an approach ensured the continuity and growth of Red Army Intelligence in France despite the arrests of its senior leadership there every few years.

Dallin describes the period between 1928 and 1932 as the "heyday of Soviet intelligence activity in France."[29] In part, this reflected the relatively low priority given to counterespionage by French security forces, which were primarily concerned with subversion at home and in the colonies. Another problem was that the *Sûreté*, and probably military counterintelligence as well, assumed after 1927 that known French communists would still be closely connected to Soviet espionage organs. Consequently, they invested most of their counterespionage efforts on generally futile surveillance of people who had been expressly forbidden by Moscow to have any contact with the Soviet intelligence services.

The increasing professionalism and skill of Soviet intelligence officers were, of course, also important factors in the general success of Fourth Department penetration of France. The foremost example of this was the career of "General Muraille." This charismatic figure, who was described by a French communist as "an amazing man, an adventurer of a high order," was a forty-five-year-old veteran Bolshevik in 1929. Muraille had served as a Red Army commissar during the Soviet-Polish War, and shortly thereafter transferred to the Red Army Intelligence Directorate. Cultured, sophisticated, multilingual, and cosmopolitan, Muraille was an intelligence officer in the best tradition of the early Fourth Department. Throughout the 1920s he carried out a variety of RU tasks abroad, including intelligence missions to China. He managed to elude the French police following the exposure of the Cremet-Uzdanski *apparat* in the spring of 1927, and Moscow Center thereafter assigned him to rebuild an illegal residency in France.

Muraille presented himself to the PCF leadership as a "talent scout" for the Comintern in search of promising young men and women from the Party's youth organizations who might profit from an all-expenses-paid education at a CPSU school.[30] His contact was Henri Barbé, the PCF's liaison to the Comintern, and, by the mid-1930s, head of the French Politburo. With the full support of his French comrades, Barbé enthusiastically put Muraille in touch with promising young people affiliated with the Party. Muraille recruited several of them as agents. Precisely how many he recruited, and how many of them knew that they were actually working for Red Army Intelligence, remains unknown; probably the number of "conscious" agents was very few. The PCF leadership eventually became suspicious, and predictably protested to Moscow about Muraille's activities.

In 1931, the Comintern, no doubt on Moscow Center's orders, ordered Barbé to come to Moscow "to report on the situation." According to Barbé, the meetings he had with Comintern leaders O. Piatnitsky and D. Manuilsky proved less than satisfactory. Far from sharing his concern about the exploits of Muraille and Red Army Intelligence, the Comintern high command, and then Moscow Center, told him he should cease whining and be more cooperative. Barbé even claimed that a man he described as "Berzin" tried to recruit him. The Frenchman turned him down. The two parted on civil terms, but nothing had been resolved. Indeed, the chief of the Fourth Department's legal residency in Paris, "André," later made a similar offer to Barbé that met with similar rejection.[31]

Muraille's network in France, meanwhile, was busily gathering information on diverse military targets, including the French air force and navy. For naval espionage, a key priority for espionage in France, Muraille employed a strategy using "floating agents." They moved from port to port, establishing themselves among the local community by joining workers' organizations or opening small shops that provided cover for visits to naval bases, taking advantage of the highly radicalized maritime workers of Europe's ports. The *Razvedupr* acquired extensive intelligence on French torpedo and submarine technology and deployments, port defense facilities, and, in one case, the blueprints for a French aircraft, which were stolen, photographed, and then replaced.[32]

All the while, French counterintelligence tried to keep up with the Soviets. On numerous occasions, they apprehended one or two junior members of a minor network, but Muraille continually evaded arrest until April 1931. At his trial, he offered a creative explanation for the evidence against him, which was designed to appeal to French sentiment. His basic defense was that the charges stemmed from misunderstandings over a failed love affair. Muraille apparently knew his audience well, for the court found his tale compelling enough to grant him a clemency of sorts; his sentence was only three years. Upon his release in 1934, he was deported from France, and thereafter disappeared.

Another major RU network in France centered on the curious phenomenon of the "*rabkors*," or "worker-correspondents." Begun during the heady days of cultural and social liberation associated with Lenin's "New Economic Policy" (NEP), the idea was to replace the bourgeois press corps of the past with a new breed of proletarian reporter. This movement started in the press, and thousands of young Soviet men and women were encouraged to participate. The impossibility of having untrained writers pass as educated commentators, however, soon became apparent. Indeed, the chief beneficiary of this movement in the USSR was the OGPU, which found that these young people were especially eager to report on despised or corrupt local officials and Party members. Outside the Soviet Union, however, the Comintern-sponsored *rabkor* movement retained its intellectual pretensions and popularity well into the 1930s. This may have reflected the patronage of Lenin's sister, Maria Ulianovna, who was a strong supporter of the *rabkors*; she even published a book in 1928 entitled *The Rabkor Movement Abroad*.[33]

The Soviet intelligence organs quickly saw opportunity in this unorganized enthusiasm. Sometime in 1928 or 1929, Muraille, together with PCF leader and INO agent Jacques Duclos, set up a commission to review *rabkor* reports and sift out anything that had intelligence value. This commission was created to appear as a legal communist organization. Its membership included a liaison with the Comintern, Izaia Bir. The commission's stated purpose was to keep the workers of France and the rest of the world informed about the warlike intentions and preparations of Paris. Bir had in actuality been a *Razvedupr* officer since at least the mid-1920s. He was born in Poland around 1904, but sometime in the early 1920s he was stripped of his Polish citizenship for refusing military service. It was probably shortly thereafter that Bir emigrated to Palestine, one of many militant young European Jews attracted to the Zionist movement at that time. In Palestine he became associated with other Jewish expatriates who later rose to prominence in the Comintern or Fourth Department, including Alter Strom, Leopold Trepper, Leo Grossvogel, Hillel Katz, and Sophie Posnanska.[34]

Longing to make their mark in the world, many of these estranged young intellectuals eventually returned to Europe, where they were co-opted by the Soviet intelligence services. The Fourth Department, which had always held a much stronger ideological appeal than the OGPU, got the lion's share of these capable recruits. Izaia Bir was one of the first of these, and one of the most gifted. In the mid-1920s, he returned to France, ostensibly to study engineering, but almost at once he began working for the RU. In 1929, at the age of twenty-five, Moscow Center considered Bir experienced enough to assign him to Muraille's *rabkor* commission. He was also given the task of organizing an agent network for collecting *rabkor* information. Together with Alter Strom, who was responsible for recruitment and organization, Bir managed a network that provided Moscow Center, and, through Duclos probably the INO, with much information for almost three years.[35]

The *Sûreté* eventually learned of the existence of an extensive spy ring being run by a skilled and fortunate agent. In fact, they had been aware of Bir's activities for some time, and the French police knew his method of operation, though not his actual identity, well enough to give him a code name, "Phantomas" (the Phantom), after a character from a popular contemporary mystery novel noted for his daring and ability to elude the police. Police began to assemble a picture of his operations by linking together chance arrests of individuals who turned out to be associated with the "Phantom," suspicious events, and an odd but systematic connection between Soviet agents and the style of their suits.[36]

Most of the senior people in this network had known each other from their *kibbutzim* days in Palestine. Although he denied it in his memoirs, Leopold Trepper almost certainly was one of Bir's key lieutenants, ordered by Strom to come to France in 1930 to join the group. Twenty-eight years old in 1932, he was also the network's oldest member.[37] His subsequent assignment to investigate the causes of the network's exposure and destruction by the French police, given him personally by Berzin, certainly supports this conclusion, as does the fact that he considered many of the senior people in Bir's organization his closest associates; Strom, he wrote, was his "childhood friend."[38]

Bir's main resources were the staffs of the communist journals *L'Humanité* and *Bulletin d'Information*, the latter of which was expressly created as a front for this purpose, and PCF chiefs in the provinces who forwarded what they considered to be useful *rabkor* reports to the "commission" in care of Bir or Strom. In 1928, *L'Humanité* had access to 1,200 "worker correspondents"; by 1934 the number had risen to 4,000.[39] One of the most prolific suppliers of *rabkor* information was a young communist named Riquier who worked on the editorial staff of both publications. Riquier remained unaware of the real identity of the ultimate beneficiary of his labors until 1932.

Together, Bir, Strom and Trepper managed the flow of information, sorting out valuable data and forwarding it directly to the legal residency in Paris or by courier to Berlin.[40] Intelligence collected by Bir's *apparat* included reports on the organization and strength of French forces stationed abroad, data about French war production capabilities, and technical information on naval guns and torpedoes. This network also infiltrated several French arsenals and factories, including an ordnance depot at Brienne-le-Château and an anti-aircraft gun factory in Tours.

However, the French police eventually caught up with Bir, too. The precise circumstances surrounding the arrests of Bir, Strom, and the others remain unknown. David Dallin reports that, as had happened earlier in both Britain and France, one of the network's "unconscious" agents grew suspicious and went to the authorities. In this case, the "weak link" turned out to be Riquier. Realizing by February 1932 that his hard work was actually on behalf of Moscow, Riquier approached the French police and offered to help break up the RU ring. In June Bir, Strom, and five French communists were arrested, although Trepper escaped. They were tried and convicted by November. Most of those involved received sentences of three years in prison, a term that by then had become "standard in Soviet espionage cases in French courts," and were amnestied after one.[41]

The fact that there were relatively few arrests, and that the sentences for those convicted were so light, may indicate just how little the *Sûreté* actually discovered about the activities of "Phantomas" and his network. In fact,

Dallin ascribes the leniency of the French courts to widespread naiveté about Soviet espionage among the French authorities. This may have been more a factor in the sentencing than in the subsequent amnesties, for Paris might have arranged the latter partly as a gesture of good will prior to the conclusion of a Franco-Soviet nonaggression pact in May 1933.[42]

The immediate results of the network's partial collapse were clear enough. The *rabkors*, now under more intense scrutiny by the police, were no longer a lucrative source of intelligence. Much of Bir's network, however, survived.[43] Bir's successor was a "Yugoslav" Fourth Department officer named "Markovich." Whether he was promoted to run the entire French residency or simply a chief of a subordinate network who was acting as temporary director is unclear. Unlike Bir and his predecessors, however, Markovich seems to have supervised the *apparat* from Berlin, not Paris.

The key people in Markovich's network included Lydia Stahl, Octave Dumoulin, and a group of expatriate Romanians from Bessarabia, who were particularly useful because of their passports. The director of the network in Paris may have been one of these Romanians, Benjamin Berkowitz. Dumoulin, as noted previously, had been an RU agent since at least 1923.[44] Lydia Stahl's real name was Lydia Chkalov. She had been married to a member of the Russian nobility; following the revolutions, they moved to New York City, where she became a naturalized citizen and worked at the Stock Exchange. After a series of personal tragedies, she returned to Europe in the early 1920s and was recruited in 1921 in Finland by the Fourth Department. She was especially valued because of her American passport. For most of the 1920s, Stahl lived in Paris, where she studied oriental languages in preparation for future RU assignments. She equipped her apartment with a photography studio, which she used to develop film of secret documents; she also on occasion served as a courier to Berlin, frequently taking along copies of her photos.[45] In addition to Stahl, at least three other American citizens were prominent in the Markovich *apparat*: Pauline Jacobson-Levine, and the husband-wife team of Robert Gordon Switz and Marjorie Switz, a.k.a. Marjorie Tilly. Jacobson-Levine had earlier worked with Stahl in New York, and was also associated with an American communist underground "meeting place" known as "The Gallery," whose patrons included future Fourth Department agent Whittaker Chambers.[46]

The careers of Switz and his wife were in many ways unique for RU officers. Switz joined the Communist Party of the United States (CPUSA) and was subsequently recruited into Red Army Intelligence sometime in the late 1920s. One of his earliest assignments was to run a small but important RU network in Panama. When U.S. Army counterintelligence discovered the ring by accident in 1933, they arrested a hapless young corporal, but Switz and his other agents got away (see next chapter). Moscow Center then instructed the Switzes to learn the basics of photography in New York. In July 1933, they were assigned to Markovich's network. Although Dallin claims that Switz took over at least part of the *apparat* from Markovich, this seems unlikely given Switz's relatively junior status in the *Razvedupr* and his limited experience (Chambers also specifically says that this resident was a Romanian).[47]

The newly rebuilt residency did not last long. The combined effort of years of investigation enabled the French police to more rapidly identify and track the activities of Soviet intelligence. By late 1933, they were closing in on the Markovich *apparat*; their inquiries were furthered by the inevitable "weak links" at the bottom of the organization and by the suspicions of those who came into contact with its members. Markovich's residency also apparently suffered from a bad case of demoralization, and was "on the point of inner collapse when the French police pounced." The causes for this are unclear, but may have been related to the arrests of its previous residents, including Bir and Strom. Chambers also implies that Markovich's "neurotic" personality was a factor.[48]

The *Sûreté* eventually closed in on both Stahl and the Switzes; Robert Switz was observed meeting Markovich in Paris. Shortly before Christmas 1933, the arrests began; twelve at first, including Berkowitz, the Switzes, and Stahl. Those of Dumoulin and several others soon followed, although Pauline Levine escaped. Over the next three months, the arrests continued, and much of the Fourth Department operation in France came crashing down. One major reason for the extent of the disaster was that Switz, for a variety of complicated reasons, decided to cooperate with the French authorities, and based on his information the *Sûreté* was able to achieve what it had failed to do since 1927: dismantle an entire RU illegal residency.[49]

By July 1934, twenty-nine people had been arrested and 200 more were under investigation. A year passed before the trials began; in the meantime the Popular Front government and the growing menace of Nazi Germany significantly altered the state of relations between Moscow and Paris. The French courts were again lenient—no sentence exceeded five years—and most of the sentences were eventually reduced. The Switzes, who had cooperated with the prosecution, were released and went into hiding, first in Austria and then, after the *Anschluss*, in the United States.[50]

GREAT BRITAIN

Soviet fear and suspicion of Great Britain did not diminish with the rise to power of a Labour government and the consequent resumption of diplomatic relations in October 1929. The depth of Stalin's paranoia about the British "ruling circles" is well demonstrated in a letter he wrote to V. M. Molotov in September of that year: "the [Ramsey] MacDonald government is the *vanguard* of the *capitalist* governments in the work of 'humiliating' and 'bridling' the Soviet government with 'new,' *more* 'diplomatic,' *more* disguised, and thus *more* 'effective' methods."[51]

Following the police raid on Arcos in May 1927 and the suspension of diplomatic relations, Moscow Center seems to have shut down what remained of its legal residency in Great Britain, moving most of the Red Army Intelligence apparatus targeted against its "main adversary" to Holland. British counterintelligence was on the alert, and for years Moscow Center classified Great Britain as a "denied area."[52] Nevertheless, the RU residency in Holland scored some remarkable successes, including the first major Soviet penetrations of the British government.

Red Army Intelligence, as well as the Comintern and the INO, were forced to rely exclusively on illegal networks for operations in Britain, many of which had managed to survive the Arcos fiasco. Indeed, unknown to the British authorities, some of the Arcos-based illegal residencies continued to operate in Britain for some time, and the Cambridge INO and RU residencies remained undetected for years.[53] With the notorious exception of the INO/OGPU "Cambridge Five" network, however, virtually nothing is known about these illegal residencies, no doubt largely because of lingering security concerns in both Moscow and London. It seems likely, however, that following the raid, Arcos became an almost exclusively INO and OGPU operation. The Arcos headquarters was moved to Bush House (later the home of the BBC World Service). Another major source of intelligence in Britain after 1927 was the OMS, which continued to gather information and maintain close contacts with RU illegal residencies there.[54]

Much of the Fourth Department's organization in Western Europe, including the networks in Britain, were directed from 1927 on by the major illegal residency in Amsterdam. NKVD files from the 1940s confirm that the primary responsibility of the RU residency in Amsterdam was to organize espionage against the British.[55] Elisabeth Poretsky suggested that the RU decided not to rebuild a residency in Britain itself because Britain was "not an immediate neighbor of the Soviet Union" and, therefore, not viewed as a direct military threat. This assertion is patently false, as we have seen. A more satisfactory explanation for the decision to operate against the British from Amsterdam is the Soviet respect for MI5 and Scotland Yard.[56]

Some of the most famous RU officers of the interwar era worked in the dangerous environment of Great Britain. Richard Sorge was sent there briefly in 1929 by the OMS in order to report on the Labour Party and British left-wing political and workers' movements. He was recalled to Moscow early in 1930, where he joined the Fourth Department and was given a crucial assignment in China.[57] In addition, both Ignace Poretsky and Walter Krivitsky were charged with running Red Army Intelligence operations against Britain into the mid-1930s.

The *rezident* in Amsterdam in the late 1920s was Max Friedman, a.k.a. "Maximov" and "Maximov-Unshlikht." He was distantly related to the RU deputy chief Unshlikht, through whom, according to Elisabeth Poretsky, he got the posting to Holland. Friedman was an example of those valuable intelligence officers the RU preferred to keep far from Moscow because of their unorthodox views—Friedman was not a communist. He was a good case officer, however, and his "cosmopolitan background" facilitated his recruitment of several agents from among the liberal intelligentsia and art world elite in Britain and northwest Europe. These included "the poetess Henriette Roland-Holst, an old friend of Rosa Luxemburg," and a sculptor named Hildo Crup. In addition, Friedman developed a solid working relationship with the Dutch Communist Party (DCP), which, despite the reorganization of 1927, remained a very important resource for his successor, Ignace Poretsky. Two of the more prominent RU agents from the DCP were H. C. Pieck and Henryk Sneevliet (a.k.a. "Maring"), who was a communist representative to the Dutch Parliament and leader of the railworkers' union.

Sneevliet had served with the Comintern in China in the early 1920s, working closely with Soviet representatives A. Joffe and M. N. Roy. While in China, he met and married a Ukrainian woman. On his return to Holland, Sneevliet formed his own network, at the direction of the OMS. By the time Poretsky arrived in Amsterdam in 1928, this network had been co-opted by Friedman's residency.[58] Sneevliet's successes enabled him to provide Poretsky with a "list of addresses in England."[59]

In 1928, Moscow Center sent Poretsky to take over from Friedman and set up a front for running a long-term penetration operation from Holland directed at Britain. Friedman had already established a "small art gallery" in Amsterdam. According to Elisabeth Poretsky, although Ignace considered taking over Friedman's front, he eventually decided that another art gallery would be "too conspicuous" (especially given the connection between Friedman and the Dutch art world), so he decided to open a wholesale stationery shop instead. The Poretskys employed Jef Swart, a member of Sneevliet's network, to manage the firm. Although Ignace protested that he knew nothing of business, like several other RU fronts, his shop nevertheless turned a profit.

Typically, few specifics are known about the RU Amsterdam residency's activities in Britain. In 1929, Poretsky or one of his agents approached an ex-Serbian artillery officer named Sava Popovitch, who had moved to England in 1917 and had been living and working in London as an artist since 1922. Popovitch had been approached in 1922, on what basis we do not know, by the head of the OMS in Britain, the notorious Indian communist C. P. Dutt. Popovitch refused to provide his services (as translator, on this occasion), and reported the contact to Scotland Yard.

Seven years later, Poretsky's RU residency renewed contact with Popovitch. This time, the Serb recalled, he was approached by "Bolshevik agents posing as art experts" who wanted him to supply plans "of the latest British tank," naval training manuals, secret RAF documents, and "confidential industrial information." It remains unclear why Moscow Center believed Popovitch could or would supply them with this information; perhaps he still maintained useful contacts among both military circles and the CPGB. It is also possible that the OMS dossier on him was inaccurate; it is certainly obvious that the Soviets were unaware of his earlier report to Scotland Yard.

In any event, by the spring of 1930, after meeting with a certain "Herr Stahl" (no apparent connection to Lydia Stahl) in both Berlin and Amsterdam, Popovitch again decided to inform the authorities. The fact that he met with them at all suggests some sort of connection between him and the Soviets. What information, if any, Poretsky got from Popovitch is unknown, as is the ultimate fate of the Serbian artillerist *cum* artist, although he did manage to get his story published in May 1930 in the *Daily Mail*. Scotland Yard made no arrests on this occasion, but the *Mail* published sketches of "Herr Stahl" and another RU agent named "Maguire." These may have been the sketches that Elisabeth Poretsky believed compromised her husband's work in Great Britain.[60]

More significant results were achieved by a Fourth Department network run by Hans Galleni. Galleni also ran his network out of an artists' supply shop in Amsterdam. Red Army Intelligence probably recruited Galleni from the Swiss Communist Party in 1921. He was fluent in several European languages, and had previously carried out assignments in France, Belgium, and The Hague. In Holland, his contact with the RU Amsterdam residency was probably one of Friedman's agents, Henri Pieck.[61]

Knowledgeable sources credit Galleni as the first Soviet intelligence officer to penetrate the British Foreign Office. Ironically, this was not the result of careful planning and deliberate targeting, but rather sheer luck. A "disgruntled" former British army captain named E. C. Oldham, who at the time was a clerk in the Foreign Office, walked into the Soviet Embassy in Paris in 1928 and volunteered his services. Understandably suspicious, the Soviets opened a file on Oldham but took no further action. After a few months, during which time he had presumably been vetted by Moscow Center, Galleni approached Oldham in London.

In what was undoubtedly an extraordinary espionage coup, Oldham turned over to Galleni "details of Foreign Office communications procedures and codes." (It is interesting to note that this was about the same time, 1929–30, that the *Spets otdel* was set up in Moscow.) Oldham continued to provide the RU with information about British diplomatic communications and Foreign Service personnel until 1932, when for unknown reasons he resigned from the government.[62]

This penetration of the British Foreign Office was followed by an even more dramatic success. Sometime in early 1930, Pieck managed to recruit a Foreign Office cipher clerk, Captain John King. After the recruitment, Pieck handed King over to a more senior Fourth Department officer, probably

Galleni. King's espionage lasted for almost nine years.[63] His work on behalf of the Soviets was only discovered in the wake of Walter Krivitsky's defection in 1937.

Krivitsky was ignored by both American and British counterintelligence authorities until after his book, *I Was Stalin's Agent*, was published in early 1940. Two years after his defection to the West, Krivitsky was finally interviewed by MI5, and provided the British authorities with their first clue about King and his activities.[64] After due surveillance, King was arrested in a pub in 1939. He gave a full confession, and was sentenced in October 1939 to ten years in prison, of which he served about six. The proceedings of the trial, and virtually the entire record of the case, have remained sealed; the full extent of the damage Captain King did to Britain's national security may never be publicly revealed.[65]

Several authorities have concluded that the RU recruited other agents in the Foreign Office, probably two or three.[66] To date, however, no solid information has surfaced confirming these suspicions, and in some case the suspected parties have been exonerated.[67]

Poretsky's tour as chief of the Amsterdam residency came to an early and unexpected end. This resulted from two unrelated circumstances. First, Jef Swart, the stationery firm's manager, ended up having an affair with Sneevliet's wife, who moved in with Swart. Both Swart and Sneevliet soon departed the company of the Poretskys, and both the business and the intelligence work consequently suffered. Of more significance, however, was Poretsky's failed attempt to develop contacts with the Irish Communist Party (ICP).[68]

Although the ICP was created in the early 1920s, its internationalist nature did not appealed to many Irish, and by 1925 it had for all practical purposes ceased to exist. Still, the RU had, as standard procedure, established tentative contacts with the ICP. According to Elisabeth Poretsky, probably sometime in early 1929 ICP representatives traveled to Holland to meet personally with Poretsky.[69]

If this indeed was the case, then we must surmise that such an immensely risky operation must have been carried out on higher authorization, from Moscow Center at the very least; perhaps even higher. This conclusion is further supported by Elisabeth Poretsky's claim that this meeting took place despite the fact that her husband "never took these Irish contacts seriously." Unfortunately, as she wryly observed, "Scotland Yard did." According to her, Scotland Yard tailed the Irishmen to Holland, and observed them meeting with Poretsky himself, not one of his subordinates.[70]

One consequence of this was that the British authorities made accurate sketches of Ignace Poretsky, which then appeared in the British press. With his identity publicly exposed, his ability to function as the Amsterdam resident was severely impaired. He decided to go to the Fourth Department residency in Berlin to be re-assigned. He was ordered to return to Moscow for debriefing, and the Poretskys left Amsterdam in the autumn of 1929. He would never leave Russia as an RU officer again.[71] His successor as chief of the Amsterdam residency was Walter Krivitsky, who by the mid-1930s became the chief of the RU Western European Division, and a key figure in Fourth Department operations in Western Europe, including Spain.

Krivitsky's operations against Great Britain over the next few years remain completely shrouded in mystery. We do know that after 1933, the Amsterdam residency increasingly focused on the growing threat of Nazi Germany. Amsterdam eventually proved to be a major site for Fourth Department illegal operations against the Third Reich. Great Britain, however, with the exception of RU penetration of scientific research, became almost exclusively the province of the OGPU, as it assembled and ran the most notorious espionage network of the twentieth century, the "Cambridge Ring."

CONCLUSION

Although general trends characteristic of the period between 1928 and 1933 are perhaps not as obvious as for the years before, we can nonetheless discern important if subtle changes in the course of RU espionage operations. The most significant of these was the gradual emergence of professionalism, manifested in increased emphasis on training and the theoretical study of intelligence, and more sophisticated security procedures, including better insulation between Moscow Center and local communist parties. The results of this trend may be reflected in the fact that the illegal residency in France lasted, more or less intact, for six years, and that King's espionage in Great Britain went undetected for nine years.

These years also saw the Fourth Department embrace and develop new means of intelligence gathering. The rapid growth of the *Spets otdel* after 1930 was an important part of this diversification, as was the inspired, if short-lived, experiment in turning hundreds of enthusiastic young would-be communist journalists into "unconscious" agents through the *rabkor* movement.

Yet these developments did not occur in a vacuum. Another major trend during these years was the growing proficiency of French and British counterintelligence, which were now more alert to the threat of Soviet-sponsored espionage, and much more adept at ferreting out entire Soviet residencies in preference to isolated networks. In France, this meant that, although the RU illegal residency lasted much longer than its predecessors, when its destruction came it was all the more thorough. And in Great Britain, Soviet successes were a direct consequence of the efficiency and skill of Scotland Yard and MI5, which forced Moscow Center to rapidly and drastically improve the sophistication of its agent operations. The synergistic nature of this process continued to shape the course of Fourth Department espionage, even as the focus of its efforts turned to Nazi Germany and Japan.

NOTES

1. Piotr Wandycz, *The Twilight of the French Eastern Alliances, 1926–1936: French-Czechoslovak-Polish Relations from Locarno to the Remilitarization of the Rhineland* (Princeton: Princeton University Press, 1988), p. 48.

2. Dallin, *Soviet Espionage*, p. 40.

3. Pick, as far as I have been able to determine, was the first RU defector. For more on his fascinating career, see Corson and Crowley, *New KGB*, pp. 441–442.

4. Fischer, *Stalin*, p. 579; Heller and Nekrich, *Utopia*, p. 215; Andrew and Gordievsky, *KGB*, p. 112.

5. Corson and Crowley, *New KGB*, pp. 288, 414 (on Oras), 441 (on Bekenovsky).

6. American communist leader Benjamin Gitlow, who was there at the time, provides a useful and interesting account of the "war fever" gripping Moscow following the assassination of Voikov; see Benjamin Gitlow, *I Confess: The Truth about American Communism* (New York: E. P. Dutton & Co., 1940), pp. 433–436.

7. Lih, Naumov, and Khlevniuk, *Stalin's Letters*, pp. 133–134.

8. Samuelson, *Soviet Defence*, p. 54.

9. Ibid., p. 56.

10. Heller and Nekrich, *Utopia*, pp. 215–216.

11. Ibid., pp. 204–207; Dimitri Volkogonov, *Stalin: Triumph and Tragedy*, trans. by Harold Shukman (New York: Grove Weidenfeld, 1991), pp. 133–144; Dmitri Volkogonov, *Trotskii: politicheskii portret*, vol. 2 (Moscow: Novosti, 1992), pp. 65–108.

12. From an article written by Stalin in June 1927; quoted in Andrew and Gordievsky, *KGB*, p. 113. Andrew and Gordievsky provide perhaps the most thoughtful discussion of the "war scare" (pp. 112–114); see also Corson and Crowley, *New KGB*, pp. 92–95.

13. S. M. Belitskii, *Operativnaia razvedka* (Moscow: Gosudarstvennoe izdatel'stvo otdel Voennoi Literatury, 1929). This work was supervised by A. M. Nikonov, chief of the RU's Third (Analysis) Section. In this instance, *operativnaya* may be best translated as "practical" or "applied," rather than "operational" in the sense of the level of military art, for the text devotes similar attention to the role of intelligence at all three levels of warfare: tactical, operational, and strategic.

14. Dallin, *Soviet Espionage*, p. 41 fn.

15. Ibid., pp. 40–41; and Andrew and Gordievsky, *KGB*, p. 122.

16. Dallin, *Soviet Espionage*, pp. 40–41; Suvorov, *Soviet Military Intelligence*, pp. 18–19.

17. Christopher Andrew, "Secret Intelligence and British Foreign Policy," in *Intelligence and International Relations*, p. 18.

18. Corson and Crowley, *New KGB*, p. 69. Polish Military Intelligence (Department 2 of the Polish General Staff) had been breaking into Soviet military and diplomatic radio traffic since the Soviet-Polish War. Some of the Polish intelligence officers responsible for decryption of Soviet sigint were later involved in the earliest efforts to crack the German "Enigma" device. See Richard A. Woytak, *On the Border of War and Peace: Polish Intelligence and Diplomacy in 1937–1939 and the Origins of the ULTRA Secret* (Boulder, Colo.: East European Quarterly, 1979), pp. 8–9; see also chapter 7.

19. Andrew and Gordievsky, *KGB*, pp. 112–113.

20. Andrew, "Introduction," in *Intelligence and International Relations*, p. 2.

21. Andrew and Gordievsky, *KGB*, p. 89. There are repeated references to "Special Section of Ogpu" decryptions in Agabekov's work, *OGPU* (see for example p. 168).

22. Kahn, *Code-Breakers*, p. 362.

23. Andrew and Gordievsky, *KGB*, pp. 173–174; Kahn, *Code-Breakers*, pp. 359–360.

Corson and Crowley claim that since the "earliest KRO [GPU counterintelligence] and INO agents," "all personnel directly involved in the control of clandestine communications . . . have been Chekists"; Corson and Crowley, *New KGB*, p. 69. This needs to be clarified. The Fourth Department ran its own clandestine communications, as the GRU also undoubtedly still does. These may in some circumstances be monitored by state security, but Red Army Intelligence has always had its own cipher clerks and communications specialists. Notable examples include the various radio operators for the illegal networks of Richard Sorge and the Red Orchestra, as well as Igor Gouzenko, a GRU cipher clerk at the Soviet Embassy in Ottawa who defected to the Canadians in 1946.

24. For more on Soviet sigint and Japan, see next chapter.

25. Akhmedov, *In and out of Stalin's*, pp. 84–85. Probably the first dedicated facility for training Soviet agents in the art of clandestine radio communications was set up by the OMS in the Moscow suburb of Mytishchi in 1925; see Andrew and Gordievsky, *KGB*, p. 93.

26. Akhmedov, *In and out of Stalin's*, p. 85.

27. Akhmedov notes that the Fourth Department political officers emphasized that the United States was the chief adversary, as it was the "base of world capitalism"; see his *In and out of Stalin's*, p. 86.

28. For example, the Germans were always reluctant to share with the Soviets any of their developments in chemical warfare, repeatedly insisting that they simply had nothing new to report. Fourth Department intelligence on French poison gas research, much of which was obtained through penetration of the laboratory of a certain "Dr. Bushe," coupled with extensive RU information on the German chemical industry proper, gave the lie to German claims and tended to reinforce Moscow's suspicions. See Dyakov and Bushuyeva, *Red Army*, p. 232; TsGASA, f. 33987, op. 3, d. 295, l. 1–2.

29. Dallin, *Soviet Espionage*, p. 49.

30. Ibid., pp. 42–43.

31. Ibid., pp. 46–47. Given Barbé's description of the man he met, it was almost certainly *not* Berzin.

32. Ibid., pp. 43–44.

33. Ibid., pp. 50–53.

34. Ibid., p. 55; Höhne, *Codeword*, p. 85.

35. Höhne, *Codeword*, p. 85.

36. In 1937, when Trepper was sent by Berzin to Paris to investigate the exposure of Bir's "Phantomas" network, Stigga, at the time the RU chief of operations in Western Europe, cautioned him to take care about the clothes he wore, for "several of our agents [in France] were exposed because of the pleat that a Warsaw tailor used to put in the middle of the jacket collar"; see *Great Game*, Trepper, p. 78. This is reminiscent of Suvorov's account of the arrests of *Razvedupr* operatives in the Baltic states, which resulted from their inability to tie a necktie correctly; see Suvorov, *Soviet Military Intelligence*, p. 13.

37. Höhne, *Codeword*, p. 85.

38. Trepper, *Great Game*, pp. 26–27.

39. These figures are quoted by Dallin from a Soviet source, the *Small Soviet Encyclopedia*, and so may very well be exaggerations. The same source claimed that in 1934 the American *Daily Worker* in New York had 800 *rabkors*, while the British *Daily Worker* had 600. Dallin also observes that there were "thousands" in Germany by 1933 in his *Soviet Espionage*, p. 52.

40. From about 1928 until 1933, the Soviet Embassy in Paris had been without an official military attaché. Most probably this was a lingering consequence of the 1927 diplomatic crisis; ibid., p. 54.

41. Ibid., pp. 55–56. Leopold Trepper, however, in memoirs first published in 1975, claimed that the Riquier story was a concoction of the *Sûreté*; see Trepper, *Great Game*, pp. 80–81. Trepper's account is incorrect in a number of important respects. For a discussion of Trepper's account and other relevant issues, see Leonard, *Kremlin's Secret Soldiers*, pp. 196–197.

42. Dallin, *Soviet Espionage*, pp. 56–57.

43. Isolated arrests, hinting at the extent of continued RU penetration of France, continued up to late 1933 and early 1934, when the illegal residency was again crippled by the authorities; ibid., pp. 57–59.

44. Dallin describes him as the group's "paymaster and financial operator"; Ibid., p. 61. See also Whittaker Chambers, *Witness* (Washington, D.C.: Regnery Gateway, 1980), p. 387.

45. Dallin, *Soviet Espionage*, pp. 60–61.

46. Chambers, *Witness*, p. 387.

47. Dallin says that Markovich came to Paris in August 1933 to turn over "part of the machinery" to Switz. This would have been about a month after the American couple arrived in France; Dallin, *Soviet Espionage*, pp. 63–64.

48. Chambers, *Age of Conflict*, p. 387.

49. For a discussion of Switz's motives, see ibid. See also Dallin, *Soviet Espionage*, pp. 65–66.

50. Ibid., pp. 66–67, 399–400. Dallin maintains that the Switzes feared Soviet reprisals, and "had every reason to fear for their lives"; ibid., p. 400. On the other hand, Chambers oddly notes that the CPUSA, apparently on orders of Moscow Center, arranged for money to be sent clandestinely to France to fund Switz's court costs, even after it was widely known that he had betrayed the Party and the Fourth Department; see Chambers, *Witness*, p. 387 Robert Switz died in 1951, as far as we know of natural causes.

51. Lih, Naumov, Khlevniuk, *Stalin's Letters*, Letter 47, 9 September 1929, p. 178.

52. Corson and Crowley, *New KGB*, p. 418.

53. The RU illegal residency may have been based in Lewisham; ibid., p. 148.

54. Shipley, *Hostile Action*, p. 51.

55. In August 1945, the NKVD referred to Walter Krivitsky as "the traitor to the Homeland, former resident of the intelligence administration of the Red Army in England." Although it is possible, it seems unlikely that Krivitsky ever actually ran his residency on British soil; certainly some indication of this would have appeared over the years. It is more probable that this document refers to Krivitsky's Dutch residency. See Genrikh Borovikh, *The Philby Files: The Secret Life of Master Spy Kim Philby*, ed. and intro. by Phillip Knightly (Boston: Little, Brown and Company, 1994), p. 243.

56. This was tacitly acknowledged by Elisabeth Poretsky when she noted that "the Netherlands were much more easily accessible from the rest of Europe, and seemed much safer to the Soviets" in *Our Own People*, p. 73.

57. Shipley, *Hostile Action*, pp. 56–57.

58. Poretsky, *Our Own People*, pp. 77–80.

59. Shipley, *Hostile Action*, p. 57.

60. Ibid., pp. 57–58; Poretsky, *Our Own People*, p. 84.

61. Pieck was described as a "genuine artist"; see Shipley, *Hostile Action*, p. 59. See also Corson and Crowley, *New KGB*, pp. 417–418.

62. A year later, he apparently committed suicide in his home in Kensington. There is no indication that he was ever arrested or charged, although he may well have been questioned and kept under surveillance; see Shipley, *Hostile Action*, p. 59.

63. West, *MI5*, *passim*; Wright, *Spycatcher*, p. 328; and Shipley, *Hostile Action*, p. 59. Galleni, it should be noted, would at the time have been the only RU officer with experience at running a British Foreign Office agent.

64. Gordon Brook-Shepherd, *The Storm Petrels: The First Soviet Defectors, 1928–1938* (London: Collins, 1977), pp. 166–170.

65. West, *MI5*, pp. 73–74.

66. For example, see Shipley, *Hostile Action*, p. 59.

67. The most notable examples are Richard "Dickie" Ellis, Guy Liddell, and Roger Hollis, all of whom had senior positions at one time or another in MI5 or MI6. Peter Wright strenuously argued that Ellis was the "Fifth Man" in the Cambridge ring (this turned out to be John Cairncross), and Peter Costello maintained Liddell was a RU penetration agent. Others have accused Ellis of working for the Nazis. In addition to Costello and Wright, who discuss their charges at length throughout their books, see Shipley, *Hostile Action*, p. 59.

68. Poretsky, *Our Own People*, p. 84.

69. Ibid.

70. Ibid.

71. It was during his assignment in Amsterdam that Poretsky also recruited Hede Massing, formerly married to the German Comintern-turned-RU officer Gerhardt Eisler. Massing developed into an important and successful recruiter herself, and this became her specialty. Massing worked in both Western Europe and the United States, where she recruited State Department official Noel Field, and ran Whittaker Chambers' network (including Alger Hiss, who had already been recruited by Chambers) in the late 1930s. See Hede Massing, *This Deception* (New York: Duell, Sloan and Pearce, 1951), pp. 77–78. See also see Corson and Crowley, *New KGB*, p. 469; and Chambers, *Witness*, *passim*.

CHAPTER 5

Espionage, 1928–1933: Part 2

Significant RU operations against the United States and Japan did not begin until relatively late in the 1920s. In the case of the United States, this was a reflection of the fact that, from the Soviet perspective, although it was an industrial giant, the United States was simply not a great enough threat to warrant investment of scarce resources. Covert operations in the United States were also complicated by the early confusion and squabbling among American communists that worked to make conditions for espionage especially risky. Moscow Center's interest in America had increased dramatically by 1928, however, as the drive to prepare for the Five Year Plan made industrial and technological espionage a priority.

In contrast, Russia had for decades regarded Japan as a serious threat to its interests in the Far East. Nevertheless, until the mid-1920s, the Soviets were preoccupied with the defense of their western and southern frontiers. As internal political struggles in Japan led Tokyo to pursue increasingly aggressive policies by the late 1920s, Moscow Center built up its agent networks in the Far East, and in particular in Shanghai. Two important factors determined the nature and place of these deployments. First, the twin disasters in China, the raid on the PMC and Chiang Kai-shek's ruthless attack on the CCP, forced the RU *apparat* to concentrate in Shanghai, which was still an international "treaty port" with a large and relatively radicalized working class and a strong Comintern presence. The other factor was the efficiency of the Japanese police, which prevented any substantive Soviet penetration of Japan before that of Richard Sorge in the mid-1930s. As a result, the Fourth Department found it necessary to target Japan from adjacent regions, especially Shanghai, Manchuria, and Korea.

Although penetration of these two countries occurred later, it was also undertaken by a more experienced and professional intelligence service. It was no accident that some of the Fourth Department's greatest triumphs came against Tokyo and Washington.

THE UNITED STATES

Moscow Center did not establish a full-scale residency in the United States until sometime in 1928–29. This was partly due to the fragmentation of the American communist movement. During the first few years, the American comrades were so preoccupied with disputes over ideology, organization, and leadership that Moscow simply had no coherent entity with which to deal. Indeed, between 1919 and 1923 most Soviet and Comintern interaction with American communists was focused on trying to shape a single unified party out of the chaos.[1] It was not until 1923 that a unified communist organization finally emerged, largely due to Moscow's prodding. This was the Workers' Party, which in 1929 officially changed its name to the Communist Party of the U.S.A. (CPUSA).[2]

Immigrants from eastern and southeastern Europe made up the majority in early communist organizations in the United States. These included a particularly zealous group of Latvians based in Massachusetts, some of whom later rose to prominence in the ranks of Red Army Intelligence.[3] Many of these immigrants had long associations with radical and revolutionary groups like the IWW (the Industrial Workers of the World, also known as the "Wobblies"), and therefore had considerable experience in underground work. In fact, when the first two American "communist" parties were founded in 1919, out of a total membership of some 34,000, only about 4,000 spoke English, and "not until the 1930s were the majority of American communists English-speaking and native-born."[4]

Moscow could also rely on the Comintern networks concentrated in ports like New York, New Orleans, and San Francisco (described in chapter 3). These provided access to American communists for the purposes of opportunistic espionage, and even provided useful intelligence in their own right. Intelligence was also provided through the front organizations set up initially in Europe by both the INO and the *Razvedupr*, particularly the various businesses operated by Julius and Armand Hammer, who, among other things, helped the Soviet intelligence services "launder" money and other valuables.[5] Other useful fronts included William Z. Foster's Trade Union Educational League, the Young Workers' League, the Friends of Soviet Russia, and the American Committee for Russian Famine Relief.[6] Most early Comintern operations in the United States may in fact have been directed from Berlin by Willi Münzenberg.[7] Following the establishment of Arcos, Soviet money destined for clandestine American operations usually went through London and then Canada on its way to the United States. After the raid on the Soviet trading center in London in 1927, however, Berlin once again became the base for Comintern activity in America.[8]

Given the dangerous international situation, both real and imagined, confronted by the Soviet Union in the early 1920s, it simply did not view the United States, firmly committed to a policy of isolationism, as a major threat.[9] Moscow Center, therefore, concluded that commitment of scarce "professional" intelligence personnel to the United States was both unnecessary, and, given the confusion among the communists there, of little value. Nevertheless, a small Fourth Department presence, operating mostly under cover of the Comintern maritime networks, was established in the United States by 1923. There may even have been some *Razvedupr* personnel associated with the Russian Soviet Government Information Bureau, the "unofficial Soviet Embassy" in the United States.[10] Their mission was familiar: to "collect data regarding the U.S. armed forces, especially technical information that would accelerate Soviet industrial development for military purposes."[11]

By 1924, early Soviet trading offices in America, including those started by the Hammers, had been consolidated into the "Amtorg" (American Trading Organization) company. Organized similarly to Arcos, Ltd., in London, with which it maintained close connections, Amtorg was also responsible for supporting the same types of clandestine activities. Unlike Arcos, however, the Amtorg Comintern staff found it necessary to devote most of its energies to liaisoning with the troublesome CPUSA.[12] The OGPU maintained a residency at Amtorg and, together with its intelligence-gathering branch, the INO, it seems to have been the dominant presence there. There was also a small RU staff, perhaps under the direction of Felix Wolf, a.k.a. "Nikolai Krebs," but ultimately subordinate to the OGPU resident. These officers were assigned to carry out "conventional military intelligence missions," "directed toward military and industrial espionage," which were facilitated by Amtorg's policy that any company wishing to do business had to submit to an on-site inspection of its plants and facilities.[13] Fourth Department officers at Amtorg also played a key role in acquiring shipping and naval intelligence.

The first Fourth Department resident in the United States was Wolf/Krebs, who ran the American station under Amtorg cover from 1924 to 1929.[14] Wolf had been a Fourth Department officer since at least 1923, and had served as a military attaché at the Vienna Embassy at about the same time that the Poretskys were assigned there. Shortly thereafter, Moscow Center assigned him to direct the newly established RU residency in New York City. Another Red Army intelligence officer who probably operated out of Wolf's residency was Dr. Philip Rosenbliett, who was later Whittaker Chambers's RU contact.[15]

After RU penetration of the United States increased dramatically in 1928–29, several officers served at one time or another in the Amtorg illegal residency throughout the 1930s, including Hede Massing; Alexander Pavlov; Valentin Markin (later OGPU residency chief in New York); Walter Grinke (known to American agents Chambers and Elizabeth Bentley as "Bill"); Nicholas Dozenberg ("Arthur"); Dr. Valentine Burtan (most notorious for his role in the RU counterfeiting operation described below); Boris Bykov; the Switzes; and a man known as "Stashevich." In 1927, Moishe Stern, who had served earlier in China and was later known as "Zilbert" in New York and "General Kleber" in Spain, took over the Fourth Department Amtorg residency, which he directed until 1931.[16]

THE "CHRISTIE" TANKS

The Amtorg RU residency provided the base from which the Red Army coordinated efforts to obtain U.S. tank technology. These may have begun in October 1928 when I. A. Khalepski, a leading Soviet tank expert and a close friend of Tukhachevsky's, entered the United States on a visa arranged by Amtorg.[17] His declared purpose was to negotiate a deal with the Ford Motor Company, a rationale apparently often used with the connivance of Ford to justify the entrance of Red Army officers into the United States.[18]

Khalepski used his association with Amtorg and Ford to facilitate his study of American weapons development. At first, he was particularly interested in artillery. Over the next six months, he spent most of his time touring arsenals and observing weapons tests at the Aberdeen proving grounds. During his stay he became familiar with the work of J. Walter Christie, who was experimenting with a series of advanced tank design prototypes that incorporated an innovative suspension system. His M-1928 impressed not only the U.S. War Department but Khalepski and the Polish army, as well. When Christie developed a new design that he called the M-1930, Moscow sent Khalepski back to America to get it.

Christie had several deals in the works, and was simultaneously negotiating with the U.S. War Department, the British, and the Poles. American bureaucratic confusion, coupled with the miserly attitude toward defense spending characteristic of the interwar years, severely complicated Christie's efforts to sell his invention to Washington. In the meantime, seemingly endless legal haggling contributed to the government's indecision and confusion on the issue of technology exports. Christie decided to wait and see who would be the first to come up with the cash. This turned out to be the Soviets, who arranged through the RU section at Amtorg to purchase two of his M-1930s. Still unsure of the legality of this transaction, Christie arranged for the vehicles, which were "completely equipped and ready to fight except for mounting the guns," to be shipped as "tractors." On 24 December 1930 the "tractors" left New York for the USSR.

The consequences of this particular RU coup were profound. Christie's revolutionary suspension system made possible the modern, fast, well armored, and well armed tank. This and other features developed by Christie were incorporated in almost every Soviet tank design in the 1930s, most notably the *bystrokhodnii tank* (fast tank), or BT series. They also led directly to the highly successful T-34 series of tanks, assault guns, and tank destroyers produced during World War II. By the end of the war, variants of Christie's suspension appeared in tanks designed in Poland, Germany, the United States, and Great Britain.[19]

The first major independent *Razvedupr* residency in the United States was established in 1929 by another Latvian, Alfred Tilton, a.k.a. "Joseph Paquett," a friend and protégé of Berzin, and Lydia Stahl, who Krivitsky described as "one our best agents."[20] Both were veterans of the French illegal residency. Another agent-turned-officer recruited by Tilton was Nicholas Dozenberg.

Born in Latvia in 1882, Dozenberg and his family moved to the United States in 1904. Dozenberg had been in radical socialist organizations since before the war, including the Left Wing of the Lettish Workers Society of Boston, and once served as secretary of the Malden branch of the Socialist party. In 1921, he joined the American Communist Party (precursor to the Workers' party) and was assigned to propaganda and publishing projects. Four years later, Dozenberg unsuccessfully ran for the office of alderman of Chicago's Twenty-eighth Ward. Soon thereafter he was in charge of the CPUSA's publishing house. Although dedicated to the Party, he could not make ends meet on his meager and often unpredictable salary. After requesting a better paying job, in 1927 the American Politburo put Dozenberg in contact with Tilton. Shortly thereafter, Dozenberg left the Workers' party and assumed the name of Nicholas L. Dallant, and became, in the estimation of Theodore Draper, "the first American Communist to make the transition to Soviet military intelligence."[21]

Using resources and cover provided by Amtorg, Tilton opened a shipping office as a front in downtown New York City. Dozenberg's first assignment was as a "talent scout," probably in search of suitable couriers; however, his responsibilities rapidly grew.[22] Stahl, by now an accomplished photographer, set up a clandestine photo studio and lab, the purpose of which was to copy stolen documents. Through his extensive contacts, Dozenberg arranged for the nightly use of a photography shop owned by a man named Joseph Tourin. Dozenberg then purchased a large photostat machine and set it up in the shop. Later, when Tourin made more demands, Tilton authorized Dozenberg to buy him out.[23]

In the little photo studio, Stahl took pictures of smuggled sensitive documents and sometimes developed them on the spot. When she was not working in the lab, she ran her own network of agents. One of Stahl's major coups was her acquisition of the blueprints for the British battleship HMS *Royal Oak*. These were obtained from an unidentified "cooperative and venal American officer" in Washington D.C. while they were en route to Britain from Canada. The plans apparently were stolen, photographed in Stahl's lab, and returned. British and American authorities only discovered the theft years later.[24] Stahl also obtained copies of American scientific, engineering, and technical publications, which were shipped to Moscow. Meanwhile, Dozenberg coordinated the acquisition of items specified by the "questionnaires" and other similar lists provided by Moscow Center. All of this material, including books, documents, scientific instruments, and machines, was boxed and shipped through one of the *Razvedupr*'s extensive maritime courier systems.

Dozenberg's authority continued to expand, and soon he was in charge of keeping track of expenses. On one occasion, to help Tilton raise cash, Moscow Center sent a shipment of "books"—actually, revolutionary tracts and pamphlets—to sell on the American market. The industrious Dozenberg, upon realizing that he would find no buyers for these, eventually sold them all for pulp to a paper company in New Jersey. The New York residency's chronic shortage of cash figured prominently in one of the stranger Soviet schemes of the 1930s, the decision to counterfeit American dollars.

Probably sometime in late 1930, Tilton was recalled to Moscow.[25] He was replaced by Dozenberg, who continued his amazingly swift and unusual climb from agent to senior intelligence officer. Sometime in 1929, he was called to Moscow specifically to meet with Yan Berzin, who seems to have been favorably impressed. Berzin assigned Dozenberg to assist an RU officer named John Kirchenstein in building a cover with a false identity based on a stolen U.S. passport—a process known in Soviet intelligence parlance as building a "legend."[26] Dozenberg's rapid rise in the Fourth Department was probably a result not only of his unquestionable talents but also the patronage of fellow Latvians Berzin and Tilton.[27]

STALIN'S COUNTERFEITING SCHEME

At about the same time, Dozenberg became involved in a plan to smuggle counterfeit dollars through the international banking system. The idea probably originated with Stalin (although Tilton claimed credit for it), who remained its strongest, and virtually only, supporter.[28] By the late 1920s, the expanding Soviet espionage organs were beginning to run out of money. This was the result of a combination of circumstances, including the growing international financial crisis following the crash of the American stock market in October 1929, years of profligate spending for costly Comintern and intelligence adventures, and, perhaps most importantly, the growing shortage of *valuta* (convertible currency) caused by the first Five Year Plan.[29] This situation may have led Moscow to risk counterfeiting small amounts of unspecified European currencies by 1927 or 1928. The prominent American communist Benjamin Gitlow maintained that "much of this counterfeit money found its way into the treasuries of the various Communist parties of Europe." "American money," he noted, was "the last to be counterfeited."[30]

Stalin, who had personal experience in illegal fund raising (he robbed banks and state liquor stores for the Party before the October Revolution), found the idea of counterfeiting dollars appealing for a number of reasons.[31] By "laundering" these bills, Moscow would get legitimate hard foreign currency, and cause confidence in the dollar to fall, thereby aggravating the deteriorating economic situation in the United States and fostering the growth of revolutionary forces. It would also be imminently satisfying ideologically to use such "financial judo" against the leader of capitalism.[32] It is characteristic of Stalin's grasp of macroeconomics that he would consider such an objective beneficial to overall Soviet interests.

Most sources who discuss the counterfeiting scheme, including David Dallin, William Corson, and Robert Crowley, focus on the $100,000 or so that ended up in the United States, and the isolated cases in Europe where some of these bills showed up. Krivitsky is clear, however, that the origins of the scheme lay in the need for readily convertible currency to pay for operations in China and Asia, and that that is where the vast amount of the fake money ended up. The plan consequently called for its circulation mainly in China, where the need for hard currency was especially acute owing to the destruction of many clandestine cash sources following the raid on the Peking Military Center. China was also considered a good target for circulating counterfeit bills because of its relatively primitive financial system.[33]

Experts in both the RU and OGPU, which seemed to have no qualms about the earlier forays into minting fake European currency, apparently tried to talk Stalin out of this idea. They pointed out the vast technical problems inherent in pulling off such a large counterfeiting operation, and speculated about the potential impact on Soviet diplomatic relations, still recovering from the setbacks of 1927, if the true source of the bogus money was ever discovered. Stalin dismissed these arguments as evidence of shallow imagination and timidity. The project was approved, and was set in motion probably in late 1928 or early 1929.[34]

The first requirements were to decide on the denomination of the bill to be forged, and to acquire precise data about every facet of the U.S. Treasury Department's printing process. The first question proved to be relatively easy to answer. The $100 Federal Reserve note was judged most suitable for large-scale counterfeiting (although there is some indication that a few $500 bills were also counterfeited). The second requirement, however, proved far more complicated. Both Dozenberg and one of his agents, Dr. Valentine G. Burtan, cultivated contacts at the U.S. Bureau of Printing and Engraving who were subsequently developed by an RU expert on currency engraving, J. Polyakov, who came to New York under Amtorg cover expressly for this purpose.[35] Eventually, "several [federal] employees were induced to provide technical intelligence, and one in particular actually assisted the Soviets in acquiring a large stock of U.S. banknote paper."[36]

Once the technical information and necessary materials were procured, the extensive Fourth Department clandestine documents bureau went to work. The timing of the release of the bills was also probably connected to the fact that the U.S. Treasury was planning a major revision in the currency in 1929, which would make the old $100 and $500 bills obsolete.[37] The first of perhaps millions of dollars in counterfeit bills were probably passed unnoticed in China early in 1929.[38] It may be that the bogus money was so successful in Asia that Stalin and Berzin were persuaded to try to use it in Europe later that year.

In any event, the first counterfeit $100 bill was spotted in a bank in Vienna in March 1929. A few weeks later, the phony notes appeared in Havana, where the RU attempted to pass them at several casinos. In April 1930, more counterfeit $100 notes showed up in Bulgaria. The notes detected in all these incidents shared key features, and clearly were the product of the same sophisticated forging operation. The U.S. Treasury Department quickly alerted banking officials around the world that a supply of counterfeit $100 bills was in circulation.

American forgery experts soon had a very good description of the fake notes, and early on there were even vague indications that the Soviets might be behind them. But in 1930 it seemed too far-fetched to think that such a massively illegal and clumsy scheme could be supported and directed by a national government, even the one in Moscow. After all, at the time the Soviets were actively courting American diplomatic recognition.

The first solid evidence that the trail of the counterfeiters might lead to Moscow turned up in December 1929. An RU agent named Franz Fischer, acting apparently on Tilton's orders, traveled to Berlin in order to pass some of the phony bills at the Sass & Martini Bank.[39] Fooled initially by Fischer's notes, which were interspersed with genuine ones, the bank proprietors nevertheless decided as a precaution to send the dollars to the *Deutschebank* for examination. Although German officials there initially concluded that the bills were real, almost simultaneously, the Federal Reserve Bank of New York telegrammed a warning to the *Deutschebank* to be on the lookout for forged $100 bills, the description of which exactly matched the Sass & Martini deposit. In late January, the Berlin police raided Sass & Martini. Aside from putting those essentially innocent bankers out of business, however, the authorities accomplished little of substance. But the subsequent investigation did turn up the name, though not the affiliation, of Franz Fischer, and at least enough information about him for the *Berliner Tageblatt* to note that "Franz Fischer, of Neue Winterfeldstrasse 3, who undertook to pass the counterfeit notes in Berlin, returned from Russia in March 1929."[40]

After this close call (at the time there was no direct tie to the Soviet government), Moscow Center apparently decided to stop circulating the forged money, at least for a while. Krivitsky claims that about this time he even had an argument with Berzin over the idea of a sovereign state going into the counterfeiting business.[41] No further incidents, at least in Europe and the United States, were reported for almost two years. Tilton was recalled to Moscow and re-assigned, and Dozenberg took over the New York residency.

In 1931, Berzin assigned Dozenberg to set up a new Fourth Department residency under the front of another Amtorg-connected firm, the Romanian-American Film Company. Romania was an increasingly important target for penetration, because of its geographical position, its relationship to France, and, most importantly, the assumption expressed in threat assessments that war against the USSR would be spearheaded by a joint Polish-Romanian attack.[42] Dozenberg's new business required an office in Bucharest as well as New York. He therefore traveled to Romania, where "he represented himself as an American movie mogul. . . . After several months of photographing everything in Romania he thought to be of interest to the Soviet Military Intelligence (including films of Magda Lepescu frolicking in the nude), he returned to Berlin."[43]

Dozenberg, however, was by now woefully short of funds, and by 1932 the fiscal problems confronting the RU had only gotten worse. Almost certainly with Berzin's approval, if not on his instigation, Dozenberg decided to risk trying to pass about $125,000 worth of the leftover counterfeit bills. He assigned Burtan, who still retained his enthusiasm for the project, to launder the fake money and use it as seed money to raise a further $60,000 in real currency to finance the Romanian venture.

Burtan got in touch with one of his own contacts, a con man who called himself Count Enrique von Bulow. The two of them originally hatched a scheme to circulate the counterfeit money by finding a corrupt South American finance minister with whom to go into partnership. Trips to Mexico and several countries in Central and South America in the summer or fall of 1932 turned up plenty of willing ministers, but to Burtan's naive disgust they were all more interested in getting a healthy "cut" of the profits than in helping to raise money for the revolution. After a deal with the finance minister of Guatemala fell through, Burtan gave up on this approach, and "with the inverted morality of a practiced Soviet agent he pronounced them all thieves and returned to New York."[44]

Less than a month later, von Bulow came to Burtan with another suggestion: he knew a private detective in Chicago who had connections with the underworld. Now the whole operation, always on the bizarre side, became positively farcical.[45] Burtan and the count, who seems to have been the "idea man," went to Chicago, where the detective, a man named Smiley, introduced them to a motley collection of small-time hoods and confidence men. Burtan and von Bulow fabricated the dangerous story that they were trying to launder legitimate but "hot" money on behalf of the gang founded by the notorious New York gangster Arnold Rothstein.[46] "Smiley's people" accepted this explanation without bothering to corroborate it. As Corson and Crowley observed, "the aggregate technical competence of the Chicago conspirators . . . was roughly equivalent to that of a doorknob."[47] An out-of-work bank teller named Johnson was prevailed upon to evaluate the bills. After being treated to the first real meal he had had in weeks, he pronounced the bills to be genuine and agreed to pass them through four Chicago banks. The plan went into operation in December 1932.

On a repeat visit to the First National Bank of Chicago on 23 December, Johnson, who apparently really did believe the money to be real but "hot," sported nervous behavior that aroused the suspicions of a teller, who immediately contacted the authorities. At that point, the whole operation quickly began to unravel. Johnson was arrested by the Secret Service while he was still in the lobby of the First National Bank, and "within forty-eight hours of Johnson's arrest two lawyers, one contractor, Johnson, four boulevardiers from the Croydon [Hotel], and Frank Smiley . . . offered themselves up as government witnesses."[48] The count himself was soon arrested in New York.

Burtan was now truly left "out in the cold." Dozenberg distanced himself and the residency as much as possible from Burtan, and after a few days, Dozenberg and his wife departed by ship for Moscow.[49] Now Burtan found himself in the unenviable position of being hunted by Rothstein's mob as well as the G-men. The gangsters were furious at being so ill-used, and some of them were quoted in the *New York Times* as promising that if they caught up with Burtan they would "take him for a ride."[50] Fortunately for him, the Secret Service got to him first, arresting him in New York as he was about to board a plane for Montreal.

The subsequent trial revealed almost all the details about the counterfeiting operation save one: Burtan was the only one who knew that Red Army Intelligence was behind the scheme, and he never talked. Despite Dozenberg's hasty retreat, Berzin was not willing simply to abandon Burtan, and, according to Krivitsky, the Fourth Department provided "substantial funds" for his defense. Burtan argued that he was being persecuted because he was Jewish. This failed to win him much sympathy, at least from the jury; he was convicted and received a fifteen-year sentence, of which he served ten years.[51]

Once again, potential disaster was averted for Stalin's foreign policy, this time thanks to the loyalty of Valentine Burtan. The *Razvedupr*, however, did not emerge so happily from the counterfeiting fiasco. Valentin Markin, the OGPU resident in New York and formerly a Fourth Department officer, was extremely ambitious, and for some unknown reason held a grudge against Berzin. In early 1933, Markin prepared an assessment of the damage the Burtan affair could have potentially caused, together with a more general indictment of the RU residency in the United States. He directed much of his criticism at Berzin personally. Markin returned to Moscow from New York, "ready to wage war against General Berzin and all his lieutenants in the Military Intelligence," and delivered his report to Premier V. Molotov.[52]

In an ominous development for the *Razvedupr*, Markin won his case, probably because Stalin sought to find a scapegoat to cover his own complicity in the failed counterfeiting scheme. As a result, for the first time an entire Fourth Department *apparat* was put under OGPU control. Although the Cheka and its successors had tried to obtain such authority ever since the creation of the *Registraupr* by conducting an ongoing campaign to co-opt the more skilled Fourth Department personnel into their ranks, Krivitsky noted that this "was the first time in our [RU] history that such a consolidation had been effected." Markin was made chief of the combined RU/OGPU operation in the United States, a post that he held until his death shortly thereafter, following a brawl in a nightclub in New York in 1934.[53]

THE PANAMANIAN AFFAIR

At almost the same time that Dozenberg authorized Burtan to plan an operation to circulate counterfeit money, his residency managed to achieve a minor but notorious success in Panama.[54] Sometime in 1930 or 1931, RU agents befriended a lonely young U.S. Army corporal from New York named Robert Osman, who happened to be assigned to the Headquarters Battery, First Coastal Artillery, at Ft. Sherman, Panama. In a variation of what intelligence organizations would later call a "honey trap," a young Russian girl named Frema Karry, an agent in the network run by Robert Gordon Switz and his wife, Marjorie Tilly, began a relationship with Osman that led him to fall in love with her. Osman had associated with CPUSA circles for some years, and was, in fact a member of the Communist Youth League. He therefore likely shared some ideological enthusiasm with Karry, and was probably initially approached for clandestine work on this basis.[55]

Osman was a code clerk, and thus occupied a position that was traditionally a "high value" target for penetration. Security in the office where Osman worked was notoriously lax (a fact that figured prominently in Osman's eventual acquittal), and Switz's agents managed to get hold of a number of classified documents, including war plans for the defense of Panama and the Canal Zone in the event of hostilities. This information was mailed to one of Dozenberg's "dead drops" in New York, in care of one "Herman Meyers."[56]

This arrangement probably did not go on for very long before it broke down. One of the packets ended up not in Meyers's box in New York but instead in the "dead letter file" at the Panama City post office, where a clerk, following standard procedure, opened it. Inside he found classified documents, clearly from Ft. Sherman, as well as a number of mysterious addresses and cryptic memos. Included in the packet were the "White Plan" for the defense of Ft. Sherman and a report on local anti-aircraft drills. (As a code clerk, one would expect that the most useful information he could have provided Moscow would have concerned American ciphers, but to date nothing relevant to this aspect of Osman's espionage has ever been made public.) The local post office turned these documents over to U.S. Army Counterintelligence, which quickly tied the packet to Osman based on the typewriter used and on his connection to Karry, whose name carelessly appeared in one of the memos.[57]

Osman was arrested, court-martialed, and sentenced to twenty-five years. Switz, Karry, and the other RU agents involved all escaped. Army counterintelligence officers apparently discovered nothing about their true identities or their organizational affiliation at the time. Indeed, Switz's name, which Osman never connected to his predicament, did not even come up until his retrial.

Following their son's conviction, Osman's parents sought the services of Louis Waldman, the well-known socialist lawyer who later became Walter Krivitsky's attorney and confidant. Waldman concluded that Osman's conviction stemmed mostly from the fact that he was a "Russian-Jew," and on that basis appealed the military tribunal's decision. His request for a retrial was granted by President Roosevelt, acting in his capacity as commander in chief.[58]

In the course of this proceeding, Waldman, remembering Switz's name from a deposition he had taken from Osman, noticed Switz's photograph in the 21 March 1934 issue of *Time* magazine. This appeared with the accompanying story about the conviction of the Switzes for espionage in France. Osman recognized Switz, whom he had met briefly through Karry, from the picture. After the Switzes' conviction in France, as we have seen, they became "fully cooperative," and, among other information, related the details of their involvement in the Osman case to the *Sûreté* and the FBI. Osman was eventually acquitted.[59]

The Panama affair remains an odd chapter in the story of RU activities in the United States. The decision to use such a risky dead-drop method for passing sensitive information was perhaps the most unusual aspect of the operation. As we have seen, the RU's preferred means of communication was by courier or diplomatic pouch, although it is true that the latter was unavailable in the United States until February 1933. The full extent of the Fourth Department operation in Panama also remains publicly unknown. But it is distinctly possible that the sloppy tradecraft and management displayed on this occasion by a network under the supervision of the RU residency in New York, coming as it did in the wake of the Burtan fiasco, figured in Valentin Markin's attack on Berzin, and the OGPU's subsequent co-option of the Fourth Department's American *apparat*.

Throughout this period, there is little evidence that the chief American agency responsible for counterintelligence, the Federal Bureau of Investigation (FBI), ever puzzled out the relationship between the American Communist party (which they kept a keen eye on), the OGPU, and the RU. On at least two separate occasions the FBI had access to significant information about RU operations in the United States that it either ignored or misinterpreted: after the Arcos raid in 1927, when the British government passed copies of captured documents relating to Amtorg to J. Edgar Hoover's

Bureau, and ten years later, following the defection of Walter Krivitsky in 1937. There is also no indication that the Bureau managed to identify the true affiliation of any RU officer in the United States before World War II. It was not until after the Soviets and the Nazis began to take sides in the Spanish Civil War in 1936 that Hoover seems to have taken much of an interest in counterintelligence at all. Indeed, President Franklin D. Roosevelt felt it necessary to personally direct Hoover to step up the monitoring of Soviet and German activities in the United States.[60]

Following Roosevelt's victory in the November 1932 elections, there were significant changes in the relationship between Washington and Moscow, if not in Stalin's overall policy toward the United States. As a result both of the *Razvedupr's* recent high-profile failures, and of Stalin's desire to encourage better relations with the United States and its new president, on orders from Moscow Center the RU residencies in America, now under OGPU supervision, became temporarily "dormant." Several Fourth Department officers and agents were consequently dispatched to other assignments.

In addition to Dozenberg, this group included John Sherman, like Burtan a former "Lovestonite" who sometime after 1929 was expelled from his position with the CPUSA paper, the *Daily Worker*. The Fourth Department recruited him into its ranks, and by at least 1932 he was serving as a "talent scout" for Moscow, bringing in new agents like Whittaker Chambers.[61] Sherman was briefly sent to work in Japan, perhaps in conjunction with the efforts to get Sorge's network in Tokyo started.[62] Moscow Center used other American agents, including Chambers, to help rebuild a Fourth Department *apparat* in Great Britain in the mid-1930s.[63]

The lull in RU operations in the United States inevitably gave way to renewed activity by the mid- and late 1930s. Moscow took advantage of the generally cordial feelings many American intellectuals had for the Soviet Union. As the decade wore on, the Soviet Union's supporters and sympathizers around the world increasingly believed that the USSR was the only nation willing to confront the growing menace of fascism. This view in large measure reflected widespread doubts about the future of western liberalism and capitalism during the darkest days of the Great Depression. It also happened to provide Red Army Intelligence with the opportunity to penetrate the highest levels of the Roosevelt administration, and, during the course of World War II, to place agents in an obscure research program called the Manhattan Project.

THE FAR EAST, 1928–1932

Following the destruction of Soviet hopes for a Chinese revolution in 1927, the attention of the Politburo quickly returned to the traditional main geostrategic issue in the region: the competition between Russia, China, and Japan for control of Manchuria. This rich area had by the turn of the century become the focus of Russian and Japanese expansionist plans, as the Middle Kingdom crumbled under the weight of western pressure and archaic political, military, and diplomatic policies. By 1905, Manchuria had become the chief prize in the struggle between Russia and Japan, and remained the bone of contention in Soviet-Japanese relations throughout the pre–World War II period.[64]

In addition to great power rivalry, another source of friction between Moscow and Tokyo was ideology. The Soviets believed that Japan had shown its true imperialist colors during the Allied intervention of 1918–19, when it deployed some 50,000 troops in Siberia, took over key Russian concessions and property holdings in Manchuria and China, and continued to occupy southern Sakhalin Island. Regarded in Moscow as an enemy of the Workers' Revolution second only to Great Britain, Japan remained a primary target, together with Britain, of Soviet propaganda and active measures into World War II and beyond.

Following the withdrawal of the last Japanese troops from Siberia in October 1922, and a tentatively agreed compromise on the Sakhalin question, a comprehensive treaty between Moscow and Japan was signed in January 1925. This brought about a temporary period of "normalcy" in Soviet-Japanese relations. Both powers were united in their opposition to European and American influence in the region (indeed, one constant goal of Soviet policy in the Far East was to exacerbate the existing tensions between Tokyo and Washington), and briefly even found themselves on the same side of a confrontation with Chiang Kai-shek. In July 1929, hostility between Chiang and Stalin led to a brief and bloody clash in Manchuria after the Chinese attempted to seize control of the Chinese Eastern Railroad.[65] Japan, following its own agenda in China, supported the USSR in this confrontation.

This rapprochement did not last long, however. By December 1929 the dispute between Nanking and Moscow had been resolved, largely in Stalin's favor, following a strong showing by the Red Army in the border clashes and subsequent third-party negotiations.[66] At the same time, Soviet ambitions for revolution in China, and their increasing involvement there and in Manchuria throughout the 1920s, made Tokyo increasingly wary of Moscow's policy in the Far East. Japanese suspicions were in some respects well founded. In October 1929, Stalin suggested that the Red Army stage another "revolutionary" uprising, this time in Manchuria. However, although Fourth Department operations there, which Stalin characterized as "isolated detachments being sent . . . to perform isolated tasks of an episodic nature," continued and even expanded, there is no evidence that Stalin's brainstorm was ever seriously considered.[67]

Of even larger significance, however, was the struggle going on in Japan between the civilians nominally in charge of the government and a small but politically powerful clique of ultranationalist generals and young officers. This group, concentrated primarily in the Japanese army but with supporters in the navy as well, was bent on destroying what they regarded as the alien and pernicious influence of western political ideas and institutions in Japan. Their main power base was the formidable Kwantung Army in Manchuria. These officers employed a variety of violent schemes in the mid- and late 1920s to topple the civilian government in Tokyo and commit the military as a whole to their objectives. Ultimately, they succeeded in provoking war with China through their activities in Manchuria and Shanghai.[68]

TARGET: JAPAN

After 1927, the RU faced some special challenges in trying to carry out its responsibilities in the Far East. Among the other consequences of the Peking raid of April 1927 was the exposure of many residencies and networks throughout the region. Although significant portions of the RU organization survived, probably including the residencies in Harbin and Mukden, much of it was destroyed.[69]

Japanese counterintelligence was also cracking down on Soviet espionage. At about the same time as the British raid on Arcos in 1927, Tokyo "confronted the Russian Embassy with evidence that Japanese Communists" were being financed and directed by "official Soviet agencies."[70] Increasing concern among Japanese officials about Comintern meddling, combined with the escalation of tensions between Moscow and Tokyo, led the Japanese security service in the late 1920s to step up its counterintelligence operations in Vladivostok, Harbin, and Shanghai. This effort was so effective that by the mid-1930s, the clandestine Comintern communications routes long established in China, Manchuria, and Korea, so crucial for Fourth Department operations, "had become both impractical and dangerous."[71]

Another major problem faced by Moscow Center was the nature of Japan as a target. Almost everywhere else, Moscow could rely on a ready-made group of potential clandestine operatives: the various radicals organized by the Comintern. As we have seen, indigenous communist parties generally provided the skeletons for espionage networks under the guidance of the Comintern's OMS. This was not the case in Japan. Although there had been clashes between workers and the government ever since the turn of the century, these had been few in number, and ruthlessly suppressed.[72] Japan was a small, insular nation, and the police were very capable. It was not until the summer of 1927 that a Japanese Communist Party, supported by Moscow and approved by the Comintern, was finally created.[73]

The *Tokubetsu Kotoka* (the Special Higher Secret Police, more commonly known as the "Thought Police") was quite familiar with most of the founding members of the Party, and kept them and their associates under close surveillance. The Japanese Communist Party (JCP), although remaining in more or less continuous existence in the home islands until World War II, was essentially impotent.[74] As a consequence, the usual support base for clandestine Soviet operations never developed in Japan.

One alternative pursued by the Comintern, and, later, the Fourth Department and the INO, was to get access to information in the home islands by recruiting native-born and immigrant Japanese communists in the United States.[75] This approach proved to be of mixed usefulness, for, although Moscow was indeed able to develop some good contacts, Japanese members of the CPUSA frequently left paper trails through their work for the CPUSA. Their articles for communist newspapers, and pamphlets targeted at the Japanese-American community or smuggled into Japan, often enabled the Thought Police, with a little diligent research in the American public record, to track down the communist affiliations of a suspected Party member.[76]

SHANGHAI

In the late 1920s and early 1930s, the fundamental task of Red Army Intelligence in Asia was to try and rebuild a useful *apparat*. This effort began with Shanghai, where a multitude of Soviet and communist fronts flourished, including at least three illegal Comintern and RU residencies.[77]

After 1927, in the wake of the collapse of Stalin's China policy and Chiang's assault on the CCP, Shanghai became the focal point of Soviet clandestine activity in the Far East. Essentially founded as a British-dominated foreign outpost following the Opium Wars in the mid-nineteenth century, by 1900 Shanghai had become one of the largest cities in the world, and the economic center of China. There was also a sizeable foreign presence there, and Shanghai continued to be a cosmopolitan and relatively open city until the Japanese occupation in 1937.[78]

Abysmal working conditions combined with nationalistic outrage at the status and power of the highly visible foreigners made Shanghai fertile ground for revolutionary activism. A series of spontaneous, large-scale uprisings of workers against the Chinese government and the foreign occupation began in Shanghai in the summer of 1925. What began initially on 25 May 1925 as a strike by Chinese workers at Japanese-owned textile mills quickly escalated into "an anti-British political uprising." Similar disturbances, collectively known as the "May 30th Movement," spread to other major Chinese cities in July.[79] There were three more "insurrections" in the city during the next two years, the last one in March 1927.[80]

It is therefore not surprising that Shanghai was also a meeting place for an international cadre of leftists and would-be revolutionaries, and a major center for Comintern, OGPU, and RU intrigue. Even after the raid on the Peking Military Center, the various Soviet intelligence organs retained a strong presence in Shanghai. In the PMC organization, Shanghai contained RU Residency No. 9. There were probably at least two separate Fourth Department networks already in Shanghai when Moscow Center sent Richard Sorge to the city in 1930 to organize a third, primarily targeted at Japanese activities in Manchuria.[81]

Sorge's immediate predecessor, and the senior Fourth Department officer assigned to Shanghai until his recall to Moscow, was "Jim" (who may also have been known as "Lehman"). Jim's primary responsibility, according to Sorge, was to set up radio communications between Shanghai, which seems to have been the main relay point, other RU networks in China, and Moscow Center.

Although Sorge described Jim's duties as "primarily technical, preparatory and experimental," he was also charged with intelligence gathering as a secondary task. Jim/Lehman had largely completed his organization of a radio network by the time of Sorge's arrival in Shanghai (although for some reason he was unable to set up a communications post in Canton). When he returned to Moscow soon thereafter, he turned over two of his assistants, Max Klausen and "Mischa," to Sorge, as well as the wireless post he had set up in Shanghai.[82]

Another RU *apparat* in Shanghai was headed by a major general named Frolich, a.k.a. "Theo." Sorge recalled that Frolich's primary task was to establish contacts with the Chinese Red Army "and to gather intelligence concerning it." Frolich's radio technician was a lieutenant colonel called Feldman. Completely separate from Sorge's residency, the Frolich-Feldman group made no progress, according to Sorge, and they were recalled sometime in 1931.[83] A third network was directed by "Paul" (Karl Rimm), a Fourth Department officer who was Sorge's superior and successor in China. Rimm directed his network out of a restaurant.[84] Rimm was probably chief of the RU illegal residency in Shanghai.

The RU relied heavily on the Comintern's OMS *apparat*, which by now answered directly to Moscow Center and the INO, to mask its own work in China. Most of Sorge's agents in China were previously members of the various OMS networks in Asia.[85] One such network was directed out of the *Zeitgeist* bookstore near Soochow Creek. This shop specialized in "radical German, English, and French literature," and was owned by a young German woman named Irene Wiedemeyer. It was a branch of the *Zeitgeist Buchhandlung* chain, which had its headquarters in Berlin and was an international Comintern front. Frau Wiedemeyer's bookshop was the nerve center for most of the OMS's illegal activity in Shanghai, and the major meeting place and recruiting site for the Fourth Department in the city.[86]

RICHARD SORGE'S CHINESE RESIDENCY

Richard Sorge's work on behalf of the world revolution began as early as 1918, when, as a student at Kiel University, he helped prepare the ground for the naval mutiny there by giving "secret lectures on socialism" to groups of sailors. Later he helped organize students and miners for the KPD in Hamburg and Aachen. While in Hamburg, he completed a Ph.D. in political science. Later, on the suggestion of the KPD leadership, he went to the University of Frankfurt, where he was employed first as a "private lecturer," and then became associated with the Marxist Institute for Social Research, probably in 1923 or 1924.

By this time, Sorge was fully immersed in clandestine work on behalf of the KPD and the Comintern. In January 1925, he began working as an OMS officer, charged with establishing Comintern intelligence networks.[87] He usually carried out his illegal work for the Comintern, and later the Fourth Department, as a journalist. It may have been about the time of his assignment to Shanghai that Sorge began to cultivate a pro-Nazi reputation. If so, this proved both fortuitous and prescient, for by the time the Nazis came to power, Sorge had developed excellent contacts and sources among the German press and diplomatic communities in China and Japan.

By 1929, Sorge recalled, he had come to the conclusion that in order for his intelligence work to be most effective, it had to be far removed from the political activities of the Comintern and any communist parties.[88] As we have seen, this had been a matter of debate in the RU since the early 1920s, and was official policy after June 1927. Sorge claimed that he talked this over with Piatnitsky, the chief of the OMS, who then suggested he go see Yan Berzin (inexplicably spelled "Beldin" in Charles Willoughby's English translation).[89] According to Sorge's account, Berzin agreed with this logic, and approved Sorge's request to go to Asia. This may, in fact, have been what happened. But it is more likely that Berzin's decision to send Sorge to China was a response to the worsening situation in Manchuria, the growing tensions with Japan, and the need to rebuild an effective intelligence organization in the Far East after the disasters of 1927. It is also possible that Sorge's wishes coincided with Berzin's needs.[90]

When Sorge arrived in Shanghai in 1931 he did not have to start from scratch. Moscow Center put at his disposal a radio operator specially trained at the RU cipher-radio school, "Seber" (Sepper) Weingarten, and a military specialist, "Alex," who was technically Sorge's superior. In addition, the OMS assigned to Sorge two of its agents in Shanghai, Agnes Smedley and Ruth Werner, and through them a core of Chinese and foreign agents of varying capabilities. Smedley proved to be the key to Sorge's organization in Shanghai. A well-known leftist, Smedley was a classic example of a rebellious intellectual who became obsessed with the workers' revolution.[91] Although she always denied it, as have her biographers as recently as 1988, she was a valuable asset for Soviet espionage in China. By the time Sorge got to Shanghai, she was "in the service of the Eastern Branch of the Central Committee of the Communist International," responsible for, among other things, promoting subversion among anti-British Indian groups.[92] Sorge noted that "the only person in China upon whom I knew that I could depend was Agnes Smedley. . . . I solicited her aid in establishing my group in Shanghai and particularly in selecting Chinese co-workers. . . . She was used in Shanghai by me *as a direct member of my group* [added emphasis]. She worked for me very competently."[93]

One of the people with whom Smedley put Sorge in contact was Ruth Werner, a young woman who had joined the German Communist Party in May 1926. When her husband, who sympathized with her leftist views but was unaware of his wife's covert work, fortuitously received a job in Shanghai in 1931, Werner recalled, she requested that her KPD superiors give her some political work to do in China.[94] Her request was approved, and she was told to await contact. Not coincidentally, the first significant contact she made in China was Smedley, who introduced Werner to Sorge in November 1930.[95] This was the classic pattern of recruitment into an espionage network.

Most of Sorge's agents in Shanghai seem to have been Chinese, although the Japanese played key roles, as well; some of them went on to become crucial components of his Tokyo network, including Hotsumi Ozaki. Ozaki was Sorge's "first and most important associate," and for all practical purposes served as Sorge's right-hand man in China. There were also at least two other Americans in Sorge's network besides Smedley. One was "Jacob," "a young American newspaper reporter" who, like Sorge and Smedley, used his contacts as a journalist to gather political intelligence. The other, interestingly enough, was described by Sorge as "a young employee of the American Consulate," whose name Sorge claimed to have forgotten (this seems most unlikely). Sorge assigned this mysterious agent to collect political and economic intelligence.

Max Klausen was another Fourth Department radio and cipher expert, sent expressly to work with Jim before Sorge's arrival. In September 1931 Klausen was transferred to the Fourth Department residency at Harbin.[96] Sorge was impressed with his abilities, and in 1935 arranged for Klausen to join his Tokyo group. On 4 October 1941 Klausen transmitted a series of messages that made up Sorge's most famous report, telling Moscow Center that the Japanese were planning to move east, not west, and go to war with America and Britain, not the Soviet Union. Fourteen days later he was arrested, along with Sorge.[97]

Except for Werner and the Americans, including Smedley, all of the non-Asian personnel in Sorge's network were actually Red Army intelligence officers. It also seems reasonable to conclude that the vast bulk of information came from his Chinese and Japanese agents through their contacts and friends. Personal relationships played an especially important role in intelligence gathering in China, for as Werner observed, "China did not offer anything like the same facilities for collecting information as a European country; there was 96 percent illiteracy and little published material."[98]

Sorge's responsibilities in China were extensive. He divided his assignments into two categories: those given him by Moscow Center before he left, and the "new duties, arising in conjunction with the changing political situation in the Far East, which I took up and studied of my own accord."[99] His original objectives focused on gathering intelligence about and analyzing all aspects of Chinese government and economy, including military developments, deployments, and doctrine; foreign policy; social conditions; organized and unorganized political movements; and industrial and agricultural conditions. An important secondary objective was to monitor and infiltrate the foreign presence in China, particularly that of the British, Americans, and Japanese.[100] Sorge sent many relatively small "supplementary reports" to Moscow Center. Twice, in late 1930 and in the summer of 1932, he also prepared "voluminous" studies.[101]

In these tasks, Sorge relied heavily on his Chinese agents, although he noted that in a number of instances, he personally gathered the bulk of the information. On questions of foreign policy and military affairs, Sorge also relied on his contacts in the German foreign and diplomatic community, including several *Reichswehr* advisors. Ironically, by 1930 German advisors and military "instructors" were working closely with Chiang's army, taking the place of their Red Army predecessors, even while the *Reichswehr* and Red Army maintained a close relationship. Sorge also recorded that he was able to get information from "the German and American Consulates."[102] Some of this may have come from the "young employee of the American Consulate." It may also have been one or more domestic servants, like those recruited by the PMC. Other possibilities include an associate of Smedley's, or even a conscious or unconscious agent recruited by Sorge from the small American diplomatic and military community.[103]

Indeed, a subject of growing interest to Moscow Center was the increasing German military presence in China. By late 1930 or early 1931, the Germans were not simply offering their services as advisors and instructors to Chiang's army. They were also using Chiang's good graces to do much the same thing that they had been doing in Russia since the mid-1920s: circumvent the Versailles Treaty by carrying out forbidden military tests and encouraging the growth of industries that could support a reborn German military machine. Military exercises were of necessity smaller than the similar ones carried out on Soviet soil. The main emphasis seems to have been on aviation. Sorge struck up acquaintances with a number of German pilots, who proved to be valuable sources of information.[104]

The major focus of Sorge's and Moscow's concerns, however, was the increasingly expansionist policy being pursued by Tokyo. A group of junior officers in the Kwantung Army, supported by a handful of extremist generals in Tokyo, on 18 September 1931 staged an attack on a Japanese railroad near Mukden, blamed it on the Chinese, and promptly occupied the town. The larger objective of the "Mukden Incident," to force the Japanese government to support their expansionist goals, was completely achieved.[105] Four months later, using the pretext that the anti-foreign sentiment among the Chinese had become a threat to the international community in Shanghai, the Imperial Japanese Navy deployed warships off the coast. Chinese hostility, although real enough, at that moment actually focused on the Japanese occupation of Manchuria.

On 28 January 1932, Japanese troops landed to reinforce their small marine detachment already stationed in the Japanese quarter. That night, an artillery duel signaled a full-scale outbreak of hostilities in Shanghai between Nationalist China and Japan. Within a month, 50,000 additional Japanese troops were deployed to the area, and they waged a pitched battle with Chiang's Nineteenth Route Army in the narrow streets and crowded residential and business districts of the city. On 30 January the carrier *Kaga* arrived; it was joined on 1 February by the *Hosho*. Together the two carriers launched air raids that ultimately destroyed most of the Chinese section of Shanghai.[106]

These events led Sorge to redirect his network's energies. Japanese intentions and capabilities assumed top priority. As journalists and associates of journalists, and because of what Sorge called "the unique nature of the city," Sorge and his Chinese and Japanese agents had almost unlimited access to both sides during the fighting, and were thus in a perfect position to observe, analyze, and report on the organization and tactics of the combatants. Sorge's contacts in the German delegation filled most of the gaps left by his agents.[107]

Ruth Werner's activities during this period provide an instructive glimpse into how Sorge's agents operated. One of Werner's tasks was to visit hospitalized Chinese soldiers, ostensibly as charity work. In reality, Sorge had assigned her to find out about "the mood of the soldiers, their social background, their reasons for joining the army, their impressions of the Red Army and the Japanese army in Shanghai, and what motivated them personally to fight so bravely."[108] After a few visits, Sorge, who was always immensely cautious about his agents' covers, became concerned that Werner's questions might be arousing suspicions among "the nurses and Chinese welfare ladies," and ordered her to stop going to the hospital. Sorge encouraged her not only to report information, but to analyze it as well.[109] Besides her intelligence-gathering duties, Werner provided the use of her home as a safe house, and Sorge frequently met there with agents and other Fourth Department officers, including, on one occasion, "Zilbert" a.k.a. "Kleber," Nick Dozenberg's successor as chief of the RU New York residency.[110] As dangerous for Werner and her family as this was (she had a very young son with her in Shanghai), even more potentially perilous was the fact that Sorge's *apparat* frequently stashed stolen pieces of military and industrial hardware, and occasionally even weapons, in her home.[111]

By late 1932, it became clear to Moscow Center that it would have to target Japan directly. Within a few years, the worsening situation in the Far East would even lead Stalin to temporarily assign Berzin as a deputy commander to the newly created Special Far Eastern Military District. In the meantime, Berzin ordered Sorge, with his key Japanese agents and RU radio technicians, to set up a network in Japan proper. Sorge simultaneously moved his public political views even further to the right, in order to ingratiate himself with the increasingly pro-Nazi German military and diplomatic cadre in the Far East. Within a year, Sorge was well established in Japan, where he went on to perform his most important work.

Sorge's accomplishments in the Far East were significantly augmented by the efforts of the *Spets otdel*. The success of Soviet code breaking resulted from the combined efforts of decryption and espionage. One of the most significant messages intercepted by Soviet intelligence in the early 1930s was a telegram sent by Lt. Col. Yukio Kasahara, the Japanese military attaché in Moscow, to the Japanese General Staff in March 1931. In it, Kasahara called for a quick war against the USSR, arguing that it was Japan's "unavoidable destiny to clash with the U.S.S.R. sooner or later." The Japanese attaché went so far as to imply that Japan should arrange an incident that would spark such a war. This telegram, together with others of a similar nature, combined with Japanese aggression in Manchuria and Shanghai in the winter of 1931–32 to provoke the first of the serious diplomatic crises between Moscow and Tokyo that occurred throughout the 1930s.[112]

In February 1932, shortly after the outbreak of fighting in Shanghai, in an episode reminiscent of the "Mukden Incident" five months earlier, a train carrying Japanese troops was mysteriously blown up near Harbin. Blaming Moscow for this provocation, the Japanese seized forty officials of the Chinese Eastern Railway and charged them with the attack. The Soviets in turn maintained that the bombing was the work of White Russian forces supported by Tokyo. The Kwantung Army used the incident as a pretext to complete the occupation of Manchuria in order to "pacify" the region.[113] The result was the creation of the puppet regime of Manchukuo.

Exemplifying the crisis mood in Moscow was the fact that in early March 1932, an *Izvestiia* editorial condemning "Japanese provocations" went so far as to actually cite "documents which originate from officials of the most senior military circles in Japan," including the Kasahara Telegram, which had been decrypted by the *Spets otdel*.[114] Both sides put forces on alert, and there were isolated outbreaks of fighting along the Manchurian border. Still, the situation did not yet escalate into a major military confrontation. It did, however, mark the first in a long series of small-scale armed clashes along the border. These escalated into a major but brief clash in July 1938 at Chang-kufeng, near Lake Khasan in Manchuria, and culminated in May 1939 with a major battle at Nomonhan on the Khalkin-Gol River in Mongolia.[115]

In January 1933, Sorge was recalled to Moscow, where he was "congratulated personally by Berzin on his achievements in Shanghai," and briefed for a new mission: to establish the first Fourth Department *apparat* in Japan. "For the next few years the main priority of Soviet cryptanalysis, as of Sorge's espionage ring, was to monitor the danger of a Japanese attack which was never to materialize."[116]

NOTES

1. Harvey Klehr and John Earl Haynes, *The American Communist Movement: Storming Heaven Itself* (New York: Twayne, 1992), pp. 20–38. For more on the early

history of the American communist, see Koch, *Double Lives*; Theodore Draper, *The Roots of American Communism* (New York: Viking Press, 1957); and *American Communism and Soviet Russia* (New York: Viking Press, 1960). Also see the useful summary in Klehr et al., *The Secret World*, pp. 3–19.

2. Klehr and Haynes, *American Communist*, p. 37; see also Gitlow, *I Confess*, passim.

3. Draper, *American Communism and Soviet Russia*, pp. 209–210.

4. Dallin, *Soviet Espionage*, pp. 389–390; Klehr, et al., *The Secret World*, p. 5. In 1925, out of 16,000 members, 6,400 spoke Finnish, 900 Russian, 1,400 Yiddish, and 1,000 Serbo-Croatian. English speakers numbered some 2,000; see Herbert Romerstein and Stanislav Levchenko, *The KGB against the "Main Enemy"* (Lexington: D. C. Heath and Company, 1989), p. 5.

5. Although links between the Hammer family and Soviet intelligence have been suspected for years, recently published documents prove conclusively that both Armand and Julius were fully and knowingly involved in a wide variety of illegal Soviet intelligence operations; see Klehr et al., *The Secret World*, pp. 26–30. See also Corson and Crowley, *New KGB*, pp. 280–281.

6. Powers, *Not without Honor*, p. 76.

7. Ibid., p. 75; R. M. Whitney, *Reds in America* (New York: Beckwith Press, 1924), pp. 74–75. Whitney's work was based on documents seized in an FBI raid on a meeting between American communist leaders and Comintern representatives in Bridgman, Michigan, on 22 August 1922. For a discussion of the value of Whitney's book, which was the first major anticommunist treatise published in the United States, see Powers, *Not without Honor*, pp. 76–78. For more on Münzenberg and his American connections, see Koch, *Double Lives*.

8. Gitlow, *I Confess*, pp. 388–389.

9. Corson and Crowley, *New KGB*, pp. 276–278.

10. Klehr and Haynes, *American Communist*, p. 20.

11. Corson and Crowley, *New KGB*, p. 279.

12. Chambers originally belonged to one of the "dissident" groups known as the "Lovestoneists" or "Lovestonites"; see Klehr et al., *The Secret World*, pp. 4–16.

13. Corson and Crowley, *New KGB*, pp. 278, 282.

14. "Testimony of Walter Krivitsky, Former Member, Soviet Military Intelligence Service, Through an Interpreter, Boris Shub," in "Investigation of Un-American Propaganda Activities in the United States," *Hearings before a Special Committee on Un-American Activities*, House of Representatives, U.S. Congress (Washington, D.C.: U.S. Government Printing Office, 1939; hereafter cited as Krivitsky, "Testimony"), p. 5742.

15. Corson and Crowley imply that Rosenbliett's RU work at Amtorg began in 1926; see their *New KGB*, p. 468.

16. Ibid., pp. 468–475.

17. George F. Hofman, "The United States' Contribution to Soviet Tank Technology," *Journal of the Royal United Services Institute for Defence Studies* [*RUSI*] 125, no. 1 (March 1980): 64.

By the early 1930s Khalepski was chief of the Red Army's Mechanization and Motorization Administration. He was shot in 1938 (ibid.).

18. Ford had a vested financial interest in good relations with the Soviet government at this time, since he had helped build a major automobile factory in Nizhni-Novgorod starting in 1929 (ibid.). Furthermore, by the late 1920s, Ford was running

into serious economic problems in the United States, stemming from overproduction and a huge back inventory.

19. Ibid., p. 66. For more on Christie's suspension system, see Duncan Crow and Robert J. Icks, *Encyclopedia of Tanks* (New York: Chartwell Books, 1975), pp. 18–19.

20. Krivitsky, *I Was Stalin's Agent*, p. 148. Also see Corson and Crowley, *New KGB*, pp. 468; Dallin, *Soviet Espionage*, p. 392; and Krivitsky, "Testimony," p. 5742. On Berzin's patronage of Tilton, see Poretsky, *Our Own People*, p. 124.

21. Draper, *American Communism and Soviet Russia*, pp. 209–211; Romerstein and Levchenko, *KGB*, pp. 6–7.

22. Draper, *American Communism and Soviet Russia*, p. 211.

23. Corson and Crowley, *New KGB*, p. 321.

24. Dallin, *Soviet Espionage*, pp. 392–393; Corson and Crowley, *New KGB*, pp. 321–322.

25. Tilton was almost certainly recalled because of the failure and exposure of the counterfeiting scheme, for which he seems to have become the scapegoat; see Krivitsky, *I Was Stalin's Agent*, p. 149. Dozenberg, too, was "burned" by this fiasco (see note 29).

26. Corson and Crowley, *New KGB*, p. 454.

27. Dallin, *Soviet Espionage*, p. 393.

28. Krivitsky says this directly in *I Was Stalin's Agent*, p. 136. Elisabeth Poretsky claims that the "Fourth Department wanted no part of this affair but it was forced on them by Stalin who apparently believed in the usefulness of such operations"; see Poretsky, *Our Own People*, pp. 123–124.

29. Gitlow, *I Confess*, p. 389. Krivitsky notes that the problem of the growing scarcity of *valuta*—defined by him as "gold or its equivalent"—was so great by the late 1920s that the OGPU established a special department, the "*Valuta* Bureau," which often resorted to prison and torture to persuade victims to cooperate; *I Was Stalin's Agent*, p. 136. For more on the counterfeiting scheme, see Corson and Crowley, *New KGB*, pp. 318–328; Krivitsky, *I Was Stalin's Agent*, pp. 135–158; and Dallin, *Soviet Espionage*, pp. 393–396.

30. Gitlow, *I Confess*, p. 389.

31. See, for example, Volkogonov, who also accepts Martov's assertion that Stalin even got briefly expelled from the Party once for his excess zeal in carrying out such "expropriations" in his *Stalin*, p. 11.

32. Corson and Crowley, *New KGB*, p. 320.

33. Krivitsky, *I Was Stalin's Agent*, pp. 144, 150.

34. Corson and Crowley, *New KGB*, p. 320.

35. Burtan, also known as William Gregory Burtan, was another "Lovestonite" who had been officially expelled from the CPUSA, along with Lovestone, in 1929, in part, no doubt to facilitate his new clandestine work. He remained a staunch and committed communist until his death in 1985; see Romerstein and Levchenko, *The KGB*, pp. 12–13.

36. Corson and Crowley, *New KGB*, p. 322.

37. Ibid., p. 323. The 1929 currency reform was the last time before 1996 that American $100 bills were changed.

38. In January 1930, a German attorney with communist connections, Dr. Alphonse Sack (who later represented the defense during the Reichstag Fire Trial), made the still unsubstantiated claim that $2,500,000 in "counterfeit pound and dollar

notes from . . . the Soviet State Printing Establishment at Moscow . . . was circulated in China by Soviet agents"; see Krivitsky, *I Was Stalin's Agent*, p. 145.

39. Poretsky, *Our Own People*, p. 124.

40. Krivitsky, *I Was Stalin's Agent*, p. 138.

41. Ibid., pp. 147–150.

42. Dallin, *Soviet Espionage*, p. 303.

43. Corson and Crowley, *New KGB*, p. 454.

44. Ibid., p. 324.

45. Ibid., pp. 324–327.

46. Krivitsky, *I Was Stalin's Agent*, p. 146. Rothstein is perhaps mostly known today for "fixing" the 1919 World Series. He made his reputation in organized crime, however, as a "financier" for a number of up-and-coming gangs during Prohibition. Rothstein frequently supported two or more opposing factions in the same city at once. Such duplicity seemed excessive even to the mob, however, and in 1928 Rothstein was murdered; see Virgil W. Peterson, *The Mob: 200 Years of Organized Crime in New York* (Ottawa, Ill.: Green Hill Publishers, 1983), esp. chapter 12.

47. Corson and Crowley, *New KGB*, p. 325.

48. Ibid., p. 326.

49. Dallin maintained that Dozenberg was assigned to Germany and then Romania, after which he was sent into virtual exile (like Tilton) in China; see his *Soviet Espionage*, p. 396. Later he returned to the United States, supposedly as a private citizen, but was eventually arrested by the authorities. Now "a disappointed and disillusioned Communist," he cooperated fully with the HUAC, after which he spent a year in prison for making false statements on a passport application. After his release, he changed his name, and "although he continued to live in the United States, retired into obscurity"; see Dallin, *Soviet Espionage*, p. 396. See also Krivitsky, *I Was Stalin's Agent*, p. 157; and Draper, *American Communism and Soviet Russia*, p. 212.

50. Krivitsky, *I Was Stalin's Agent*, p. 154.

51. Corson and Crowley, *New KGB*, pp. 327–328; Dallin, *Soviet Espionage*, p. 396.

52. Krivitsky, *I Was Stalin's Agent*, pp. 156–157.

53. Ibid., p. 157. Corson and Crowley cite one account of Markin's demise that claims that he was murdered on Berzin's orders; see their *New KGB*, p. 416. Poretsky, however, supports Krivitsky's version, that Markin died after a fight in a "speakeasy"; see her *Our Own People*, p. 124.

54. Dallin says the New York residency was run at the time by Mark Zilbert (a.k.a. Emilio Kleber and Moishe Stern), Dozenberg's successor, in his *Soviet Espionage*, pp. 396–398. However, as Dozenberg did not return to Moscow until January 1933, clearly the cultivation of Robert Osman and the espionage in Panama happened on Dozenberg's watch.

55. Ibid., pp. 398–400. The most comprehensive discussion of Osman's involvement in this case is in Louis Waldman, *Labor Lawyer* (New York: E. P. Dutton and Company, 1944), pp. 221–257.

56. A "dead drop" is a method of transferring information or objects that involves no actual meeting between people.

57. Waldman, *Labor Lawyer*, pp. 227–228.

58. Ibid., 223–225.

59. Ibid., p. 257.

60. Ralph de Toledano, *J. Edgar Hoover: The Man in His Time* (New Rochelle, N.Y.: Arlington House, 1973), p. 151; also see Brook-Shepherd, *Storm Petrels*, pp. 166–170.

61. Chambers, *Witness*, pp. 252, 280–283.

62. Dallin, *Soviet Espionage*, p. 391.

63. Ibid., pp. 403–404.

64. The best discussion of the problem of Manchuria in Russo-Japanese relations is provided by Dallin in *Russia in Asia*.

65. Dallin, *Russia in Asia*, pp. 260–265.

66. "Obviously our fellows from the Far Eastern Army gave them [the Chinese] a good scare. . . . I think the Chinese landowners won't forget the object lesson taught them by the Far East Army"; see Lih, Naumov, and Khlevnuik, *Stalin' Letters*, Letter 53, 5 December 1929, p. 183.

67. Ibid., Letter 51, 7 October 1929, p. 182. Stalin suggested that "we need to organize two double regiment brigades, chiefly made up of Chinese, outfit them with everything necessary—artillery, machine guns, and so on—put Chinese at the head of the brigade, and send them into Manchuria [*sic*]." He claimed that "no 'international law' contradicts this task. It will be clear to everyone that we are against war with China"; ibid. There is a striking similarity between this plan and the earlier, though much less ambitious, operation in Afghanistan described in chapter 2.

68. Meirion Harries and Susie Harries, *Soldiers of the Sun: The Rise and Fall of the Imperial Japanese Army* (New York: Random House, 1991), chaps. 13–15.

69. All of the other Soviet consulates in Manchuria and northern China were shut down by Chiang's arrests of their staffs in the summer of 1929; see Heller and Nekrich, *Utopia*, p. 251.

70. Rodger Swearingen and Paul Langer, *Red Flag in Japan: International Communism in Action, 1919–1951* (Westport, Conn.: Greenwood Press, 1968), p. 60.

71. Ibid.

72. Ibid., pp. 4–6.

73. Ibid., pp. 25–26.

74. Ibid., chaps. 4–6.

75. For more on this connection, see Swearingen and Langer, *Red Flag*, chap. 7; and Klehr et al., *Secret World*, pp. 226–232.

76. The most disastrous example was that of Yotoku Miyagi, who was conspicuously involved in CPUSA activities during the early 1930s as an émigré. When the Japanese police started to investigate Sorge's network, one of their first steps was to run extensive background checks on all Japanese who were associated with the CPUSA. This turned up Miyagi's name, and through him they eventually got to Sorge; see Klehr et al., *Secret World*, pp. 52–54.

77. For an exhaustive, if occasionally histrionic, description of communist organization and activity in Shanghai, see U.S. National Archives, Harry S. Truman Library, Papers of Harry S. Truman, White House Central Files, Department of the Army, Confidential File, 1949–50, Box No. 4, *A Partial Documentation of the Sorge Espionage Case* [hereafter cited as *Sorge Espionage Case*], Part 1, p. 29. I am indebted to Dr. Randy Sowell of the Truman Library for bringing this material to my attention. Compiled under the direction of Maj. Gen. Charles A. Willoughby, Douglas MacArthur's chief of intelligence, this document reflects both the partisan political

agenda of its editor and sponsor, as well as some of the more verbose paranoia of the post–WWII "Red Scare." Willoughby's narration aside, the document represents an impressive job of investigation, and is based on Chinese, French, and British police files and reports. Although compiled in 1949, much of this report's content has since been verified by other sources, both during and after the Cold War. This report also contains a full, translated transcript of Sorge's confession to the Japanese.

78. Chalmers Johnson, *An Instance of Treason: Ozaki Hotsumi and the Sorge Spy Ring* (Stanford: Stanford University Press, 1990), pp. 41–52.

79. Dallin, *Russia in Asia*, p. 222.

80. These are described in Neuberg, *Armed Insurrection*, pp. 133–150. This essay may have been written, at least in part, by Ho Chi Minh; see ibid., p. 19.

81. Sorge had connections to the Harbin residency, as well, although he claimed that this relationship was only for the purposes of communications (Sorge's agents used the Harbin groups' facilities to run a dead drop). The chief of the Harbin residency was "Ott-Gloemberg"; see *Sorge Espionage Case*, Part 3, File 191, "Part 1 of Translation of Statement of Richard Sorge" [hereafter cited as "Sorge Statement, Part 1"], pp. 23–24).

82. Ibid., pp. 17, 23. "Jim" later became head of the Fourth Department's Radio and Cipher School in Moscow.

83. Ibid., p. 24.

84. Ruth Werner, *Sonya's Report*, trans. by Renate Simpson (London: Chatto & Windus, 1991), pp. 60–61.

85. For a discussion of Comintern activity in Shanghai, see *Sorge Espionage Case*, Part III, "The Shanghai Conspiracy" [hereafter cited as "Shanghai"], pp. 33–54; and Johnson *Instance of Treason*, chaps. 3 and 4.

86. Werner, *Sonya's Report*, pp. 60–61; "Shanghai," p. 35.

87. *Sorge Espionage Case*," "Part 2 of Translation of Statement of Richard Sorge" [hereafter cited as "Sorge Statement, Part 2"], pp. 33–35; also see Massing, *This Deception*, p. 71.

88. "Sorge Statement, Part 1," p. 5.

89. Ibid., p. 29.

90. See Sorge's elaborate rationale for working in Asia in ibid., p. 14.

91. Werner, *Sonya's Report*, p. 39.

92. This was the conclusion of the Shanghai Special Branch of the Chinese Police; see "Shanghai," p. 36.

93. "Sorge Statement, Part 1," pp. 14, 17. Werner also makes it clear that Smedley was an active and energetic recruiter and acquirer of information for Sorge. Other sources have even suggested that Smedley had an affair with Sorge; see Johnson, *Instance of Treason*, p. 231, fn. Johnson in turn relies on Smedley's biographers for this story, as well as the conclusion that Smedley was never a Soviet agent; see Janice R. MacKinnon and Stephen R. MacKinnon, *Agnes Smedley: The Life and Times of an American Radical* (Berkeley: University of California Press, 1988). For more on Smedley's activities in Shanghai, see Leonard, *Kremlin's Secret Soldiers*, pp. 271–272, n. 104.

94. Werner, *Sonya's Report*, pp. 10, 22.

95. Ibid., p. 39.

96. Gordon Prange, with Donald M. Goldstein and Katherine V. Dillon, *Target Tokyo: The Story of the Sorge Spy Ring* (New York: McGraw-Hill, 1984), p. 21.

97. Ibid., pp. 411, 442. The popular notion, perpetuated in Soviet, Russian, and American sources, that Sorge sent a message specifically detailing Japan's plan to attack Pearl Harbor was disproved by Prange's analysis in *Target Tokyo*, pp. 409–411.

98. Werner, *Sonya's Report*, p. 80.

99. "Sorge Statement, Part 1," p. 19.

100. Ibid., pp. 19–21.

101. Ibid., p. 20.

102. Ibid.

103. There is no other evidence of U.S. diplomats serving as agents at this time (ca. 1931).

104. "Sorge Statement, Part 1," pp. 21–22.

105. Harries and Harries, *Soldiers of the Sun*, pp. 151–154.

106. Ibid., pp. 159–61; Norman Polmar, *Aircraft Carriers: A Graphic History of Carrier Aviation and Its Influence on World Events* (Garden City, N.Y.: Doubleday & Company, 1969), pp. 78–79.

107. "Sorge Statement, Part 1," pp. 22–23. The German "military instructors" were a particularly valuable source of information about Japanese tactics.

108. Werner, *Sonya's Report*, pp. 79–80.

109. Ibid., p. 46.

110. Ibid., pp. 66–67.

111. Ibid., p. 62.

112. Andrew and Gordievsky, *KGB*, p. 179.

113. The attack probably was the work of Manchurian guerrillas; see David J. Dallin, *Soviet Russia and the Far East* (London: Hollis & Carter, 1949), p. 10.

114. Unlike the similar situation involving the British GC & CS in 1927, the *Spets otdel* knew by 1932 that the Japanese were aware that their communications had been compromised. A retired American decryption officer, Herbert Yardley, revealed in his memoirs, *The American Black Chamber* (Indianapolis: Bobbs-Merrill, 1931, pp. 250–271), that the United States had broken Japanese diplomatic codes. This fact may have led Moscow to decide it had little to lose in making decrypted material public. By March 1932, Tokyo was in the process of changing over to new, and, so they hoped, more secure encryption systems, although the Japanese may have been unaware of the extent of Soviet code-breaking successes against them until the appearance of the *Izvestiia* article; see Andrew and Gordievsky, *KGB*, pp. 179–180.

115. Harries and Harries, *Soldiers of the Sun*, pp. 263–265. Sorge's network in Tokyo proved of great value during these clashes, and played an important role in guiding Moscow's actions; see Prange, *Target Tokyo*, pp. 21–23, and chap. 32.

116. Andrew and Gordievsky, *KGB*, pp. 176, 180.

center of the Revolution. Marxist theory predicted that the world revolution would begin either there or in Great Britain. Later, Lenin argued that a "colonial" uprising would eventually lead to a socialist Germany. Even after the failure of the Polish campaign of 1920 and the defeat of brief revolutionary outbursts throughout much of Eastern and Central Europe in the early 1920s, many Bolsheviks continued to believe that revolution in Germany was imminent. As we have seen, this led the Soviets to encourage, organize, finance, and arm their German comrades for this eventuality until the end of 1923. As the years went by, they still harbored the hope, albeit increasingly remote, that some fortuitous combination of events could yet bring about the German revolution. In some quarters in Moscow this belief lingered on even after January 1933, when Adolf Hitler became chancellor of Germany. If in the Soviet imagination Great Britain represented the evil genius behind all counterrevolution, then Germany remained the constant beacon of all revolutionary hopes.

Yet the difficulties of trying to maintain power in a vast, economically underdeveloped, and technologically backward nation led the Soviets to seek a more or less "normal" relationship with Weimar Germany as early as 1921. The economic ties and military cooperation that eventually resulted formed the basis for a most unlikely but surprisingly resilient partnership between Moscow and Berlin, first expressed officially in the Rapallo Treaty of April 1922.

This partnership offered Moscow the chance to receive much needed assistance in its drive to modernize. It brought German exports and government loans, gave Moscow access to the international business and diplomatic communities, and provided the Red Army with advanced weapons and the latest developments in western military thought.[2] It was also strategically useful in helping to keep Poland and the Baltic states militarily, if not diplomatically, isolated. This was crucial from Moscow's perspective for helping to check the threat posed by the "coalition of western bordering states," which was the focus of Soviet threat assessment in the 1920s.

Reservations about Moscow's revolutionary tendencies nevertheless continued to trouble German statesmen, who were quite aware of the existence, if not the extent, of many of Moscow's global efforts at subversion and espionage. This awareness did not mean that the Weimar leadership understood Moscow. As late as June 1930, German army analysts, perhaps mirror-imaging their perceptions of their own role, believed that the Red Army saw itself as a "factor for stabilization" in the Soviet Union and a force for *Realpolitik*, curbing the revolutionary impulses of bolshevism.[3] Furthermore, leaders in Berlin steadfastly believed that it was *foreign* communists in the Comintern who retained "lingering influence" on Soviet Russia.[4] In both cases, the Germans had the tail wagging the dog.

Still, from Berlin's perspective, the advantages of pursuing closer relations with the Bolsheviks outweighed the disadvantages. Germany benefited from

CHAPTER 6

Red Army Intelligence and the Weimar Republic

We have to keep our fingers tight on the gullet of the [German] Communists, but go together with Soviet Russia.
—Hans von Seeckt, ca. 1923[1]

The central role played by the Red Army Intelligence Directorate in the strange relationship between Soviet Russia and the Weimar Republic perfectly symbolized its ambiguity, for the RU was responsible for supervising and coordinating the secret military collaboration in the USSR even as it organized and carried out a massive espionage effort against Germany.

The close contact between the German and Soviet high commands had important consequences for the Red Army and its intelligence directorate. Since the end of the Soviet-Polish War, Moscow believed that the primary military threat it faced was a combined Polish-Romanian attack, supported by Britain and France. German assistance in acquiring intelligence on Polish capabilities, if not intentions, may well have proved immensely valuable. Yan Berzin also considered the close cooperation between the two armies in their exploration of new methods of thinking and fighting crucial for enhancing the military sophistication of Red Army officers. Lastly, the close contacts between high-ranking officers from Berlin and Moscow played a significant, and fatal, part in the course of Stalin's purge of the Red Army officer corps, which began four years after the end of the military collaboration.

The Soviet Union had a peculiar relationship with the other "pariah of Versailles," Weimar Germany, throughout the latter's brief, doomed existence. On the one hand, theoretically Germany still represented the ideological trade with Moscow, especially with exports that were either less competitive or were restricted in the West. In addition, publicity surrounding real and rumored elements of the Moscow-Berlin relationship allowed German politicians and diplomats to bring subtle but gradually increasing pressure to bear on the western powers to ease the restrictions of the Versailles Treaty. More importantly, the clandestine relationship with the USSR permitted the German army, the *Reichswehr*, to illegally circumvent many of the restrictions placed on it by Part V of the Versailles Treaty.

For the Soviet secret services, Germany was not only the symbolic center of the world revolution, but its organizational and administrative center, as well. The Comintern's OMS had its headquarters in Berlin, not Moscow. Germany stood at the geographical crossroads of Europe, and provided relatively easy access to key powers like Poland and France. Its ports and rail lines afforded excellent communications with the rest of the world. Furthermore, Weimar's laws against espionage were extremely lenient and poorly enforced. Its police force, although sophisticated, was frequently sympathetic, especially to efforts it believed to be directed against German enemies like Poland and France. On those occasions when the police did act against Soviet espionage, they were usually checked by the Foreign Ministry, which placed the importance of the secret collaboration with Moscow above enforcement of the criminal code. Last but most definitely not least, Germany's large and radicalized working class offered an inexhaustible supply of zealous recruits for clandestine work.

Ironically, the combination of these factors meant that Red Army Intelligence was more invisible in Germany than anywhere else. Many of its German agents worked through the auspices of the KPD, whose intelligence section (the *N-Apparat*) was completely subordinate to the *Razvedupr*. This ensured a strong additional layer of security between the RU and the German police. It is not surprising then that, until Nazi rule, Germany was the major recruiting, training, and staging center for the Comintern and the Fourth Department. Most of the *Razvedupr's* officers were either German, trained in Germany, or spoke German, the semi-official language of the communist world.

More Comintern and Fourth Department agents were busily engaged in gathering industrial and military intelligence in Germany than in any other country in the world. Moscow Center greatly preferred this approach to gathering information about German targets over the more conventional study of what a Soviet official named "Turov"—described as the "rich German literature on the militarisation of the [German] economy" between 1914–1918.[5] Responding to Turov's suggestion that such a study be undertaken, Berzin argued that these sources "did not contain any valuable information concerning the methods of militarisation or any useful statistics."[6] Berzin contended that such information was only useful from a bureaucratic standpoint, and could contribute little to any true understanding of the relationship between economics and war planning in the West. Instead, espionage promised to provide the best relevant information.

This intelligence was analyzed by the "special Military-economic Bureau" of the Fourth Department, which published its findings in a secret restricted-circulation journal called *Voenno-ekonomicheskii biulleten* (Military-economic Bulletin). This approach did not suit the economists at *Gosplan* (*Gosudarstvennaia Planovaia Komissiia*, State Planning Committee), and the journal only had three issues, ending publication in 1927. *Gosplan* officials complained in 1929 that "far too few intelligence resources had been devoted to the study of foreign experience in preparing the economy for large-scale war."[7]

By the mid-1920s, the Fourth Department led what was probably until then the greatest peacetime espionage effort ever mounted by one nation against another. Berzin was simultaneously responsible for monitoring and carrying out many of the specifics of the Soviet-German military collaboration.

The apparent contradiction between directing espionage and subversion while simultaneously facilitating close military, economic, and intelligence cooperation no doubt appealed to Soviet dialecticians. In the real world, however, such duplicity was bound to cause problems. Berlin repeatedly worried and complained about Comintern and Soviet espionage and subversion. In 1925, the *Reichswehr*'s intelligence department concluded that "Moscow is undoubtedly ready to sacrifice Germany's interests" in pursuit of revolution. It suggested that the Wilhelmstrasse (the German Foreign Ministry) follow a more western-oriented policy, for closer ties with Britain might make "easier our struggle against [the] Communist International and its bodies, and against Bolshevik agents."[8] Such protests notwithstanding, Berlin nevertheless continued to pursue the clandestine military cooperation into the Nazi era.

BERLIN CENTER

Walter Krivitsky asserted that out of the ashes of the Hamburg Uprising, Red Army Intelligence built an intelligence operation in Germany that was "the envy of every other nation."[9] Other authoritative sources have supported Krivitsky's claim.[10] Indeed, the Fourth Department was deeply committed to operations in Germany almost from the moment of its creation in 1918. The chaos created by civil war, the defeat of the German army on the Western Front, and the increasingly revolutionary situation in Germany in 1918–19 combined to lead Trotsky's infant Red Army Intelligence Directorate to concentrate its earliest "foreign" operations there.

An early *Registraupr* report on intelligence work in Germany was produced in 1920 by an otherwise unidentified officer named "Ausem." This document set out the objectives of agent operations, summarized the resources available to the RU for the years 1918–20, and made recommendations for future operations. Taken as a whole, this early intelligence report demonstrated a sophisticated and, given the resources at hand, extremely ambitious approach to the task of intelligence gathering.[11]

The first chief of a Fourth Department residency in Germany is unknown; it may have been Ausem. Alexis Skoblevsky commanded a significant RU advisor contingent there in 1923 as part of the preparations for the Hamburg Uprising, and may have also been associated with one or more Fourth Department networks. At about the same time, the residency at the Soviet Embassy was probably commanded by the ubiquitous Nikolai Krebs. Krebs's subordinates included Ignace Poretsky and Felix Gorski, who was, like Poretsky, a Pole.[12] These two were subsequently transferred to Vienna, together with Krebs, who became the military attaché there.

The RU officer serving as military attaché in Berlin in the early 1920s may have been "Jacob." Jacob later figured prominently in the clandestine shipment of arms to Chiang's Kuomintang. By 1925, P. F. Lunev was the attaché at the Berlin embassy. He was recalled to Moscow in 1928 following the exposure of *Handelsvertretung*-sponsored espionage against the German Aeronautical Research Institute described below.[13] In the early 1930s, Walter Krivitsky was the senior Fourth Department officer in Germany, and was responsible for agent operations throughout Western Europe.

By 1920, relations between Germany and Russia had begun to move toward normalization, and the Soviets soon opened an embassy in Berlin. Predictably, this quickly became a major center for Soviet espionage.[14] The official Soviet presence in Berlin was spread throughout a variety of diplomatic and commercial establishments, all of which supported several legal and illegal residencies throughout the interwar period. Berlin became a central headquarters, exceeded in importance only by Moscow Center itself, for Fourth Department, Cheka, and Comintern operations not only in Germany but also throughout much of the rest of Europe and the United States as well.[15]

One of the major bases for RU operations in Germany was, of course, the Soviet Embassy itself. The embassy housed sections from all of Moscow's clandestine services. The Fourth Department residency at the embassy probably had two primary responsibilities: liaison duty with the *Reichswehr*, as part of the covert relationship between the German and Soviet armies (see below), and penetration of the foreign diplomatic community in Berlin. Military attachés were frequently assigned to observe German military exercises, facilitate the movement of illicit cargoes between Germany and the USSR, arrange tours of German military and technological sites for senior Soviet observers, and develop cordial relationships with highly placed German officers. For example, in September 1930 two RU officers serving in a liaison capacity, "Germanovitch" and "Kotov," observed "large-scale maneuvers" by German units in Thuringia and Bavaria, and at about the same time, also met with Wilhelm Heye, Seeckt's successor as chief of the Army Command of the *Reichswehr*.[16]

Razvedupr penetration of many foreign embassies in Berlin also provided useful intelligence. In August 1925, an RU agent in the Japanese Embassy obtained a copy of a Japanese assessment of German foreign policy that was subsequently forwarded to Frunze, Voroshilov, Unshlikht, and Chicherin.[17] By the early 1930s, Red Army Intelligence also had access to reports prepared by the American ambassador to Germany, W. E. Dodd, although it is unclear whether these were derived from penetration of the American diplomatic community in Berlin or some other source.[18] RU efforts were in some cases complemented by the OGPU's INO, which also placed agents in numerous foreign diplomatic outposts in Berlin, including the British Embassy.[19]

The Fourth Department obtained intelligence surreptitiously from the *Reichswehr*'s high command, supplementing the information shared through the official covert relationship. In February 1925, for example, Red Army agents obtained a German "secret service" (i.e., army intelligence) report assessing Berlin's foreign policy options vis-à-vis the Entente powers and Soviet Russia.[20] This report was probably prepared in the context of Foreign Minister Gustav Stresemann's proposal to the British earlier that month for a western security pact. The RU also had access to conversations at the most senior level, like that of 11 December 1932, between the Hungarian envoy to Berlin, Kaniya, and the chief of the *Reichswehr*'s Land Forces Department, Col.-Gen. Kurt von Hammerstein-Equord.[21]

Red Army Intelligence obtained this information from two agents with unusual access to classified information: General Hammerstein's two daughters. They fell under the ideological influence of Werner Hirsch, the editor of *Rote Fahne*. He persuaded them that "the revolutionary front on which it was their duty to fight was the writing desk of their father."[22] Hammerstein's daughters thereafter diligently pilfered their father's desk "for years," photographing anything that looked even remotely important. They also succeeded in recording "all the conversations that went on in their father's house." The girls passed the material to Hirsch, who sent it on to his RU superiors.[23]

In addition to the embassy, there were two other major bases in Berlin supporting Soviet military intelligence operations in Germany in the early 1920s: the OMS's *Pass-Apparat*, and the German equivalent of Arcos and Amtorg, the *Handelsvertretung*. Organized originally sometime in 1919 or 1920, the *Pass-Apparat*, later called the *Pass-Zentrale*, was composed of a series of underground workshops that provided stolen, borrowed, or forged documents for use by the Comintern and Soviet intelligence. Those involved in making forged passports were called "consuls."[24] Until 1924, this operation was "small, primitive and poor," and was almost completely destroyed by a police raid in 1921. Nevertheless, while remaining a target of police raids, the *Pass-Zentrale* was rebuilt in 1921–23, surviving and even growing into the Nazi era. Even then, it managed to elude the attentions of the Gestapo for some time. Throughout its existence, the *Pass-Zentrale*'s services were essential for Fourth Department operations around the world.[25]

As in Britain, France, and the United States, the Fourth Department found the use of front organizations in Germany to be especially valuable. The reader will recall that one of the earliest self-sustaining RU business fronts, *Wostwag*, was established there in 1921 by the Mrachkovskii/Ehrenlieb brothers. The Comintern's dockworker networks also proved invaluable to Red Army Intelligence in Germany, especially in Hamburg and Kiel. In addition to providing resources for secure communications and clandestine travel, as we have seen, OMS networks in German ports also proved lucrative sources for new agents.

But the largest and, in terms of intelligence gathering, the most successful fronts, were the semi-official trade legations and "joint ventures" sponsored by the Soviet government. With the advent of increasingly close military and industrial ties between Berlin and Moscow, the Soviet Union had justification for opening a series of trade consortiums in Germany. Although also responsible for legitimate business, their most important role was as staging bases for espionage. These fronts were parceled out to the various clandestine services and were usually assigned more or less exclusively to either the INO or Fourth Department. Red Army Intelligence consequently used the following joint Soviet-German companies: *Derutra* (*Deutsch-russische Transport Gesellschaft*), ostensibly involved in the rail and steel industries; *Derop*, which provided similar access to the German oil industry; and *Garkrebo* (*Garantie-und-Kredit-Bank für den Osten A.G.*). In addition, both the Fourth Department and the INO made use of the large *TASS* (the official Soviet news agency) presence in Germany.[26]

Following the reorganization of Soviet clandestine operations in Germany after the Hamburg Uprising, the most important Soviet front became a trade legation, the *Handelsvertretung* (also called the *Russische Handelsvertretung*), established in Berlin in 1920. Operating under a fragile layer of diplomatic immunity, by the mid-1920s the *Handelsvertretung* became the most important center for supporting Soviet intelligence and underground operatives in Germany, and perhaps in all of Europe. It figured prominently in Soviet penetrations of German industrial giants like I. G. Farben, Krupp, Junkers, and BMW. The trade legation served as a staging area for numerous Fourth Department, OMS, and INO operations, including smuggling currency, both genuine and counterfeit, and confiscated valuables throughout Germany and Europe.[27] The legation's facilities included a code and cipher department and a "large high-speed photo-printing machine." The *Handelsvertretung* soon expanded, setting up similarly equipped offices in Hamburg, Konigsberg, and Leipzig.[28] The German equivalent of Amtorg and Arcos, the *Handelsvertretung* maintained close relations with both sister organizations.[29]

The Berlin headquarters of the trade legation had a backyard opening onto the Ritterstrasse, where two RU agents known as the "Loewenstein brothers" set up another front, a jewelry shop. This conveniently located enterprise served as both a Fourth Department safe house and, on at least one occasion, an escape route.[30] According to Dallin, about 50 percent of the Berlin KPD secretaries were directly employed by the *Handelsvertretung*. Other employees included numerous OMS functionaries, and several members of the *T*- and *M/N- apparats*, most of whom answered directly or indirectly to the Fourth Department. At the highest level, GPU officers supervised the activities at the legation through the "Personnel Department." The main concentration of RU officers was probably in the *Abnähmekommissionen* (reception commissions) and in the legation's "Engineering Department." The latter, under the immediate direction of the military attaché, was responsible for, among other things, coordinating the clandestine arms trade between Moscow and Berlin. The Engineering Department had close ties with Krupp, I. G. Farben, BMW, and Junkers Aviation.[31]

The activities of the *Handelsvertretung*'s Engineering Department are a perfect example of the contradictory nature of the Soviet-Weimar relationship. Even as RU personnel supervised the officially approved transfer to Moscow of arms and technology from Krupp, Junkers, and others, its officers and agents simultaneously carried out vigorous espionage against those very same companies, frequently through the auspices of the KPD. In part this may have reflected the continuing, and partially justified, Soviet suspicion that the Germans were holding out on them; the Soviets in fact leveled such charges at their German counterparts on numerous occasions.[32]

One of the "engineers" employed by the trade legation was an RU officer called "Alexandrovski," who arrived in Berlin in 1927. He was charged with infiltrating and reporting on the German aviation industry. In the pursuit of this objective, Alexandrovski and another Fourth Department employee of the *Handelsvertretung*, a Latvian named Eduard Scheibe, used the ongoing exchange of specialists between Moscow and Berlin to recruit a German aviation engineer, Eduard Ludwig, who worked in the Junkers office in Moscow in 1924–25.

Soviet representatives approached Ludwig with the offer of "a possible appointment as a university professor" in the USSR. In late 1927, Ludwig, now working at the Aeronautical Research Institute in Berlin-Adlershof, was told by the Soviet Embassy that a university position was available. Before he received this appointment, however, he had to first "cooperate" with Scheibe. Ludwig soon began taking classified documents out of the institute for copying by RU photographers. The institute's security units eventually discovered that documents were periodically missing and traced the theft to Ludwig. In July 1928, Ludwig, Scheibe, and the Fourth Department photographer, Ernst Huttinger, were arrested. "Alexandrovski" slipped out of the country.[33]

This case, and many others like it, were the consequence of a deliberate strategy authorized by Moscow Center in the wake of the publication in the summer of 1928 of *The Future War* threat assessment, which made efforts to obtain the latest western industrial and technological secrets a top priority. In

January 1929, Uborevich explained that "we must buy these [German] specialists' services, cleverly win them over to our side, in order to catch up promptly on what we are lagging behind [in]. I do not think that German specialists might prove politically worse and more dangerous than our Russian specialists, and, in any case, there is much to learn from them, with the price being hardly higher on the whole."[34] This method of agent recruitment seems to have become more or less standard for RU officers operating against German industries into the early 1930s.

Another illustrative example is that of "Herr Meyer," who in exchange for providing "commercial and technical secrets" from the Solvay chemical plant was promised a position in Russia as a general plant manager, with a salary "of 5,000 rubles a month, a rent-free residence, and 4,500 rubles for travel and moving expenses."[35] Moscow Center used this approach to lure several valuable technicians and scientists from German firms to the USSR. Other firms successfully penetrated on this basis included Siemens and Halske, Polysius cement works, and a variety of research laboratories.[36]

In addition to serving as a base for Soviet espionage against the Weimar regime, the *Handelsvertretung* supported a number of other clandestine activities, facilitating Soviet management of various KPD organizations, and serving as a staging point for deploying INO and RU "illegals" into Germany, Europe, and even the Far East. The usual procedure for the latter was to temporarily assign aliases to the operatives, derived from a combination of real and forged papers, and officially employ them for a brief time at the legation. After residing at one of the *Handelsvertretung*'s boarding houses for a few weeks, the *razvedchiki* would disappear or "submerge," and their legation identities would be inherited by other new "employees." The Soviets called this process *Operation Umsteigen* (Operation Transformation).[37]

Security at the *Handelsvertretung* seems to have been more effective than in many other Soviet trade legations, and was no doubt facilitated by the close contacts between the two governments. Although the German police had strong suspicions about activities at the Soviet Trade Legation, they apparently never succeeded in penetrating it with one of their own agents. Hans Peters, an officer of the Political Division of the state police (*Abteilung* IA; counterintelligence) later recalled that "the police did not have agents in either the Soviet Embassy or the *Handelsvertretung*," largely because "the recruiting of an agent [from within the Soviet trade mission] required considerable time, and before we enlisted him, he had to leave."[38]

One of the most notorious incidents associated with the *Handelsvertretung* occurred in 1924. Among the agents recruited by the Fourth Department's *Handelsvertretung* residency in the early 1920s was a KPD member named Hans Botzenhard, a former railway engineer who had been fired for his political activities.[39] Under the auspices of a senior KPD leader, Wilhelm Pieck (later president of the German Democratic Republic), Botzenhard got a job at the Soviet Trade Legation. He was soon working for

Red Army Intelligence through the "Military Section" of the KPD, the organization formerly charged with carrying out the Hamburg Uprising. Botzenhard's activities were uncovered by the authorities, and they arrested him in Stuttgart in early 1924.

That would simply have been the end of another typical Soviet agent were it not for Botzenhard's extreme fear of incarceration. In May 1924, while en route to Stargard from Stuttgart, he managed to escape in Berlin by luring his two-man police escort into the trade legation (he told them it was a restaurant), and then running out the back door, taking advantage of the convenient location of the Loewensteins' jewelry shop to hide. Two hours later, the police searched the premises of the *Handelsvertretung* but found nothing incriminating, just a surprisingly "large number of employees who held privileged 'service' passports."[40] The search was not an exhaustive one, however, for Foreign Minister Gustav Stresemann, mindful of Soviet sensibilities, stopped the search after two hours.

Still, this was not enough for Moscow, which immediately saw the implications for Soviet clandestine operations around the world if this search was allowed to become a precedent. Ambassador Nikolai Krestinsky made what would come to be the standard Soviet protest against police raids and searches of its legations: that they possessed diplomatic extraterritoriality, and thus were, according to international law, beyond the reach of the police. Moscow's noisy outrage was underscored by 300,000 German coal miners already engaged in a strike, who added to their previous grievances a "protest against the search in the *Handelsvertretung*."[41] The German government quickly apologized for the search, fired the police officer who led it, and, of most importance to Moscow, conceded Soviet claims of extraterritoriality, thereby also extending diplomatic immunity to a number of the trade legation's "leading officers."

This capitulation by the Weimar government—the result of a variety of domestic pressures and foreign concerns in Berlin—established a precedent applied to many other official Soviet trade missions abroad in an age when Moscow had yet to achieve widespread diplomatic recognition. Thereafter the Soviets obtained unprecedented diplomatic status for their "trade" officials and foreign business offices in France, Italy, Great Britain, the Baltic states, China, and the United States. The "Botzenhard affair" ended in a triumph not only for Soviet diplomacy but for Soviet espionage.[42]

PENETRATION OF GERMAN INDUSTRY

David Dallin observed that "never had there been such a tight network of mass espionage as that set up by the Soviet Union within German industry in the period 1928–32."[43] A major target for Soviet espionage, especially following the approval of the first Five Year Plan in late 1928, was German industry, particularly the chemical and aviation industries. Between espionage and officially shared information, it is unlikely that Germany kept many technological secrets from Moscow in the 1920s.

An important factor encouraging such brazen Soviet efforts was that Weimar authorities viewed the theft of technological secrets not as espionage—which German criminal law narrowly defined as pertaining solely to military targets—but merely as "unfair competition." Consequently, the penalty for those convicted was extraordinarily light; the maximum term of imprisonment was generally one year.[44] Nonetheless, the constant and increasingly frequent examples of "unfair competition" that came to light over the course of the 1920s led the Weimar authorities to create a special bureau charged solely with combating industrial espionage in 1929. It investigated 330 cases in 1929 and more than 1,000 cases the following year.[45] In March 1932, following a particularly sensational RU espionage case, the "Steffen affair" (see below), President Hindenburg issued a decree establishing tougher laws with much stiffer penalties (up to five years imprisonment) for the "defense of the national economy."[46]

In the wake of the misadventures experienced with the "questionnaires" described earlier, the Fourth Department tried a new approach in its efforts to penetrate German industry by the late 1920s. A number of shorter queries were now submitted to a variety of sources from several agents, so that if one "link" was exposed, the authorities would be unable to determine the larger objective. The resulting list of pilfered "loot" was impressive and eclectic: processing secrets for the manufacture of rayon and gunpowder; a knapsack military telephone (developed by Telefunken); and new vehicle components and gasoline production methods.[47]

OMS and RU penetration of German industry was, above all, opportunistic. Given the virtually inexhaustible supply of potential sources, and the extreme leniency of the German courts toward convicted agents (the stiffest sentences for espionage rarely exceeded four years, and these were almost always reduced), there was little need to cultivate professional espionage networks. By 1930, this strategy seemed to have more than justified itself, given the information acquired balanced against the investment of the resources needed to get it.

But the side effects of such blatant disregard for German national sensitivities may well have ultimately proved disastrous. In the early 1930s, cases of Soviet espionage, usually linked to the *Handelsvertretung*, became so frequent that even Soviet sympathizers in the press and government developed a cynical and suspicious attitude toward Moscow. The proverbial "last straw" came in 1931, when a series of sensational cases of Soviet industrial espionage became front-page news almost simultaneously. The climax came with the notorious "Steffen-Dienstbach affair."

Fourth Department espionage against German industry was designed to augment the information obtained through the clandestine relationship at the state level. Important achievements included extensive penetration of the facilities involved in the construction of the "Panzerkreuzer A," the first major naval unit to be built by Germany after the war. Several *Razvedupr* networks, probably organized by the Naval Directorate of the Fourth Department, converged on the naval yard almost as soon as construction was announced in 1928.[48] At the *Rhenische Metallwaren und Maschinenfabrik* in Düsseldorf, they obtained data on the design and manufacture of the cruiser's armament. Another group composed of "technicians and designers" was organized by an RU-controlled engineer named Willi Adamczik, and stole blueprints of the ship itself. The German police managed to break up all of these networks by 1930. How many others were involved is unknown, though it is "certain . . . that when the Panzerkreuzer was launched a description and photographs of many of its essential parts lay on the desks of the General Staff of the Red Navy."[49]

The RU's greatest success in penetrating German industry, however, was achieved against the chemical giant I.G. Farben, which had several subsidiary plants and laboratories scattered throughout Germany, although most were concentrated in the Ruhr. The extensive RU penetration of Farben may have been partly a natural reflection of the sheer size of the corporation, as well as its domination of the chemical industry. It may also have simply reflected the ease of access afforded to Red Army Intelligence by the numerous KPD members and sympathizers employed by or with access to the firm. From at least the mid-1920s until the early 1930s, an almost inexhaustible series of networks was organized by the KPD, OMS, and Fourth Department (all of which ultimately forwarded their results to the RU). The trade legation was the staging center for much, though not all, of this espionage. One of the earliest networks in a Farben plant was organized by Hans Barion, who was a member of the KPD Central Committee in Berlin, in 1924 or 1925. Some of Barion's agents, those with technical or management skills, such as engineers and foremen, were recruited with the promise of high-paying positions in Soviet Russia.[50]

Erich Steffen, an employee of the trade legation and leader of the Communist Revolutionary Trade Union Opposition (RGÓ) in the German chemical industry, was at the center of another massive intelligence-gathering network targeting I. G. Farben. One of Steffen's agents, Karl Dienstbach, another member of the RGO, ran a subsidiary network of about twenty-five agents scattered throughout Farben branch plants in the Ruhr.

Steffen's agents demonstrated little discretion in their pursuit of the answers to the shortened "queries"; it was just a matter of time before they asked the wrong person, who turned out to be Karl Kraft. Kraft reported the approach by one of Dienstbach's agents to the I. G. Farben security department (an organization frequently more successful in disrupting industrial espionage efforts than the police). At first, Farben security had Kraft cooperate, and gave him bogus information to hand over to Dienstbach's *apparat*. Within a few months, Farben turned the investigation over to the police, who made several arrests in March and April of 1931. Those arrested included several engineers, scientists, and technicians. Soon thereafter, another associated network in the Bitterfeld I. G. Farben plant was also exposed.

The trade legation was not the only Soviet base sponsoring espionage against I. G. Farben. The RU residency at the Berlin embassy organized still another network. The resident was Boris Bazarov, a friend of Poretsky's who had been transferred to Berlin from the Balkans. One of his subordinate officers, Mikhail Samoilov, was in charge of industrial espionage against the giant German chemical firm. This penetration of Farben was also uncovered by the police in 1931, following which Moscow Center recalled Samoilov. Bazarov, however, together with his wife, stayed in Germany, where they remained "the most important agents of the Fourth Department in Berlin" for the next few years.[51]

As many as 111 cases of treason were tried in Germany between June 1931 and December 1932, and almost 150 persons were convicted of military espionage. The vast majority of these cases involved the Soviet Union.[52] This situation led to public outrage, especially when the Soviet Trade Legation was found once again to be at the center of the Steffen-Dienstbach affair. Police demanded authority to raid and search the *Handelsvertretung* but were again blocked by Stresemann. This further aggravated public opinion. One result was that on 9 March 1932, President Paul von Hindenburg signed a "decree on the defense of the national economy," which, although only marginally increasing the penalties for industrial espionage, at least made them more easily applicable in comparison to other types of espionage. Another, more ominous, result of these trials was the increase in popular support for the most virulently anticommunist group in Weimar Germany, the Nazi party.[53]

THE *N-APPARAT*

In Germany, the RU and, to a lesser extent, the INO, often adopted the unusual policy of deploying its officers under Comintern or KPD cover.[54] This made it even easier for the Soviet government to maintain its innocence by arguing that it had no authority over either the "independent" Comintern or the KPD. Unfortunately, this strategy also complicates the already difficult task of definitively identifying specific Fourth Department networks in Germany.

Another consequence of this approach was that OMS networks assumed greater importance for Red Army Intelligence in Weimar Germany than anywhere else. These maintained close contact with RU residencies through specifically assigned liaison operatives. Indeed, until 1928 it was not uncommon for the OMS liaison officers to actually run networks on behalf of Red Army Intelligence; recall that a similar arrangement involving Jean Cremet led to a dispute between Moscow Center and the French Communist Party. The reforms following the international embarrassments of that year, although designed to distance Soviet intelligence organizations from local communist parties, had little meaning in Germany, where political extremists, and especially communists, were so numerous that the authorities could not effectively monitor their behavior anyway. In this situation, the role of the OMS was essentially to mobilize its resources "on commission" for the INO and RU. The KPD found that, not surprisingly, agents were especially easy to recruit in the Weimar Republic."[55] Many of them understood that they were working for the Comintern as members of the KPD; however, their orders actually came from Red Army Intelligence via the *N-Apparat.*[56]

The man who served as the OMS-Fourth Department liaison in Germany for most of the mid-1920s was none other than Krivitsky's former "pupil," the leader of the Hamburg Uprising and Larissa Reissner's proletarian hero of the dockyards, Hans Kippenberger. In 1927, after spending much of the intervening time in hiding, Kippenberger re-emerged and managed to get elected as a KPD deputy to the Reichstag, where he was soon appointed to the Committee on Military Affairs, an important post that he held until 1933. Although his liaison services had been of great value to Moscow Center, his position in the Reichstag no doubt proved even more lucrative, for his committee assignment gave him access to a wealth of useful information. By the time of his committee appointment, Kippenberger had in fact already become a full-fledged RU agent.[57] Among the German comrades, Kippenberger's OMS-RU organization was known as the "N" or "M-Apparatus" (terms apparently used interchangeably), and they called its members *apparatchiks.*[58]

Kippenberger's eventual successor as the chief of the *N-Apparat* was Fritz Burde, a.k.a. "Edgar" and "Dr. Schwartz." He served in this capacity from 1929 through 1932.[59] One of Burde's recruits was an aspiring Hungarian journalist and member of the KPD named Arthur Koestler, who later achieved international acclaim as the author of *Darkness at Noon.* Ernst Schneller, a member of the KPD Central Committee and a "talent scout" for the N-Apparatus, approached Koestler soon after he had applied to join the KPD in 1931.[60] At the time, he worked for one of the major publishing families in Europe, the Ullsteins. Eager to serve the revolution, Koestler was persuaded by Burde that he could do so most effectively by maintaining his position as a noncommunist journalist.[61] Koestler's subsequent contact with Burde was through a woman he identified only as "Comrade Paula."

Together, Burde and Paula tried to school Koestler in the art of conspiracy, but by his own account the young writer was not an impressive student. Apparently, he was never called upon to perform any blatant act of espionage. Instead, his assignment was to periodically dictate to Paula a report on "any bits of political information or confidential gossip that I had picked up in the House of Ullstein."[62] To Koestler, this seemed not only of questionable value, but also quite boring. Although remaining full of idealism for the cause, he devoted the bulk of his energies to a fruitless effort at winning the affections of the aloof and suspicious Paula.

When an even younger protégé started working with Koestler at the publishing house, Koestler decided, almost certainly without authorization from Burde, to recruit him. "Von E." was the "son of a high-ranking diplomat," and for a while Koestler's reports to Paula "became much livelier," for Von E. moved in a social circle that gave him access to a wide variety of political, diplomatic, and military "gossip."[63]

Von E., however, ultimately caused Koestler's undoing as an intelligence agent, for the young aristocrat began feeling guilty about his loose talk and "disloyal" behavior, and told Koestler that he either planned to shoot himself or confess his treason to the Ullsteins. The decision, he announced while brandishing a pistol, rested with Koestler. Koestler, to whom the whole episode appeared "half comic, half disgusting," had by this time soured on his own role in the *N-Apparat*. He told Von E. to go ahead and submit his confession "with my blessing and go to hell."[64] Koestler was fired from the publishing house shortly thereafter. His limited usefulness to the RU apparently ended as a result.

Sometime earlier, apparently on the verge of cutting Koestler loose, Burde tried to talk him into going to Japan, even offering to "get you the assignment through our connections" if his employers refused to sponsor him. Koestler indicated his willingness to go, but although Burde promised to check into it, the matter never came up again. After leaving the House of Ullstein, Burde cut him loose. Koestler continued to serve in Germany and the USSR as a committed member of the Party. By the late 1930s, he had once more become part of a Fourth Department network, that of Hungarian Alexander "Sandor" Rado, later a key figure in the "Red Orchestra."

Arthur Koestler's service as a *razvedchik* did not last long; by his own reckoning, about two or three months.[65] His experience is probably illustrative of that shared by the overwhelming majority of Soviet "agents" in Germany.

In addition to the various trade enterprises in Germany, Red Army Intelligence found a number of other suitable organizations and movements, most of which were legitimate, through which to operate. These included the Communist Student Organization (*Kostufra*), and the *Klub der Geistesarbeiter*, a group of "leftist intellectuals," whose early ranks included Klaus Fuchs. This organization was heavily infiltrated by agents from both the RU and the INO, who gathered intelligence at, among other places, the *Technische Hochschule* in Berlin. According to Dallin, as many as 5 percent of the faculty there "were being used by the Soviet network, most of them without knowing it."[66]

Another prominent asset for the Soviet intelligence services was the "worker correspondents" (*rabkors*), or *Betriebs Berichterstatter* ("BBs") as they were called in Germany. This movement had in fact begun in Germany, and it had expanded rapidly by 1928. The KPD's *Rote Fahne* triumphantly noted that in June 1928 there were 127 "registered" BBs; by the end of the year there were "several thousand."[67] There were more *rabkors* in Germany than in any other country outside of the Soviet Union. Throughout the late 1920s and into the early 1930s, the director of the clandestine BB network in Germany was probably the Hungarian RU officer named Bela Vago, who operated out of the *Handelsvertretung*. As in France, the BBs reported any potentially interesting information to their affiliated journal or publication (usually but not always the *Rote Fahne*). Editors sorted through this material and forwarded anything potentially useful to RU intelligence officers.[68]

Besides being an important target for espionage and subversion, the Weimar Republic also proved invaluable as a base of operations against the rest of Central and Western Europe, including Poland and Czechoslovakia. This was of course of immense importance, since the Red Army regarded Poland as the major military threat throughout the 1920s. As we have seen, following the Hamburg Uprising in 1923, and reflecting the growing clandestine cooperation between Moscow and Berlin, much of the RU apparatus based in Germany and directed at other nations was relocated to Vienna.[69] Residencies in Berlin remained senior in the chain of command to the other stations in Europe, however, and the city continued to increase in importance as the main clandestine transit center between Moscow and Europe. On special occasions, usually in the wake of the destruction of a major *apparat*, the Fourth Department residencies in Berlin would even temporarily take over networks in another country. The illegal residencies based in Germany, cloaked by multiple layers of Comintern and KPD cover, became increasingly devoted to espionage against the Weimar Republic itself.

Espionage against these high priority targets was facilitated by the Weimar authorities, who, although diligent in trying to break up Comintern networks in Germany, "appeared to have almost no interest in the Soviet intelligence agencies," which they believed were operating solely against the Allied powers.[70] Given the antipathy for Poland shared by Berlin and Moscow, and the fact that both governments even exchanged intelligence on Poland, this is not terribly surprising. Nonetheless, the fact that much of the Comintern's resources, including the KPD, were actually subordinated to the Soviet intelligence organs meant that this German perception was dangerously naive.

THE CLANDESTINE PARTNERSHIP

I regard it necessary that our future joint work with the Germans be guided by the following main statements: to use their tactical and operative [operational] experience of the world war and further development of such experience (participation of our specialists in German military games, maneuvers, etc.) and also to use Germany's most important technical innovations in communication, artillery, aviation, [and] tank engineering, both technically and tactically.
—Unshlikht to Stalin, 31 December 1926[71]

The *Razvedupr*, and Berzin personally, played a central role in the clandestine cooperative relationship between the German and Soviet armies. To fully appreciate the significance of that role, a brief review is necessary. The rocky relationship between the Red Army and the *Reichswehr* can best be understood as consisting of three distinct periods: 1919–22, 1922–28, and 1928–33.[72]

The first period was characterized by tentative moves toward covert collaboration, in the form of unofficial and secret meetings, transfer of funds, and troop movements, signifying the efforts of some in Berlin and Moscow to find a solution to the loss of territory suffered by each power as a result of defeat in war and the nationalist revolutions sweeping Central and Eastern Europe. The major focus of resentment and hostility in both capitals was, predictably enough, reborn Poland.[73] This mutual antipathy toward Poland remained the essential cement binding Moscow to Berlin throughout the Weimar period. It would later resurface as the basis for collaboration between Hitler and Stalin, culminating in the Non-Aggression Pact of 23 August 1939, and the subsequent dismemberment of Poland by the Nazis and Soviets.

The second period, and the one most thoroughly discussed in the literature, lasted from the Rapallo Treaty until 1928, and was characterized by the attempt to illegally train and equip the *Reichswehr* with Soviet assistance.[74] Although there were plans to build several factories in Russia by firms like Junkers Aircraft and the Stolzenberg Chemical Company, none of these progressed very far in the face of the combined forces of the anxieties of German industrialists, relentless Soviet red tape, and Moscow's paranoia.[75] Instead, by 1926, efforts at collaboration were concentrated at three installations built in the USSR with German funding and technical expertise: a chemical weapons research and training facility called "Tomka," established near the town of Volsk bordering the Volga German Autonomous Republic; a tank school at Kazan; and an air warfare training and testing center at Lipetsk.

These efforts were slow to produce any meaningful results. They suffered from poor planning, delays, and ongoing logistical problems, all of which caused much recrimination on both sides. German officers were often frustrated by what they regarded as inefficient management and cumbersome transportation. The Soviets, for their part, never lost their suspicion that the Germans, who remained in Moscow's view not only capitalists but also militarists, and, in many cases, even fascists, were withholding vital information from them in a deliberate effort to sabotage Moscow's efforts to modernize.

Further complicating this situation was the fact that from the mid-1920s on, "leaks" reached first the British and then the German press about the activity in Soviet Russia; these jeopardized the whole operation. The worst flap began in late December 1926, when aspects of the secret collaboration in chemical warfare became a major news story and political scandal in Berlin.[76] This overlapped with the 1927 "war scare" and helped bring Soviet-German relations to their lowest point during the Weimar era.[77]

The third period, lasting from 1928 until the final termination of the collaboration in the fall of 1933, was characterized by increased emphasis on joint military exercises, training and planning, intelligence sharing, and officer exchanges. Exchange of senior officers for the purposes of professional training had in fact begun as early as 1926, when for the first time two Red Army officers, identified only as "Svechnikov" and "Krasilnikov," were admitted as senior students into the German Military Academy.[78]

In many respects, this third period had the greatest impact on the future of each army. Such joint operations promoted close, almost comradely, relationships between many senior officers on each side, although this was clearly more the case for German officers, who never really grasped either the ideological nature of the Red Army or its relationship with Germany. The ultimate source of this amity, of course, was their mutual hatred of Poland. Command-level officers were exposed to each other's military culture, a process that facilitated creativity and innovation, and encouraged sophisticated operational thinking. This proved to be a key element in the success of "blitzkrieg."[79]

For the Red Army, however, this close association with the German high command proved much more ominous. The personal contacts developed between several senior Red Army commanders and their German counterparts eventually helped establish the justification and pattern for Stalin's purge of the Red Army. Almost every Soviet officer who visited Germany or worked with the *Reichswehr* became a casualty of Stalin's paranoia.[80] This was an important factor in the decimation of the Fourth Department as well, which was at the center of the secret military collaboration.

One major task of the Fourth Department was to cooperate with *Reichswehr* intelligence in sharing intelligence on subjects of mutual concern. Moscow thereby gained access to important new information and sources. For example, *Reichswehr* military attachés in nations where the Soviets had little or no official presence gathered a great deal of information on foreign military developments, much of which was shared with Moscow. Significant intelligence was passed to the Soviets on military developments in England and Czechoslovakia, and German intelligence on the U.S. military was so extensive that it led one Soviet official to conclude that "the achievements of American military techniques are greatly accessible to the Reichswehr."[81] Poland, however, remained the most important subject for intelligence collaboration.

The details of the intense secret war waged between Poland and the Soviet Union during the interwar years still remain almost completely unknown. Red Army Intelligence appears to have had some access to sensitive documents prepared by the Polish army's Second Bureau (military intelligence) in 1920 during the Soviet-Polish War, but, on the whole, what little information there is suggests that Polish counterintelligence was quite efficient at breaking up RU networks.[82] Indeed, the only known specific examples of documents pertaining to Polish military capabilities in Soviet possession are all in German, and are very likely translations provided Moscow by *Reichswehr* intelligence. Still, RU threat assessments contained extensive information about Poland. Some of this intelligence may have been obtained indirectly, perhaps from French or German sources.

Direct Fourth Department penetration of Poland seems to have had limited success. In the early 1920s, Moscow Center ordered Ignace Poretsky and another officer named Jacob Locker to recruit agents from Polish army units stationed near L'viv. They managed to organize a network of nine officers and NCOs, all of whom were either sympathizers or members of the Polish Communist Party. This network gathered intelligence for an "assessment of over-all Polish strength" as well as "information on individual units, their deployment, and their national composition"—the exact kind of information used in threat analysis.[83] Elisabeth Poretsky alleged that such intelligence was widely and readily available throughout the ranks of the Polish army through bribery.

This *apparat*, however, apparently did not last very long. Elisabeth Poretsky noted that the Polish police were "very quick in making arrests," and her husband and Locker were both soon caught and tried. Ignace Poretsky was sentenced to five years, but escaped to Germany after eighteen months during a massive Polish railway workers' strike. Locker's immediate fate is unknown, but he was working for the RU again by the mid-1930s.[84]

Elisabeth Poretsky maintained that Polish counterintelligence began to adopt French techniques that enabled them to manage "long-drawn-out investigations and surveillance carried out in a professional manner, which could lead to the arrest of an entire network of agents and ensure relative security for some time to come."[85] If true, then we can only conclude that the pupils soon surpassed their teachers. The Fourth Department was always able to assemble a solid underground organization in France because of the plentiful availability of Party members and sympathizers. No such similar situation existed in Poland, where the Polish Communist Party was outlawed, small, and fragmented by feuding between nationalist and pro-Comintern factions.[86] The combination of effective Polish counterespionage and a paucity of cooperative sources may in fact have led Moscow Center to regard Poland throughout most of the 1920s as a "denied zone," like Great Britain after the Arcos raid. This in turn may have contributed to Moscow's paranoia about Polish intentions, and would help to explain the willingness on the part of the security-obsessed Soviets to entertain German suggestions for covert collaboration in intelligence gathering against Poland.

Moscow and Berlin began sharing intelligence on Poland on a very limited basis as early as the Soviet-Polish War. Throughout the summer of 1920, Trotsky apparently kept the German military attaché in Moscow, Major Wilhelm von Schubert, informed about Tukhachevsky's drive into Poland; part of Trotsky's purpose was to assure Berlin through Schubert that regardless of Soviet success in Poland, Soviet Russia intended to respect "the old German borders from 1914."[87] In March 1925, the chief of the Red Army Chemical Department, Ya. Fishman, reported from Berlin that the *Reichswehr*'s secret service had provided him with intelligence on the deployment of Polish regiments.[88] And in 1929, Gen. Werner von Blomberg shared with Uborevitch extensive information obtained through German military espionage against Poland, including what Blomberg described as a Polish "attack plan" for war against the Soviet Union.[89]

Nevertheless, available evidence suggests that the first official discussion of the possibility of significant intelligence operations occurred in late 1928. The reasons for such an apparent delay are not clear. The most likely circumstance under which the Soviets would contemplate such a move would be if the demand for intelligence about Poland suddenly transcended the means of the Fourth Department to supply it on its own. This may have resulted from the collapse of key networks, like those in France, and/or the increased demand for precise information necessitated by the complex war planning undertaken by the end of the decade in association with the first Five Year Plan.

In any event, documents show that the idea of joint intelligence operations was initiated by Yan Berzin's opposite number in the *Reichswehr*, Oscar von Niedermeyer. Berzin reported to Voroshilov on 28 December 1928 that the Germans had proposed, among other things, the "establishment of contacts in the intelligence activity of the two armies against Poland, exchange of materials on Poland, and a meeting of the leaders of the two intelligence services for joint consideration of materials on the mobilization and deployment potential of the Polish Army."[90] Berzin recommended to Voroshilov that Moscow agree to an exchange of information on Poland between the Fourth Department and *Reichswehr* intelligence, and he fully supported the proposal for joint talks on Polish mobilization and war preparation. He drew the line, however, at establishing actual organizational contacts with what was, after all, a capitalist and militarist secret service.[91] Berzin's recommendations were approved in their entirety by the Central Committee sometime in early 1929.[92]

The Soviets were also concerned about the ability of their German partners to keep the covert cooperation secret. The flap in 1926 in the Reichstag over the chemical weapons shipments was the most obvious example of what the Soviets considered to be poor German security. Indeed, the 1929 Central Committee report also specifically resolved to "demand from the Germans better security and enhanced conspiracy in [the] course of cooperation between the two armies, as well as guarantees that leaks to the press of any information concerning this cooperation will be prevented."[93]

Little evidence is available about the relative value of any information exchanged on Poland under this agreement. It may be that on balance the Germans got the better end of the deal, for it seems likely that whatever they chose to share with Moscow was probably already obtained by the RU through its agents in the German army and government. This conclusion is supported by a conversation between Voroshilov and von Heye's successor, Gen. Wilhelm Adam, held on 19 November 1931. At one point, Adam noted that "our intelligence activity against Poland is very unsatisfactory. Thank you for the materials we got from you, and I am asking for cooperation in acquiring them in the future." Adam went on to observe that "we know that your intelligence provides much better information than ours."

Voroshilov: . . . It's very pleasing to hear such praises of our intelligence men, but I am afraid they do not quite deserve them.

Adam: There is a proverb, "Only a bad man gives more than he has in his pocket."

Voroshilov: . . . I would like to assure you that everything most valuable and most important is passed to you.[94]

Liaison between the two intelligence services continued at least as late as March 1932.[95]

Intelligence operations against Weimar Germany were immeasurably enhanced by the high level cooperation between the two governments. RU officers had access to the senior echelons of the German army and the most sensitive quarters of German industry. These "legitimate" efforts were structured to complement espionage. Officially approved liaison trips to Germany by Soviet attachés and technical experts often proved invaluable for identifying what the Germans preferred to keep hidden. This allowed the Fourth Department to target its espionage more efficiently.

For example, in a January 1929 memo, Fishman instructed Red Army officers scheduled for a tour of German factories "to be very persistent and demand to be shown everything. There must be no closed doors for us. In case they refuse to show anything, our comrades must say that they will report this in Moscow. Thus we shall have (1) one extra argument against them; (2) appropriate information for the Fourth Department."[96] The uneasy nature of the relationship was clear when Fishman himself later visited Germany. He pressed his hosts for information about their latest research on chemical weapons; they denied that German technology had made any advances over what was used in the world war, and assured Fishman that the assertion that "we have discovered a new substance in the postwar period is not true. Neither our industry that works for peaceful purposes only, nor (as we are informed) any other state in the world have [*sic*] ever succeeded in creating a substance fit for our purposes." Fishman noted in his report that much of this statement was demonstrably false; for example, the Fourth Department was already aware of new chemical weapons being researched in French laboratories.[97] Soviet suspicions were reinforced when during the course of a meeting with *Reichswehr* chemical specialists a German scientist carelessly remarked that "'nobody will let real secrets out, but will keep them to themselves.'"[98]

On another occasion, Lunev, the Soviet military attaché in Berlin, was given a tour of the Hertz "optics plant" in 1925. Although allowed by the Germans more or less unrestricted access, the facility and its operations were so highly sophisticated and technical that Lunev doubted whether he could competently evaluate them. He observed that "to derive a piece of important information during an ordinary inspection is possible only for a good expert."[99] Lunev's assessment of the Hertz plant revealed its importance for Soviet military-industrial development, and identified it as a target for espionage. Moscow Center was consequently able to deploy numerous operatives against the plant.[100]

The German presence in Soviet Russia also naturally offered an important opportunity for espionage. By at least 1931, the Fourth Department succeeded in penetrating German diplomatic communications between Moscow and Berlin, and it may even have had access to the reports of the German ambassador, Herbert von Dirksen, on an almost regular basis.[101]

MANAGING THE COLLABORATION

A formal organizational structure for managing the joint military endeavors was established sometime after March 1926. Von Seeckt was in overall charge in Berlin, while Unshlikht assumed similar authority in Moscow. Lunev was the Soviet liaison in Berlin; his German counterpart in Moscow was Colonel Litt-Tomsen.[102] RU Chief Yan Berzin was responsible for actually organizing and supervising joint operations in the Soviet Union. His responsibilities included monitoring and reporting on all aspects of the three joint installations, and arranging the movement of German personnel and equipment into, out of, and through Soviet territory, and he even supervised some of the early factory construction efforts.[103]

Berzin's German counterpart was Oskar von Niedermeyer. Niedermeyer had been in charge of the first major German military mission to Moscow in 1921, and at the end of 1923 he organized the *Zentralle Moskau* (the German "Moscow Center"), the headquarters for Berlin's operations in the USSR until 1932. Niedermeyer kept this position for the duration. He was a well-known figure even before his first visit to Moscow. During World War I, his exploits in Turkey and the Middle East made him a semilegendary figure in Germany, where he was known as "the German Lawrence." After the war he became chief of *Reichswehr* intelligence. Niedermeyer had access to the highest policy-making circles both in the German Foreign Ministry and in the German army, and was a close confidant of Seeckt's.[104]

Berzin periodically submitted assessments of the joint operations to Voroshilov. One, dated December 1928, included an extensive background history on the origins and course of the clandestine relationship, an analysis of German motivations and objectives, and an assessment of the overall value of each area of cooperation.[105] He noted that "the existing enterprises [i.e., the chemical testing facility and the aircraft and tank experimental centers] have not been of very much advantage to us so far."[106] However, he did regard the officer exchanges to be of immense value: "the most appreciable results are yielded by our officers' maneuvers' observation and field trips as well as by their attending academic courses in Germany." Elaborating, he observed that "by studying the organization of individual branches of the service, the arrangement of staff work, methods of instructions and training as well as development of military thought, our officers not only acquire a good amount of useful knowledge and broaden their outlook, but also get some stimulus to examining certain problems."[107]

Expressing an opinion that may have later come back to haunt him, Berzin went on to maintain that by participating in such experiences, Soviet officers were "enriching their knowledge" and acquiring "so-called 'military culture.' Other west European armies being presently inaccessible to us, it is both expedient and necessary to retain this possibility of perfecting the professional grounding of a number of our officers."[108]

Specialists in various fields involved in the joint operations reported to Berzin, who then reported to Voroshilov. For example, P. I. Baranov, from the Red Air Force, and chemical expert Fishman each reported on relevant developments in Germany and managed to personally tour key sites.[109] However, their primary task in the context of the German-Soviet collaboration was to monitor the German activities at, respectively, the air school in Lipetsk and the Tomka chemical weapons testing center. Berzin seems to have personally overseen the operations of the tank facility at Kazan.[110]

In addition to his role as de facto supervisor of these operations, Berzin as RU chief provided peripheral support for the joint collaboration. For example, the RU arranged the transportation of personnel and equipment between the two countries, a task facilitated by the Fourth Department's covert shipping networks in the Baltic. German military personnel, dressed as civilians and carrying false passports, were smuggled into the USSR, probably through the extensive Comintern and RU maritime networks in the Baltic ports.[111]

Improvised services were also provided when necessary, as when three German pilots died in plane crashes near Lipetsk. Their bodies "were crated, declared spare parts, and slipped into the port of Stettin with the collusion of the local German customs officials."[112] Red Army Intelligence also organized the smuggling of crucial equipment. Before the necessary machine tools were finally shipped into the Soviet Union in the late 1920s, whenever the British motors that powered most of the aircraft used at Lipetsk needed factory overhaul, the Fourth Department routinely snuck them in and out of Great Britain for repair, apparently without arousing the suspicions of the British authorities.[113]

Although the military collaboration between the Red Army and the *Reichswehr* continued into the early 1930s, the end was in sight with the growth of Nazi power in the Reichstag and the appointment of Hitler as chancellor in January 1933. Already in mid-January, before Hitler was even officially sworn in as chancellor, German officials informed their Soviet counterparts that the joint installations must be shut down by autumn.[114]

Berzin consequently supervised the dismantling of the installations built on Soviet territory. Throughout the summer of 1933, he submitted to Voroshilov progress reports on this task that included inventories of equipment and facilities that the Germans agreed to leave behind.[115] On 31 August, he informed RKKA headquarters that "the liquidation of the 'friends' enterprise is taking place as quickly as possible and will be finished by September 20–30."[116] And on 14 October he reported to Voroshilov that "in compliance with your order . . . the activity of the 'friends' is completely stopped, their property is exported to Germany, and the personnel of their enterprises has left the USSR."[117]

At a final banquet held to celebrate the partnership, German officers and diplomats toasted their Red Army counterparts, and "underlined the great significance of the continuation of friendly relations between the Reichswehr and the WPRA [Red Army] in some new form."[118] Within eight years, many of the Germans present would be using the training and experience gained during the clandestine collaboration in battle against the Soviet Union. Within six years, almost all of their Red Army hosts would be dead.

NOTES

1. Hilger and Meyer, *Incompatible Allies*, p. 125.
2. For an analysis of the economic aspect of the relationship between Germany and the Soviet Union, see Haigh et al., *German-Soviet*, especially chap. 5.
3. Olaf Groehler, *Selbstmörderische Allianz: Deutsch-russische Militärbeziehungen, 1920–1941* (Berlin: Vision Verlag, 1992), p. 64.
4. Hilger and Meyer, *Incompatible Allies*, p. 108.
5. Samuelson, *Soviet Defence*, p. 38.
6. Ibid., p. 38.
7. Ibid., p. 39.
8. Dyakov and Bushuyeva, *Red Army*, pp. 50, 53; TsGASA, f. 33987, op. 3, d. 98, l. 153–7.
9. Krivitsky, *I Was Stalin's Agent*, p. 64.
10. See Poretsky, *Our Own People*, p. 58.
11. For a thorough analysis of this document, see Leonard, *The Kremlin's Secret Soldiers*, pp. 280–282.
12. Poretsky, *Our Own People*, p. 58.
13. Dallin, *Soviet Espionage*, p. 114.
14. Ibid., p. 77.
15. Ibid., p. 29.
16. Dyakov and Bushuyeva, *Red Army*, p. 23. Heye held this position from 1927 to 1930; see Gordon A. Craig, *The Politics of the Prussian Army, 1640–1945* (New York: Oxford University Press, 1964), p. 431.

17. Dyakov and Bushuyeva, *Red Army*, pp. 54–56; TsGASA, f. 33987, op. 3, d. 98, l. 73–6; see also Dyakov and Bushuyeva, *Red Army*, p. 119 n. 19. The author and even the ultimate nationality of this document remains a mystery, although the most likely guess is Japan; Dyakov and Bushuyeva, *Red Army*, p. 119 n. 19.

18. Ibid., pp. 288–290; TsGASA, f. 33987, op. 3, d. 504, l. 63–77.

19. See, for example, Dyakov and Bushuyeva, *Red Army*, p. 91; TsGASA, f. 33987, op. 3, d. 70, l. 153–62.

20. Dyakov and Bushuyeva, *Red Army*, pp. 49–53; TsGASA, f. 33987, op. 3, d. 98, l. 153–7.

21. Dyakov and Bushuyeva, *Red Army*, p. 118; TsGASA, f. 33987, op. 3, d. 497, l. 2–5.

22. Dallin, *Soviet Espionage*, pp. 112–113.

23. Ibid., p. 113.

24. Poretsky, *Our Own People*, p. 186.

25. Dallin, *Soviet Espionage*, pp. 92–93.

26. Ibid., p. 86.

27. Ibid., pp. 77–79.

28. Ibid., p. 81.

29. Massing, *This Deception*, p. 54.

30. Dallin, *Soviet Espionage*, p. 79.

31. Ibid., pp. 78–79.

32. See the exchange of November 1931 between Voroshilov and *Reichswehr* chief Gen. Wilhelm Adam, in Dyakov and Bushuyeva, *Red Army*, pp. 106–107; TsGASA, f. 33987, op. 3, d. 375, l. 22–40.

33. Even Lunev, the military attaché at the time, was recalled, although it is unclear whether or not this was because the Germans had linked him to the Alexandrovski-Scheibe ring; see Dallin, *Soviet Espionage*, pp. 113–114.

34. Ibid., p. 248; TsGASA, f. 33987, Op. 3, D. 295, l. 141–83.

35. Dallin, *Soviet Espionage*, pp. 104–105.

36. Ibid., pp. 106–108.

37. Ibid., p. 82.

38. Ibid., p. 82.

39. Unless otherwise noted, the information on Botzenhard comes from ibid., pp. 79–81.

40. Ibid., p. 80.

41. Ibid.

42. For more on Botzenhard's subsequent fate, see Dallin, *Soviet Espionage*, pp. 80–81.

43. Ibid., p. 76.

44. Ibid., p. 103.

45. Ibid., pp. 76–77.

46. Ibid., p. 110.

47. Ibid., pp. 104–105.

48. This was the "pocket battleship" *Deutschland* (later the *Lützow*); see Nathan Miller, *War at Sea: A Naval History of World War II* (New York: Scribner, 1995), p. 29.

49. Dallin, *Soviet Espionage*, pp. 114–115. The Sänger-Hofmann ring was eventually caught in May 1931 through the efforts of a self-styled "agent provocateur" named Hans Schirmer (ibid.).

50. This roughly corresponds to the period during which Hans Kippenberger's brother, Willi, may have been carrying out espionage on his behalf (ibid., p. 104). If so, then, given Hans Kippenberger's affiliations, this was indeed for all practical purposes a Red Army Intelligence network.

51. Ibid., p. 83. Bazarov was assigned to the United States in May or June of 1935, where he served as the chief of the Fourth Department residency that later ran the networks to which Hede Massing, Whittaker Chambers, Noel Field, and Alger Hiss belonged; ibid., pp. 404–405.

52. Adolf Ehrt, *Bewaffneter Aufstand* (Berlin-Leipzig: Eckart-Verlag, 1933), p. 64. As Dallin points out in *Soviet Espionage*, p. 77, Ehrt was a Nazi, and therefore his numbers should be regarded with due skepticism. Nevertheless, these particular figures come from before the Nazi era, and are probably reliable.

53. Dallin, *Soviet Espionage*, pp. 107–110.

54. This may explain Richard Sorge's claim that he was working for the OMS in Britain and Germany while simultaneously recruiting agents for the Fourth Department (see chap. 5).

55. Dallin, *Soviet Espionage*, p. 88.

56. Poretsky, *Our Own People*, p. 53.

57. Ibid., pp. 87–88; Krivitsky, *I Was Stalin's Agent*, pp. 56–57. After the Nazis came to power, Kippenberger fled to the Soviet Union. There, in 1936, he was charged with being a German spy, and, exhausted after several months of interrogation and torture, he "confessed." " 'There is a nail in my head,' he kept repeating. 'Give me something that will put me to sleep'" (ibid., p. 57). He was presumably shot sometime shortly thereafter.

58. Arthur Koestler, "Arthur Koestler," in *The God that Failed*, ed. by Richard Crossman (New York: Harper & Brothers, 1950), pp. 26–27; Alex Weissburg, *Conspiracy of Silence*, trans. by Edward Fitzgerald (London: Hamish Hamilton, 1952), p. 26; Massing, *This Deception*, pp. 75, 80–81.

The "N" may have stood for "*Nachtrichtungsdienst*," or "secret service," and the "M" may have been for "*Militärische*," or "military." Only German agents seem to have used the word *apparatchik* for a member of an espionage network. The usual Russian word for an intelligence officer was *razvedchik*, and an agent was an *agent*. *Apparatchik* has usually meant a professional communist bureaucrat.

59. Massing, p. 83; Weissberg, *Conspiracy of Silence*, p. 26; Koestler, "Arthur Koestler," pp. 28–29.

60. Schneller was head of the KPD's Agitprop Department. Koestler also asserts that Schneller was "the head of the 'Apparat N,'" a position in fact held by Burde; Koestler, "Arthur Koestler," p. 26.

61. Ibid., pp. 26–28.

62. Ibid., p. 31.

63. Ibid., pp. 32–33.

64. Ibid., p. 40.

65. Ibid., pp. 35–36, 37.

66. Dallin, *Soviet Espionage*, pp. 84–85. On Fuchs, see also Robert Chadwell Williams, *Klaus Fuchs, Atom Spy* (Cambridge: Harvard University Press, 1987), pp. 13–15.

67. Dallin, *Soviet Espionage*, p. 86.

68. Ibid.

69. Poretsky, *Our Own People*, p. 58.

70. Ibid., p. 58. The German police referred to the RU as "Klara" and the GPU as "Greta"; together they were known as the "two girls." Dallin, *Soviet Espionage*, p. 77.

71. Dyakov and Bushuyeva, *Red Army*, p. 58; TsGASA, f. 33987, op. 3, d. 151, l. 18–23.

72. As far as I am aware, no one else has broken down the period of German-Soviet military collaboration into these periods. I employ this approach here because (1) it seems to most accurately reflect the perceptions of the Soviet, and, to a lesser extent, the German officers involved, and (2) the documentation strongly supports the conclusion that the objectives and policies pursued by each side distinctly varied over time.

73. On the early contacts between the Soviet government and Weimar Germany, see Hilger and Meyer, *Incompatible Allies*, chap. 1 and pp. 49–51; Dyakov and Bushuyeva, *Red Army*, pp. 13–14, and Erickson, *Soviet High Command*, pp. 144–150.

74. See for example Groehler, *Selbstmörderische, passim*; Erickson, *Soviet High Command*, pp. 247–255; Fischer, *Stalin*, pp. 527–535; and Barton Whaley, *Covert German Rearmament, 1919–1939: Deception and Misperception* (Frederick, Md.: University Publications of America, 1984).

75. See for example Haigh et al., *German-Soviet Relations*, chap. 5. Numerous scholars, including Fischer, have described this aspect of the German-Soviet cooperation as the "rearmament" of the German army; see Fischer, *Stalin*, p. 527. This is the implication of the Russian title of D'yakov and Bushueva's work, *Fashistskii mech kovalsya v SSSR* (The Fascist Sword Forged in the USSR). Yet the evidence clearly shows that little was accomplished in the actual production of war material for Germany. A by no means atypical example is the experience of Junkers Aircraft. The Junkers factory was begun in Fili in 1925, and by 1927 was in such disrepair that Voroshilov wrote to Stalin that it

is kept badly; snow lies in the shops as a snowdrift, machine tools are rusting. Airplanes are losing their value every month since they are removed from one place to another, disassembled and assembled, and, as a consequence, they cease to be new airplanes.... All these circumstances ... strongly require the most decisive measures to be taken for liquidating the concession and reaching an understanding concerning cancelled agreements for bombers. (Dyakov and Bushuyeva, *Red Army*, p. 147; TsGASA, f. 33987, op. 3, d. 249, l. 57–9)

76. Fischer, *Stalin*, pp. 529–536.

77. See Dyakov and Bushuyeva, *Red Army*, p. 247; TsGASA, f. 33987, op. 3, d. 295, l. 141–83.

78. From a progress report by Berzin to Voroshilov dated 24 December 1928 in Dyakov and Bushuyeva, *Red Army*, p. 70; TsGASA, f. 33987, op. 3, d. 98, l. 71–8.

79. German participants included Wilhelm Keitel, Walther Model, Erich von Manstein, and Walter von Brauchitsch, all of whom studied in Moscow in 1931, and Heinz Guderian, who taught and experimented at the tank facility at Kazan; Dyakov and Bushuyeva, *Red Army*, pp. 21, 25.

80. The controversy surrounding the role played by Reinhard Heydrich's SD in supplying the NKVD with incriminating evidence against Tukhachevsky and other Red Army commanders has a significantly new meaning in light of the close collaboration between the officers of the two states before 1933; see, for example, Donald

Cameron Watt, "Who Plotted against Whom? Stalin's Purge of the Soviet High Command Revisited," *The Journal of Soviet Military Studies* 3, no. 1 (March 1990): 46–65.

81. From Report of I. P. Uborevich to Voroshilov, dated 13 January 1929 in Dyakov and Bushuyeva, *Red Army*, p. 240; TsGASA, f. 33987, op. 3, d. 295, l. 141–83.

82. Ibid., pp. 32–33, State Archives, Main, f. 1703, op. 1, d. 441, l. 80.

83. Poretsky, *Our Own People*, pp. 44–45.

84. Ibid., pp. 51–52. By 1937, Locker was stationed in "the Far East." His subsequent fate remains unknown; ibid., p. 186.

85. Ibid., p. 45.

86. Anatole C. J. Bogacki, *A Polish Paradox: International and the National Interest in Polish Communist Foreign Policy 1918–1948* (Boulder, Colo.: East European Monographs, 1991), chap. 1.

87. Groehler, *Selbstmörderische*, p. 30.

88. Ibid., p. 216; TsGASA, f. 33987, op. 3, d. 98, l. 664–5.

89. Groehler, *Selbstmörderische*, p. 61.

90. Dyakov and Bushuyeva, *Red Army*, pp. 73–74; TsGASA, f. 33987, op. 3, d. 98, l. 71–8.

91. Dyakov and Bushuyeva, *Red Army*, p. 75.

92. Ibid., p. 87; TsGASA, f. 33987, op. 3, d. 329, l. 146–7, d. 295, l. 69–70 (this is the citation given by the authors).

93. Dyakov and Bushuyeva, *Red Army*, p. 86.

94. Ibid., p. 108; TsGASA, f. 33987, op. 3, d. 375, l. 22–40.

95. Ibid.

96. Dyakov and Bushuyeva, *Red Army*, p. 231; TsGASA, f. 33987, op. 3, d. 295, l. 1–2.

97. Dyakov and Bushuyeva, *Red Army*, pp. 231–232.

98. Ibid., p. 236; TsGASA l. 13–15.

99. Ibid., p. 53; TsGASA, f. 33987, op. 3, d. 98, l. 70–1.

100. See, for example, Dyakov and Bushuyeva, *Red Army*, pp. 227–229; TsGASA l. 633–5.

101. See Dyakov and Bushuyeva, *Red Army*, pp. 102, 109; TsGASA, f. 33987, op. 3, d. 70, l. 267–9, l.253–8. This of course worked both ways, and German military intelligence took full advantage of the *Reichswehr*'s presence in the USSR, as Berzin noted in a report in late December 1928. Still, most of the German efforts were of the sort usually carried out by military attachés, and Berzin regarded this as a relatively minor security threat, since it was not "directed at procuring and collecting secret documents," but was a type of "espionage" that was "less dangerous than the clandestine one, for it confines itself only to fixing what one sees and does not yield documentary data." Cited in Dyakov and Bushuyeva, *Red Army*, p. 72.

102. Dyakov and Bushuyeva, *Red Army*, pp. 18–19.

103. No source gives a precise date on when Berzin was given this assignment.

104. Hilger and Meyer, *Incompatible Allies*, pp. 194–195.

105. Dyakov and Bushuyeva, *Red Army*, pp. 68–75; TsGASA, f. 33987, op. 3, d. 329, l. 146–7, d. 295, l. 69–70.

106. Ibid., p. 71.

107. Ibid., pp. 71, 254; TsGASA, f. 33987, op. 3, d. 87, l. 125.

108. Hilger, *Incompatible Allies*, p. 71; TsGASA, f. 33987, op. 3, d. 329, l. 146–7, d. 295, l. 69–70. Berzin arranged the exchange of nine such groups of Red Army officers in 1931; see Hilger, *Incompatible Allies*, pp. 264–269; TsGASA, f. 33988, op. 3, d. 202, l. 122–24.

109. Respective examples include Hilger, *Incompatible Allies*, pp. 150–154; TsGASA, f. 33987, op. 2, d. 295, l. 4–11, a report by Baranov to the Fourth Department summarizing the operations at Lipetsk (undated, but probably 1928 or 1929), and Hilger, *Incompatible Allies*, p. 183; TsGASA, f. 33987, op. 3, d. 295, l. 79, a summary prepared by Berzin of the work done at "Tomka" up to January 1929.

110. This is implied by Hilger, *Incompatible Allies*, pp. 164–170; TsGASA, f. 33987, op. 3, d. 295, l. 58–64. See also Hilger, *Incompatible Allies*, p. 173; TsGASA, f. 33987, op. 3, d. 295, l. 80. In addition, another Soviet source notes that in the mid–1920s Berzin "completed" a "tank school" and "served in armored units of the Red Army"; see Gorchakov, "*Yan Berzin*," p. 134.

111. Whaley, *Covert German*, p. 79.

112. Dyakov and Bushuyeva, *Red Army*, p. 159; TsGASA, f. 33987, op. 3, d. 504, l. 3.

113. Ibid.

114. For example, see Dyakov and Bushuyeva, *Red Army*, pp. 160–161; TsGASA, f. 33987, op. 3, d. 504 l. 52–3.

115. Ibid. See also Dyakov and Bushuyeva, *Red Army*, pp. 177–178; TsGASA, f. 33987, op. 3, d. 504, l. 105.

116. Dyakov and Bushuyeva, *Red Army*, pp. 190–191; TsGASA, f. 33987, op. 3, d. 458, l. 101–4.

117. Dyakov and Bushuyeva, *Red Army*, pp. 190–193; TsGASA, f. 33987, op. 3, d. 504, l. 160–5.

118. Dyakov and Bushuyeva, *Red Army*, p. 193.

CHAPTER 7

Analysis and Threat Assessment

Threat assessment is the defining function of any intelligence organization, for the most clever and resourceful agents are worth little if the nation they serve suffers a surprise enemy attack. The most important task of the Fourth Department was to supply the Soviet leadership with timely, accurate, and useful information about potential military threats. Furthermore, in the Soviet case, the central role of such analysis in shaping economic and foreign policy considerably magnified its importance. The diverse threads of Red Army Intelligence operations became most directly entwined with national policy in the realm of threat assessment.

THE CONTEXT FOR ANALYSIS

RU assessments were prepared by its Third Section. The Third Section had about a dozen or so geographical divisions staffed by about fifty people. The division chiefs were often seasoned field officers; in 1926, for example, the chief of the Central European Division was Walter Krivitsky, at the time a veteran of seven years of agent operations.[1] The head of the Third Section throughout much of the 1920s and early 1930s was A. M. Nikonov, who went to the analysis branch after Yan Berzin replaced him as RU chief. The Third Section was responsible for compiling "material gathered by Intelligence agents throughout the world and [publishing] secret reports and special bulletins for about twenty ranking leaders of the Soviet Union."[2]

One of the regular publications of the Third Section was the economic intelligence journal *Voenno-ekonomicheskii biulleten* (Military-economic Bulletin). Another important serial, published in one form or another from at least 1921 on, was *Voennyi zarubezhnik* (Foreign Military [Affairs]). Like its tsarist predecessor, *Sbornik glavnogo upravleniia*, this restricted circulation journal contained articles about foreign military developments. *Voennyi zarubezhnik* seems to have been published more or less consistently throughout the period between 1921–1941.[3] The journal contained sections devoted to Soviet analyses of foreign military developments, bibliographical surveys focusing on particular problems or issues, translations from the foreign military press, and a section devoted to reporting miscellaneous news, sometimes accompanied by Soviet commentary.

All intelligence organizations, regardless of their ideological orientation, must live, work, and think in the real world. For Soviet Russia in the 1920s, that world was definitely a hostile one. Economically primitive, technologically backward, and, at first, diplomatically isolated, the Bolsheviks were forced to focus most of their energies on the simple goal of survival. The recently concluded war with Poland revealed just how vulnerable Moscow was to even a moderately sized military power.

Marxist-Leninist ideology provided the context from which the Kremlin viewed the domestic and foreign threats it believed were arrayed against it. The implacable hostility of the capitalist "ruling circles" was orchestrated by the most powerful imperialist nations, in particular Great Britain. By definition, therefore, any foreign event that harmed Moscow's interests was taken as further evidence of the counter-revolutionary conspiracy led by London. Given Soviet belief in the scientific nature of the progress of history, the explanative power of coincidence, stupidity and plain bad luck were irrelevant.

Such a simplistic view of the nature of cause and effect tended to reinforce the xenophobia common to most of the Bolshevik leadership, especially Stalin. This fear and suspicion of the outside world had deep roots in Russian history and culture, and was exacerbated by Moscow's diplomatic and cultural isolation. With little access to, and less understanding of, the real centers of political power in the rest of the world, especially the western democracies, Soviet leaders retained a view of international relations much more applicable to the world before the world war than after it. In this view, the ruling aristocracies of Europe were replaced by the no less hostile, or omnipotent, "imperialist ruling circles," and the masses remained faceless pawns subject to the manipulation of the forces of progress or reaction.

This interpretation also helped shape a central Soviet assumption: the imperialists would soon start another major war, this time with the objective of destroying the USSR. The precise form and timing of this war remained unknown, but no one in the Soviet leadership doubted its inevitability. Consequently, intelligence gathering and analysis assumed great urgency for state planning on every level, for, as Soviet military and political leaders repeatedly argued, it would require the entire human and material resources of the workers' state to defeat the coming capitalist onslaught.

One final general assumption is implied throughout the threat assessments prepared during this period. The "future" war would not come unexpectedly like a "bolt from the blue." Although not specifically elaborated in early assessments, the scenarios they described always assumed that there would be enough warning for a complete or nearly complete mobilization of first-echelon (i.e., the most combat ready) units. Moscow's uncertainty about the precise nature of this "warning" may help explain what to many western observers often seemed like irrational Soviet overreaction. However, the Soviets evidently expected an imminent armed conflict to be preceded by a period of particularly dangerous crises (for not even the events precipitating the 1927 "war scare" were sufficient to qualify). Given this assumption, the Soviet leadership believed that although the Red Army might suffer tactical or even operational surprise, the imperialists would never be able to achieve strategic surprise.

Although Red Army Intelligence, like many other such organizations before and since, certainly found it necessary to tailor its assessments to the views of its superiors, there is little evidence to suggest that during the course of the period covered by this work, intelligence officers *deliberately* reshaped their reports to fit an ideological perspective they disbelieved or viewed as inappropriate. This state of affairs changed, of course, as the last vestiges of "democratic centralism" within the Soviet leadership were replaced by the "cult of Stalin" in the mid-1930s.

EARLY THREAT ASSESSMENT

Virtually no examples of Red Army threat assessment on a strategic level from 1921 through 1925 have yet appeared in open sources. Indeed, it may be that no systematic approach to this subject was taken until 1927; as John Erickson notes, Voroshilov himself claimed that "before 1927 no comprehensive Soviet war-plan existed."[4] This was partly a reflection of the fact that the very nature of the defense of the regime was still the subject of intense debate between those who saw the world revolution as the only real guarantor of socialism's survival, and those who favored building the Soviet state into a fortress. Complicating the picture was the fact the early 1920s were characterized by a series of foreign and domestic crises, including the rebellion at Kronstadt and fighting in Bessarabia and Georgia.

Nevertheless, some important and recurring patterns in Soviet analysis show up very early. An assessment submitted to the Revolutionary Military Council in January 1920 by former Red Army Commander in Chief I. I. Vatsetis, presumably based upon information provided by S. I. Aralov, the original head of the *Registraupr*, contains what may be the first discussion of the possibility of a joint Polish-Romanian attack on Soviet Russia. Indeed, from the end of the Civil War on, Moscow saw in the West's attempt to establish a *cordon sanitaire* along its western frontier the threat of a hostile

Polish-Baltic-Finnish-Romanian bloc.[5] As we shall see, this dominated Soviet strategic planning and RU threat assessment throughout the decade.

Vatsetis predicted that a Polish-Romanian attack would likely overrun the economic and administrative centers of Soviet Russia in the west, and that therefore these should be moved to the Urals as soon as possible as a precaution. The tone of this suggestion clearly indicated great urgency, which, given the international situation at the time and the perilous state of Soviet defenses, was not wholly without justification.[6] Vatsetis's other purpose was to warn the Soviet leadership against pursuing a plan calling for the replacement of the experienced, professional Red Army with a broad-based militia. To bolster his argument, Vatsetis noted that between them the Poles and Romanians could field the equivalent of twenty divisions. The kind of militia-based army being proposed in Moscow would be wholly incapable of defeating an attack by these forces. Vatsetis called instead for an army of at least twenty divisions, composed of a first-echelon standing force of ten divisions and a second echelon of fully trained and rapidly deployable reserves formed into another ten divisions.[7]

Already present in this document are several elements typical of later Red Army threat analyses. First was the assumption that an attack on the USSR was not only inevitable, but also likely to come in the near future. Second was the idea that the counter-revolutionary coalition would be built around Poland and Romania. Indeed, the so-called P-R scenario remained a constant element of Soviet assessment before the Nazis came to power. Lastly, we see in Vatsetis's forecast a document intended to affect not just military planning, but also the socioeconomic policies of the state.

The RU seems to have first begun producing strategic threat assessments in association with comprehensive war planning. Both of these processes were eventually made possible in part because the Red Army finally created a rudimentary system of military organization and mobilization by 1924–25.[8] With immediate defense needs met, the Red Army leadership turned to the more long-term questions of doctrine and training, industrialization, and the nature of future conflicts.[9] At about the same time, the RU's involvement in revolution and insurgency gradually gave way to growing professionalism and espionage; consequently, by the mid- and late 1920s a body of useful intelligence for long-range strategic analysis started to become available.

One of the earliest of these estimates, called simply "Report on Defence Materials," was prepared under the supervision of Tukhachevsky in 1926 as background for the 1927 war plan. The decision to produce this report reflected growing unease in Moscow over the course of events abroad. A distinctly more hostile government, led by the Conservative Party, came to power in Great Britain; Pilsudski assumed power in Poland in the spring; and, despite assurances from Berlin to the contrary, the Soviets feared that the Dawes Plan might draw Weimar Germany back into the imperialist fold, greatly increasing the threat to the USSR's western frontier. At the same time, those in the CPSU who favored the strategy of building socialism in one state began to dominate policy, and resolved to embark upon a course of rapid, centrally directed industrialization. As a result, "the desire to overcome the Red Army's technical backwardness welded together the objectives of the military and the industrialists."[10]

This report focused almost exclusively on threats along the USSR's western border; although it took note of the growing menace of Japan, its main concern with respect to the Far East was the generally poor state of communications in that theater, and it called for an improvement in the infrastructure necessary to support operations there.

The analysis proceeded from the ideological premise that the major historical trends of the time, identified as the "expansion of the Soviet economy, the fragile 'stabilization of capitalism', and the growing revolutionary movement in Europe" all combined to increase the overall likelihood of an attack on the Soviet Union.[11] This attack would be launched by a coalition formed around a Polish-Romanian alliance that would include the "western neighboring states" of Latvia, Lithuania, Estonia, and Finland.[12] The Fourth Department estimated that the total wartime force of this coalition would be about 112 infantry divisions and 9 cavalry divisions (see Table 1 in appendix B). Such an immense operation would almost certainly be fully supported, at least in terms of money and material, by Great Britain and "other Great Powers" (i.e., France). This meant that the longer the war lasted, the more the relative strength of the coalition would grow. In fact, such support could conceivably enable the populations of these states to field a much larger force, one that might be the equivalent of 165 infantry and 15 cavalry divisions.[13]

The Red Army, in contrast, would have to fight almost exclusively with what it was able to mobilize before the war and during the initial period. Unable to receive support from what the assessment characterized as an "embryonic" industrial base, and burdened with an inadequate transportation infrastructure, the Red Army faced certain defeat, "unless the European revolution will come to our rescue."[14]

It was therefore absolutely necessary, the report continued, that everything possible be done to build up Soviet industry. Until then, the best the Soviets could hope for was to capitalize on their initial superiority in numbers by rapidly carrying out massive mobilization in conjunction with the precise use of rail lines to prepare a decisive blow before the enemy could complete its own mobilization. By quickly defeating one or more of the weaker states in the coalition, and capturing key territory, the Red Army might hope to disrupt British efforts to supply the coalition forces in the field. The "prime strategic task" in such a scenario would therefore be "to disorganize the supply of British weapons and equipment." Failure to achieve this objective would have "truly 'threatening'" consequences for the survival of the workers' state.[15]

The minimum force judged necessary for this strategy of "victory through mobilization" was 120 infantry and 18 cavalry divisions. But, as the report noted, as of late 1926, even though the Red Army planned to mobilize 111 infantry divisions for war, the Soviet Union was still incapable of actually supporting more than 91. This led to the conclusion that "at present, neither the USSR nor the Red Army is ready for war. . . . A successful defence of our country is possible only if we can disrupt the 'force composition' of our enemies during the initial period. . . . Only after several years of successful industrialization will our capacity for a protracted war increase."[16] This reasoning may have been an important factor in the decision to build substantial preparations for carrying out partisan warfare in the frontier and on Soviet soil.

Nevertheless, as we saw in chapter 4, in his 1927 report *Otsenka mezhdunarodnogo i voennogo polozheniia SSSR k nachalu 1927 goda* (Assessment of the International and Military Situation of the USSR at the Beginning of 1927), Berzin dismissed the likelihood of an imminent imperialist attack on the Soviet Union, although he also noted with concern the worsening situation in the Far East. Chiang's assault on the Chinese communists was gaining momentum and "Japanese imperialist policy" threatened to upset the fragile peace between Tokyo and Moscow. Japanese designs on Manchuria were also plainly evident. Berzin cautioned that "in general, in the Far East a very serious military-political situation has arisen," and advised that "maximum attention be paid to the strengthening of our political influence on the liberation forces in China."[17]

Berzin argued that Soviet diplomacy should be employed to buy time for strengthening the Red Army and Soviet industry. In the Far East, this could be accomplished by promoting discord between the United States and Japan and encouraging the failure of British-Japanese talks on a China settlement. In the West, he called for Moscow to ensure that Finland remain neutral in case of war, possibly by signing a unilateral pact with Helsinki; the Soviets should also take steps to sabotage a possible Polish–Baltic states security agreement.

The conclusion to the 1927 threat assessment was essentially the same as it had been in 1926: "In general, our international position in the West has worsened, and chances for an armed operation by our Western neighbors have increased." At the same time, he took rare notice of the practical difficulties of such an operation when he noted that "unresolved conflicts between our neighbors, and between Poland and Germany, as well as the difficulty of common action by the West European Great Powers to support our neighbors in a war against us, make military action in 1927 unlikely."[18] The importance of these conflicts was nevertheless greatly underestimated, and the Fourth Department continued to see western behavior as essentially the result of a monolithic policy formulated by the "imperialist" ruling circles and orchestrated by London. Indeed, as we shall see, this caveat wholly disappears from subsequent analyses.

THE FUTURE WAR

The single most important, and most influential, work prepared by the RU's Third Section during the interwar years was probably *The Future War*. The origins of this study lie in a directive issued by Tukhachevsky in 1926 to several Red Army departments charging them with studying "the probable characteristics of future military conflicts."[19] In actual fact, only the Fourth Department seems to have completed this task. The principal authors were Berzin, Nikonov, and Y. Zhigur, a specialist in chemical warfare.[20] Only eighty copies were prepared, and the work was completed in May 1928.[21]

The study was composed of six major parts and was divided into twelve chapters, which were in turn subdivided into numerous sections. Part I discussed the "General Situation," and focused on the ideological basis for evaluating the international situation.[22] Part II studied "Human Resources and Their Utilization," describing the demographics of the probable enemy coalition states.[23] Part III considered "Economic Factors," explored the likely requirements for arms and ammunition in the future war, and analyzed the capabilities of the various coalition states to produce these under wartime conditions.[24] "Technical Factors" were the subject of Part IV, which was split into Parts-IVa and IVb. These comprised a comprehensive discussion of the technological state of all aspects of warfare, including tank design, the use of chemical weapons by aircraft, transportation, and naval power.[25] Part V evaluated the internal "Political Factors" in the coalition states, and consisted of a heavily ideological discussion of the class and national antagonisms present in coalition states.[26] Part VI was in many ways a policy-oriented summary of the previous material; it was entitled "Operational and Organizational Problems."[27]

In establishing the Marxist-Leninist basis for evaluating the correlation of forces, the authors categorized all capitalist states as belonging to one of four groups, distinguished by the probability that they would go to war against the USSR. The first group, those dedicated to the destruction of the socialist state, was of course led by Great Britain, and in particular the Conservative Party, and also included France, Italy, Poland, Romania, Finland, and the Baltic states. The second group comprised states likely to follow the lead of the first group: Czechoslovakia, Belgium, Hungary, Bulgaria, and Yugoslavia. In the third category were states that because of "their geographical position or other reasons are not interested in war with us": the Scandinavian states, Denmark, Switzerland, Austria, Albania, Persia, Latin America, Spain, and Portugal. The last group was made up of states on friendly terms with the USSR: Turkey, Afghanistan, "revolutionary China," and Mongolia.[28]

Germany, the United States, and Japan were considered to be essentially part of the second group for the purposes of threat forecasting.[29] Japan's ambitions in the Far East obviously clashed with those of the USSR. Germany, although not expected to be among the actively belligerent powers in the future war, was fundamentally tied to the West both economically and in terms of class interests. Under the right circumstances, it would even join the British-led anti-Soviet bloc. However, since any attack on the Soviet Union would be led on the ground by Poland, Germany, depending on the course of the conflict and the positions of the Great Powers, could almost certainly be expected to remain neutral, and might even take advantage of the situation at Poland's expense. Likewise, the authors concluded that while the United States would not actively participate in any British-sponsored anti-Soviet operations, it also would not oppose them.[30]

The first group would pursue a three-pronged strategy against the USSR in the future war: active military operations in the form of an attack; economic blockade; and aggressive class-warfare (propaganda and repression). The study outlined three broad variants of an attack scenario, distinguished by the participating states and the principal axes of attack. The first variant involved an attack by the western bordering states with the material and economic support of Britain and France; this had been the standard threat scenario dominating all RU assessments since at least 1926.[31] The second variant was similar to the first, but involved the active participation of British and French military forces.[32] The third, and most apocalyptic, scenario was of an all-out global attack on the USSR. In addition to the attack by the western bordering states, the British would advance across Turkey, Persia, and Afghanistan, and the "reactionary" Chinese and Japan would attack in the Far East.[33]

The last variant, although obviously the most disastrous, was also considered the least likely. Given the study's insistence on the urgent need to prepare for the first variant, they probably regarded the last as hopeless unless a cataclysmic series of revolutions shook the capitalist states.[34] The most likely variant in the immediate future, defined as the five-year period between 1928–32, was the first.

This variant of the future war would assume one of three scenarios. The first scenario was the worst-case situation, and involved a concerted attack by Poland, Romania, Latvia, Lithuania, Estonia, and Finland. In the second, the coalition was the same, except Finland would remain neutral. The third scenario was an attack by Poland and Romania, while the Baltic states and Finland remained neutral. Although the first scenario was apparently not necessarily more likely than the others, the authors argued that it was absolutely essential and prudent to use it as the basis for military and industrial planning.[35]

A reasonable picture of wartime personnel requirements emerged from an analysis comparing known and estimated contemporary reserve strengths with those from 1914. The results indicated that the future war would put an immense strain upon the economies, and societies as a whole, of the belligerents. These stresses would occur rapidly, as well, for the first period of the war would see the highest casualty rates.

Wartime mobilization would produce the following deployments (equivalent peacetime estimates are given in Table 2 in appendix B):

Country	Peacetime	After 1 month	6 months	1 year
Poland	30	60	70	70
Romania	24	32	39	46
Latvia	4	6	5	—*
Estonia	3	4	5	—*
Finland	4	7	8	9**
(no comparable data for Lithuania was provided)				
TOTAL:	65	109	127	125

*The assumption was that these countries' units would be effectively destroyed within a year of combat.
**Finland was estimated to be capable of eventually fielding thirteen infantry divisions.[36]

The study considered the maximum force levels, however, to be achievable only if the coalition states were willing to put a dangerous level of stress upon their economies and societies; the ability of these states to maintain these force levels in the field over time was highly questionable.

The Fourth Department's predictions of probable casualties were based on extensive statistical analysis of the world war. Factors incorporated into this analysis included the impact of automatic weapons and chemical warfare, the intensification of casualties during the maneuver periods at the beginning and end of the war, and disease. Casualties were predicted to run as high as 60 to 70 percent in combat units during the first (maneuver) period of the future war; the engaged armies could experience overall losses as high as 35 to 40 percent during this stage. Poland was expected to have relatively higher casualties, as was the USSR, because they would be the principle combatants (see Table 3 in appendix B).

The study concluded that manpower resources available to the belligerents would be sufficient for them to maintain more or less full-strength armies in the field for between two and a half and three years, assuming they drew upon males between eighteen and forty-five years of age for military service. If some or all of the belligerents expanded the pool of eligible males to include seventeen through fifty year olds, the coalition could maintain its strength for an additional one to three years.[37]

The Fourth Department analysis of the role of tanks in future combat is illustrative of the study as a whole. The authors began with a brief historical analysis of the performance of tanks in the world war. They noted that these early vehicles characteristically suffered a very high proportion of losses, although this declined over time, from 63 percent for the British attack in September 1916 to 30 percent for a later British attack on 8 August 1918.[38] More importantly, their impact on the battlefield increased markedly, to the point that in August 1918 a 600-tank British attack led to the destruction of seven German divisions and the loss of 400 guns.[39]

The authors next considered the views of contemporary foreign military theorists, including British writer J.F.C. Fuller. They agreed with his assertion that the greatest problem facing modern armies was the threat of positional warfare, and that motorized military movement offered the potential solution.[40] However, they took issue with his prediction that future conflicts would be decided by relatively small, corps-size combined-arms units.[41] Since the primary enemy in the future war would be Poland, and since Poland represented the biggest threat in terms of armor, the study analyzed Polish views on the use of tanks. It noted that the Poles considered the main purpose of tanks to be as support for infantry. The Poles believed that surprise was essential for the success of tank assaults, and so intended to launch these with no artillery preparation. On the defense, tanks would serve as a key element in any counterattack. For exploiting a breach in enemy defenses, however, the Poles favored armored cars, as they believed their French-supplied Renault tanks were too slow for effective pursuit.[42]

All of the western bordering states in fact used Renault tanks, although their peacetime strengths were not especially impressive. Poland had 250, and Romania 100; Latvia had a total of 25 Renaults and British Mk. Vs, as did Estonia; Lithuania possessed a total of 20 Renaults and Mk. Vs; and Finland had 35 Renaults. These numbers however were expected to increase dramatically in wartime with French and British reinforcements.

The study noted that modern armored vehicles had developed into three distinct types. Light tanks and armored cars were designed for rapid, independent operations, like exploitation of a breakthrough or reconnaissance. Infantry tanks, on the other hand, were intended to support infantry assaults on prepared and fortified positions, and were consequently heavily armored, well armed, and slow with a correspondingly smaller radius of action. The Fourth Department analysts noted that many western writers were "skeptical" about the idea of the infantry tank; they argued that its slowness and restricted mobility would make it an "excellent target" for enemy artillery, a concern which to some extent the Soviet analysts shared.[43] However, although the authors agreed that tanks in general were most vulnerable to artillery, as of 1928 "sufficiently effective" antitank weapons had yet to be devised. In the absence of such weapons tanks would remain the most decisive means of attack.[44]

The discussion of the role of tanks in the future war closed with recommendations for Red Army tank requirements. They suggested two types of tanks: The first was a "heavy maneuver tank," designed to support infantry operations, operate jointly with cavalry and motorized units, and form independent detachments for pursuit. The second type was a "light maneuver tank" for operations in support of cavalry and motorized units, reconnaissance, and participation in joint operations with heavy tank units.[45]

The study argued that the future war would have four major impacts on general political conditions. First, it would be a total war, and would involve unprecedented mobilization of the entire populations of the belligerents; consequently, millions of workers would serve in the army. Second, the demands of conscription and economic restructuring would cause immense economic dislocation that would, in turn, place huge strains on the social fabric of the warring states. Third, the success of the war efforts of the belligerents would depend on the total mobilization of the workers in industry and transportation. And fourth, new technology "permitted the realization of active operations not only on the combat front, but in the deep rear of the enemy"; one specific example was aerial chemical attack. The effect of such blows would be to severely shake the social fabric of the enemy state, setting the stage for a "colossal morale shock in the [civilian] population."[46]

The study went on to evaluate the specific political situations in the western border states. Poland, for example, was likely to suffer from enormous social stress during the war, primarily due to the hostility of its working class and national minorities.[47] The bourgeoisie, although presently opposed to Pilsudski's "warlike" policies due to their desire for more developed economic ties with the USSR, would inevitably support the regime wholeheartedly in the future war, and energetically set about repressing any signs of internal opposition by the working class. The Red Army authors believed that the "oppressed majority of workers," together with the poor peasants and the national minorities, were universally opposed to Pilsudski. The economic position of Poland was unsteady at best, and was expected to deteriorate over time, despite attempts by western states like Great Britain and the United States to encourage growth through large-scale loans.[48] Unrest and radicalization could be expected to increase as the war dragged on, and the authors predicted that "the state organs of Poland will not display sufficient internal force and firmness, in particular if the war assumes a protracted character."[49] The greatest possibility for a successful workers' revolution in the future war, concluded the analysts, existed in Finland. The working class there was judged to be a "significant force, imbued with a revolutionary mood and friendliness for the USSR."[50]

The study next considered the moral-political condition of the armies of the western bordering states, with the exception of Lithuania. In Poland, the army suffered from severe class and national antagonisms, and it was only the harsh discipline of the aristocratic officers that ensured their obedience. These inherent antagonisms were not expected to be of much significance in the first period of the future war. But over time, casualties and mobilization would greatly increase the percentage of national minorities in the army. In this situation, national antagonisms would "accelerate and possibly be expressed in a more open form."[51]

The moral-political state of the Romanian army was significantly more brittle. This weakness was, however, not the result of class or national antagonisms. Although the "repressed" peasants made up the vast majority of the enlisted ranks, they were politically unsophisticated and thoroughly "cowed" by their officers. Instead, the greatest threat to the stability of the Romanian army was its own poor combat capabilities. Red Army analysts expected Romanian unit cohesion to decline precipitously under the stress of combat and high casualties. Although this would put great stress on Romanian society, as in Poland, this did not mean that revolution was an automatic result.[52]

The troops of the Latvian and Estonian armies, in contrast, were considered to be essentially "monolithic" in their support for their respective regimes. The Estonians could be expected to fight "stubbornly" against the Red Army. Likewise, the Latvian army would serve as a "model for the defense of the bourgeoisie in Latvia." Only heavy and sustained battlefield casualties could create a situation in which "we could realistically say there are contradictions in the social order" in either of these countries.[53]

The prospects for the deterioration of the Finnish army were much more promising. Although the Finns would fight resolutely in the first period of the future war, the conflict would inevitably aggravate class and national hostilities. A protracted war would put immense strains on the army and the social fabric. As in Poland and Romania, losses would inevitably lead to a higher proportion of the oppressed groups, in this case the workers, in the army. As a consequence the moral-political situation in the Finnish army would become increasingly unstable.[54]

On the whole, moral-political conditions in the probable coalition states were expected to deteriorate over time under the impact of growing internal class and nationality antagonisms. Therefore, these conditions would work to the advantage of the Soviet Union. Significant disruption of the social structure of the belligerent states would not likely occur in the first period of war, however, nor would these antagonisms necessarily lead to revolution by themselves.[55] Therefore, victories by the Red Army were essential.

The authors repeatedly emphasized the crucial connection between battlefield success and the growth of revolutionary momentum in the anti-Soviet coalition. "Each military success of the Red Army will promote still greater exacerbation of the internal-political situation and undermine the moral stability of the [enemy] army and population." Indeed, this process was all but inevitable, for "only catastrophic defeat of the Red Army could possibly hinder . . . the process of disintegration."[56]

The Red Army analysts reasoned that "millions" of workers would become involved in the future war through the efforts of Britain and other imperialist great powers to support the anti-Soviet coalition. Under these conditions, the combination of "serious" military victories and intense political work among the armies and proletariate of the enemy would likely transform the war into "a civil war, into revolution."[57] Given this development, the war would probably "be decided" in one or two years at most, for by that time the enemy states would begin to collapse from internal stress. This would happen, the study added, long before the military and economic resources of the belligerents were exhausted.

In order for this result to be achieved, however, the authors cautioned that the Soviet Union must also be prepared to endure the same sorts of stresses. They emphasized that only by following the "correct" approach to building the economy and managing internal politics would the Soviet masses "undoubtedly display sufficient endurance and prove willing to suffer the heavy casualties" necessary to achieve complete victory.[58]

Part VI in many ways represented the heart of the Red Army's analysis of the military context of *The Future War*. It consisted of an examination of the operational and organizational features that were expected to characterize strategy and military art in the future war, and concluded with far-reaching recommendations for Soviet military planning. The work of important Soviet theoreticians, like Triandafillov, figured prominently in this analysis, and in the arguments formed by the authors we can recognize the shape of what would—by the mid-1930s—be known as "Deep Operations" theory.

The application of mechanization to modern warfare made possible rapid advances and the exploitation of breakthroughs in the first, or maneuver, period of the future war. However, the lines of communications of both sides would be degraded by poor roads and insufficient transport capacity; this in turn would severely restrict the depth and duration of offensive operations. The use of new "methods of destruction of railways," together with the problem of outpacing supporting forces, would further exacerbate this problem, slowing the tempo of advance, eventually bringing it to a complete halt.[59]

Based on the experience of the world war and the Civil War, the study estimated the average depth of individual modern operations to be 400–500 kilometers. After such an advance, the attacking units would be exhausted, dispersed, and out of supply. At this point, the enemy would certainly counterattack before the advancing forces had an opportunity to regroup or prepare for the next operation. Therefore it was crucial that attacking elements retain sufficient strength to receive and crush the inevitable counterattack.[60] Otherwise, confusion in the rear areas of the advancing armies, an overburdened supply chain, and the consequent collapse of offensive momentum would set the stage for protracted positional warfare.[61] Such a conflict would inevitably cause the internal collapse of the belligerent states, but it would also put dangerous stress on the USSR, and perhaps lead the great imperialist powers to directly commit their military forces.

The study concluded that in the first period of the future war it might be possible to defeat Latvia, Lithuania, and Estonia with a concentrated and well-timed blow, after which they could be rapidly conquered and "sovietized." However, the larger states, especially Poland, could not be defeated by one strike, but only through a series of consecutive operations that would not only inflict heavy losses in the field but also serve to exhaust their material resources, eventually precipitating the "social-political" shock that would herald the collapse of their regimes.[62]

CONCLUSIONS ABOUT *THE FUTURE WAR*

The authors of the study summarized their main arguments in the last ten pages. Their chief objective here appears to have been to establish the rationale for massive investment in military-industrial growth. The study as a whole served as the "basis for the views of the military leadership concerning the economic development required for the new kind of warfare that was expected."[63] The focus, therefore, was on "questions about the military organization of the USSR," for the latter conditioned the former.[64]

Once again, the RU analysts emphasized that the future war would assume the character of a "great war," much more similar to the world war of 1914–18 than the Civil War. It would begin with a period of maneuver, during which a decisive outcome might be achieved against one or more of the smaller coalition states. It would probably grow into a protracted war, however, characterized by intervals of positional warfare that, if neither side possessed the combat means to break through the other's defenses, would inevitably turn into stalemate.

In any event, the war would almost certainly be decided by the course of internal political-economic events in the belligerent states. Military action could decisively affect those events, but battle alone would not win the war (except under very improbable circumstances and only during the first period of the war). In the moral-political sense, then, the future war would be a war of attrition. It was crucial therefore that the USSR develop the capability to endure such a conflict. If it could do so, then victory should be inevitable, for the western bordering states would certainly overextend themselves by deploying larger forces than their material bases could support.[65]

The Soviet Union must take care not to make the same mistake. It needed to set in motion *in peacetime* the ability to produce military supplies and equipment in quantities greater than those consumed during the world war. Steps had to be taken to prepare the civilian population for war, both in terms of training reserves and civil defense. New weapons and military technologies needed to be researched or "acquired," tested, manufactured, and liberally distributed to combat units. Officers and enlisted men had to be trained and prepared to fight in the conditions created by the impact of these technologies on the battlefield. It was necessary to prepare transportation networks, including both rail and surfaced road networks, to support rapid movement of supplies for continuous operations. All of these tasks were urgent, for the future war would likely come in a matter of a few years.

Overall, the study's authors observed that with respect to technology, Soviet scientific research was very weak, especially in the field of "military work." It was therefore important to strengthen efforts at obtaining such technology from other powers, in order to make "broad utilization of foreign achievements."[66] This of course translated into the intensification of industrial and technological espionage after 1928, as has been described in earlier chapters.

Red Army field commanders also had to understand the nature of the war that was coming. The authors noted that in the past, far too much emphasis had been placed upon the glorious exploits of the Civil War. With the exception of the maneuver phase in its first period, however, the future war would be much more like the world war. This fact had to be indoctrinated into the Red Army command at all levels. Such an effort would be facilitated by dedicated historical study of the world war and the Civil War based on careful and thorough research of archival material, carried out under the guidance of the RKKA staff.[67]

The Future War considered that the most difficult operational problem confronting field commanders was the determination of the correct depth and tempo of contemporary offensive operations. This calculation reflected a complex combination of factors, chief among which was the coordination of the rate of advance, the supply capacity of the rear and the forward movement of railheads, and the radius of action of vehicles and units. The depth and tempo of these operations also had to be configured to withstand an enemy counterattack at their most vulnerable stage, when the attacking forces had reached the limits of their current advance and were in the process of regrouping and consolidating their gains. Mastery of this problem was judged to be "the summit of contemporary operational art."[68]

The ability to resolve this problem was especially crucial, given the fact that contemporary combat means all but precluded the possibility of "operations of annihilation." Consecutive operations were necessary to sustain an offensive. These had to be carried out by "rapid mobile blows," delivered by combined arms groups composed of cavalry, armored cars, motorized infantry units with organic motorized artillery, and heavy tank units, all supported by heavy weapons.[69]

On the defensive, the Red Army should in retreat take measures to destroy lines of communication (especially rail lines) in order to hamper the enemy's ability to sustain its own offensive momentum, even though this would prove to be a problem once the Red Army went back on the attack. The study insisted on the need for specialized and well-equipped railroad engineer units that could carry out both rapid demolition and speedy reconstruction of rail lines.[70]

The analysts concluded the study by once again emphasizing the grave danger positional warfare held for the Soviet state. To prevent this situation, it was

urgently necessary to strengthen the means of attack of the Red Army and to secure . . . in time of war sufficient amounts of weapons, firepower, ammunition and other items for conducting uninterrupted active offensive operations. Without such a guarantee we will continue to face the threat that the future war will assume a positional character. Avoiding this to a significant degree depends on the direction of the construction of our military strength and the development of our industry and its preparations for war.[71]

The Future War represented the most exhaustive study prepared by the Fourth Department during its first fifteen years. It had an immense impact on the course of Soviet industrial policy, and for the next several years served as the primary source for the Red Army's approach to questions of military production.[72] Its discussion of strategic and operational problems represented the cutting edge in Soviet military thought. Although it underwent periodic revision, and its scenarios were somewhat modified, especially after the Japanese occupation of Manchuria in 1931, *The Future War* remained the fundamental basis for Red Army war planning and threat assessment until Adolf Hitler became chancellor of Germany in January 1933.

POST–*FUTURE WAR* THREAT ASSESSMENTS

Describing and evaluating Fourth Department threat analysis between 1928–32 is complicated by the fact that, as the planning and execution of the first Five Year Plan proceeded, an increasingly diverse group of Soviet departments developed a vested interest in the subject of threat forecasting, in particular *Gosplan*. Indeed, war forecasting seems to have become something of a cottage industry during this period.

Threat assessments also played a central role in the infighting within the Red Army high command between Tukhachevsky, who initiated *The Future War*, supported the idea of offensive warfare, and favored intensive peacetime military preparations, and Voroshilov, who supported a program of more modest growth in military-industrial strength, and suspected Tukhachevsky of being an alarmist at best and a "militarist" at worst.[73] Both sides may have used Fourth Department data to support their positions; however, given the fact that Tukhachevsky's most important work on this question, *The Future War*, was actually written by senior RU officers, it is reasonable to suppose that the opinions and conclusions therein represented the official views of the Red Army Intelligence Directorate. The sources for Tukhachevsky's subsequent threat analyses, however, are problematical, for, as noted earlier, by the spring of 1927 the RU was no longer directly subordinate to the Red Army

Staff but to Voroshilov's Commissariat for Defense.[74] For the present purposes, therefore, we shall only consider those assessments presumably authored by the Fourth Department.

The year 1928 was especially crucial for threat analysis and war planning, probably because of the looming Five Year Plan scheduled to begin in 1929. Counting *The Future War*, no fewer than three major threat assessment reports were completed between May and November of that year. Voroshilov ordered a new threat analysis in the spring of 1928, some four months before the completion of *The Future War*, as part of the Red Army proposal for mobilization requirements at the end of the Five Year Plan.[75] Not surprisingly this assessment essentially repeated the conclusions of *The Future War*.

On balance, the report concluded, the correlation of forces in the west was "unfavorable and deteriorating over time." The probable enemies were, once again, the western neighboring states, in particular Poland and Romania. The numbers cited were predictably very close to those cited in *The Future War* (see Table 4 in appendix B). This assessment focused on the policies of Pilsudski, which the *Razvedupr* believed posed a "concrete" and immediate threat of a Polish-Romanian attack, supported by France. This specific threat dominated military planning during the first Five Year Plan, and affected "decisions concerning the transport network and the infrastructure in the western Ukraine, Belorussia and Crimea."[76]

Another Fourth Department assessment prepared by Berzin appeared in November 1928; this may also have incorporated some of the analysis from the spring report. This was entitled *Military Preparations against the USSR and the Main Question of Strengthening Defence*. Berzin predictably singled out the Polish-Romanian threat as the most serious immediate danger. He also once more noted with concern the increasing menace posed by Japan. Berzin referred to the "well-known plans and attempts of the military clique in Japan for enormous conquests on the Asian continent (China, Manchuria and the Soviet Far East)." However, he also concluded that Japan was unlikely to threaten Moscow's interests militarily in the absence of any serious "internal trouble" in the Soviet Union.[77] This assessment also discussed in vague terms a possible British threat to the oil fields at Baku via an attack from India and Afghanistan.[78] That same month, Unshlikht warned the plenary session of the Central Committee that not only had "French generals . . . been travelling in Poland, Romania and the Baltic states, apparently to prepare a coordinated attack on the Soviet Union," but the British were engaged in actively "supporting Ukrainian separatism or a Ukrainian union with Poland."[79] Nevertheless, none of these reports concluded that war was imminent.

The evidence suggests that by 1928 the RU was producing at least one major threat summary per year in association with annual war planning, although specific examples of Red Army Intelligence threat assessment for the years 1929–1932 have yet to surface. Still, Red Army war plans, notably those prepared by A. A. Svechin and B. M. Shaposhnikov, were no doubt based on those assessments, and reflected the assumptions and conclusions formulated in 1926 and described in detail in *The Future War*.[80] The only major change in the 1932 assessment was increased attention to the threat of Japanese expansion into Siberia and the Soviet Far East.

In 1930, for example, in a letter to Molotov, Stalin noted that the threat from a Polish-Romanian-Baltic coalition was imminent and would materialize in an attack, probably aimed at Leningrad and Ukraine, as soon as the Poles "have secured" the alliance. Reflecting threat assessments and war plans that must have been very similar to those described above, Stalin asserted that to be sure of defeating such an attack the Red Army needed to field 150 to 160 infantry divisions, or "40 to 50 divisions more than are provided for under our *current guidelines* [emphasis in original]." It is also interesting to note that Soviet intelligence agencies had apparently not been able to ascertain whether or not this alliance had already been formed.[81]

CONCLUSION: THE ACCURACY OF RU THREAT ASSESSMENT

Intelligence agencies are inevitably subject to a variety of forces beyond their immediate control that shape their observation and interpretation of the world in which they work. We would naturally expect these to be even greater in a society like the Soviet Union, in which totalitarian rule and rigid ideology imposed their own weight upon analysis. Still, even by 1932 Stalin had not yet managed to fully consolidate his power on a personal level, and there was still room among the leadership of the Communist Party and Red Army, albeit ever shrinking, for disagreement in the spirit of "democratic centralism." The ongoing and occasionally vitriolic doctrinal disputes in the army's high command provide ample evidence for this. Marxist-Leninist ideology nonetheless clearly played an important role in shaping Fourth Department threat assessment.

In order to evaluate the overall quality of the RU's analytical efforts, it is important to bear in mind that intelligence analysis occurs on qualitatively different levels. In the West, these have long been distinguished by the two fundamental questions intelligence analysis seeks to address: what is the enemy *capable* of, and what is it *likely* to do? In intelligence jargon, these are respectively known as "capabilities" and "intentions" assessment.[82]

Determining capabilities is intrinsically a much more objective process than is discerning intentions. It ranges from technical descriptions of weapons performance to "bean counting," that is, calculating the number and types of military units and equipment possessed by a foreign power—for example, the number of tanks in a particular unit or deployed at a particular place. This is objectively quantifiable information, and can be more or less precisely measured, depending on the intelligence assets available.

At this level, Fourth Department analysis seems to have been fairly reliable, although given the havoc visited upon the archival records of many of the states in Eastern Europe over the last five decades we may never be able to fully evaluate the accuracy of Soviet capabilities assessment in the 1920s and 1930s.[83] Nevertheless, some measure of the general "ballpark" accuracy is possible by looking at comparable figures from World War II, although this approach has very little validity beyond raw manpower estimates, for numbers and types of weapons were dependent over time more on economic, political, and technological factors than on population demographics.

In September 1939 the Poles had 280,000 men organized into thirty infantry divisions and eleven cavalry brigades, with about 3 million trained reservists.[84] Although demographic conditions had changed considerably by then, figures on the Romanian army from 1942 are also reasonably close to RU estimates; by the summer of that year the Romanians had about 350,000 men deployed in thirty-three divisions.[85] Finland had ten highly trained but poorly equipped divisions at the start of the "Winter War" in November 1939.[86] These numbers, especially in terms of combat divisions, are very roughly equivalent to those in Tables 2 and 3 in appendix B, particularly when we take into account population growth and geopolitical changes. The Baltic states, of course, were occupied in June 1940 as a result of one of the secret protocols of the Nazi-Soviet Non-Aggression Pact.

The more hypothetical the capability assessed, however, the more subjective the analysis. For example, estimating the number of divisions a foreign power may currently deploy is relatively simple. But determining the number that might be mobilized in the event of war is much more complicated, even with access to the enemy's mobilization plans, because the theoretical nature of the estimate forces analysts to make a number of unverifiable assumptions. Even more difficult is the attempt to predict the number of divisions an enemy power might be able to mobilize over the course of several months or years, for this relies on a complex judgment of the enemy's demographic, social, political, and economic situation under hypothetical circumstances. This is why intelligence organizations usually follow the rule of thumb in threat assessment of assuming the worst case scenario. The Red Army Intelligence Directorate was no exception.[87]

Ideology clearly had a significant impact on RU capabilities analysis. As we have seen, for example, it considered that the capacity of the western bordering states to raise and support troops in the field to be fundamentally dependent on their class compositions. Poland was expected to field so large an army that, given its class and ethnic "antagonisms," the strain would disrupt its economic and social equilibrium, and topple Pilsudski's regime into chaos and revolution. This is not to argue that such predictions were necessarily wrong; indeed, their very hypothetical nature renders such a criticism moot. The point is that the combination of serious military defeat and high casualties would tend to undermine the stability of any state, regardless of its "class or national antagonisms."

The level of analysis that most seriously suffered from ideological assumptions, however, was intentions assessment. In the case of the RU's threat assessments prior to 1933, one of the most crucial mistakes it repeatedly made was to underestimate the strategic preoccupation of virtually every European state, especially France, with Germany. For instance, the French consistently sought to manipulate the "Little Entente," the alliance between Yugoslavia, Czechoslovakia, and Romania directed at Hungary, into an instrument for curbing German resurgence. France's relationship with Poland was also essentially based on both of those powers' fear and mistrust of Berlin.

The British likewise focused on the relationship between France and Germany on the Continent, and as the decade progressed came to lead the call for moderation of the Versailles restrictions on the latter in order to decrease the prospects for confrontation between Paris and Berlin (and to lure Germany away from Moscow's embrace). France's foreign policy therefore became increasingly dependent on Britain. As a result, to a great extent the actions of the rest of the European states entwined with France and came to rest upon London. Moscow was in a sense correct to see a British lion lurking in the background of European diplomacy; what it missed altogether, however, was that this lion, although not cowardly, was pacifistic and very, very cautious.[88]

The Soviet Union, by contrast, was regarded by most European observers as being, for the immediate future anyway, militarily incapable of offensive action anywhere but perhaps on its southern borders.[89] To the extent that the USSR represented a threat, it was either only in the context of a hostile Germany or as a source of subversion.

More to the point, Soviet analysis ignored the unparalleled postwar obsession of Western Europeans (and Americans, for that matter) with pacifism. It is relevant to note that perhaps the single most popular act of many governments in the 1920s was to sign the Kellogg-Briand Pact, which ostensibly outlawed war as a legitimate instrument of national policy.[90] The pacifism that pervaded postwar France, notwithstanding support for occupation of the Rhineland (which ended five years earlier than planned), ultimately led the French high command to conclude by the late 1920s that the only military policy the public would support was one of strict strategic defense based on a line of fixed fortifications along France's eastern frontier.[91] It is absurd to imagine that these same generals would participate in, let alone encourage, an attack on the Soviet Union. It is almost as impossible to suppose that Paris would support an independent Polish attack, either.

In the case of Poland, the Soviet perception of Pilsudski as "an implacable enemy of Russia" colored both their response to his coup of May 1926 and their views of Poland as a military threat.[92] Indeed Pilsudski, probably more than any other western leader, viewed the Soviets as the most dangerous enemy. He promoted the strategic maxim of "Eyes East" in the Polish high command. And Polish war planning in the 1920s (and for much of the 1930s, as well) was built on the assumption of war with the USSR.[93] The key to this strategy, however, and the central fact overlooked by the Fourth Department's assessments, was that Warsaw's strategic position depended on France's relationship with Germany. Polish leaders understood that they could not survive a two-front war without an immediate French attack against Germany; similarly, Warsaw understood that Germany would not likely pass up the opportunity to take advantage of a Polish-Soviet conflict if free of the threat of French intervention. As the decade progressed, and Franco-German rapprochement proceeded apace, Pilsudski faced the increasing threat of war on two fronts. The Poles also had grave and growing reservations about the reliability of their partners in Paris and Bucharest.[94] Indeed, Polish concerns about their allies, and Germany, even led them to seek an independent agreement with Moscow, and after tough negotiations a Polish-Soviet non-aggression pact was signed on 25 July 1932.[95]

Even more subtle and complex factors were at work to make an attack by the western powers extremely unlikely. Another error pervading Red Army threat assessment was a Marxist-Leninist model of capitalist behavior emphasizing the almost absolute power of the "ruling imperialistic circles." As a result, the Fourth Department almost completely neglected the complicated and central roles that the press, public opinion, bureaucratic infighting, and political partisanship all played in shaping the policies of the democracies. Berzin's observation in the 1926 report that these factors served to lessen the chances for a combined attack on the USSR in the near future still reflected a vast underestimation of their impact, and such caveats seem to thereafter disappear altogether from RU analysis.

In Great Britain, for example, strategic policy had as its primary goal the preservation (but not expansion) of the empire. Maintaining authority and control in the Dominions and India took up much of the time and energy of the British government. At home, political, economic, and social divisions also served to make decisive action in the realm of foreign affairs most difficult. A government taking such action was likely to be voted out in the next election. Further exacerbating this problem was intense bureaucratic infighting among the Treasury and the services, each of which offered competing strategies for preserving Britain's greatness.[96] Underlying all of this was a public mood that was second to none in its revulsion to the bloodletting of the world war and its advocacy of pacifism and disarmament.

Given that the likelihood of an attack by the imperialist powers was much more remote than Red Army Intelligence ever supposed, was their assessment of the probable enemy coalition nevertheless correct? This question is more problematical. From the perspective of Moscow Center, there was reason to believe that such a coalition was being prepared, if in fact it was not already a reality. Romania and Poland had a defensive alliance, and Soviet suspicions were aggravated by Poland's repeated insistence that any security agreements between Moscow and Warsaw include the Baltic states and Romania.[97] There is no evidence, however, that anything like military cooperation, let alone coordination, took place between Poland, Estonia, and Latvia.

In fact, in the early 1920s the Poles did invest much energy in trying to form a defensive "Baltic bloc" that would be under the guidance of Warsaw. This project never bore much fruit, however. Finland identified its interests with Scandinavia; Lithuania and Poland had tense relations with each other; and Latvia and Estonia saw an alliance with Poland as less desirable with the absence of Lithuania. Furthermore, these small states also had to "be on guard not to arouse too much displeasure in Moscow." As a result, the best Warsaw could achieve was a "loose agreement" signed on March 1922 in which Poland, Finland, Estonia, and Latvia agreed "not to enter into any coalitions directed against each other." Subsequent conferences affirmed that the signatories had "common interests and concerns," and Estonia and Latvia signed a mutual defensive treaty in November 1923. This was the full extent of the "Baltic coalition."[98]

The Soviets seem to have been aware that such a bloc had not yet in fact been created. As late as 1927 Berzin still hoped that Soviet diplomatic efforts could scuttle any sort of Polish-Baltic security arrangements. A few months earlier, in late September 1926, the USSR and Lithuania signed a treaty that "had an anti-Polish edge to it."[99] Even by 1930, as the letter from Stalin to Molotov described earlier indicates, Moscow remained uncertain if a "bloc" had been formed.

Poland's actual allies also proved troublesome. The Warsaw-Bucharest relationship was fraught with complications, not the least of which was the Poles' low opinion of the Romanians.[100] Furthermore, Romania's ongoing dispute with Hungary over Transylvania dominated Romanian foreign policy, preventing French efforts to build a system of collective security to contain Germany.

The relationship between the French and Polish armies formed during the Soviet-Polish War was essentially institutionalized in the wake of the formal alliance established in 1921, and included close cooperation between the military intelligence agencies of Warsaw and Paris. One of the most significant manifestations of this occurred in 1931 when senior French military intelligence officer Gen. Gustave Bertrand provided the Poles with documents that finally enabled them, after years of work, to crack an early version of the German Enigma encryption device by 1933.[101] Nevertheless, the mood and polices of Paris described above precluded the possibility of its participation in (and probably support for) any offensive war.

It is unreasonable to expect that Red Army Intelligence should have been aware of every nuance of these threads of intrigue, suspicion, and acrimony. After all, much of this evidence was top secret and remained unknown for years, even to the parties concerned. Still, the inescapable conclusion remains that Fourth Department threat assessment, unable to transcend ideology, the cultural and diplomatic insularity of the CPSU leadership, or ingrained Bolshevik paranoia, seems to have failed to perceive, let alone understand, any of the forces and circumstances that combined to make any attack on the USSR in the 1920s by the "capitalist powers" virtually impossible. In fact, the RU always judged that the "objective conditions" favoring an imperialist attack were increasing; first, because of the relative weakening of the USSR's overall geopolitical situation, and then, by 1931, because of its growing strength.[102]

Regardless of its objective validity, the fundamental views expressed in Red Army Intelligence threat analysis were almost universally shared by the Soviet leadership, and consequently served the crucial institutional objective of providing a comprehensive and consistent context for strategic planning, and helped define Soviet production and force structure goals. And its sophisticated military-technical and operational analyses contributed to the development in the mid-1930s of the Soviet operational art ("Deep Battle") and the doctrine of Deep Operations.

In an ironic and yet wholly characteristic way, then, the threat assessments prepared by Red Army Intelligence perfectly reflected its unique duality as both an instrument for promoting the revolution and a professional intelligence organization.

NOTES

1. The Third Section also employed noncommunist intelligence officers; see Krivitsky, *I Was Stalin's Agent*, pp. 159–160.

2. Ibid., p. 159.

3. Since 1972, this journal has been called *Zarubezhnoe voennoe obozrenie* (Foreign Military Review). I am grateful to the Foreign Military Studies Office at Ft. Leavenworth, and in particular Dr. Tim Sands, for access to a fairly complete run of this journal on microforms.

3. Erickson, *Soviet High Command*, p. 288.

4. Jan Karski, *The Great Powers and Poland, 1919–1945: From Versailles to Yalta* (Lanham, Md.: University Press of America, 1985), p. 123.

6. See Klyatskin, *Na zashchite*, pp. 428–429; see also John Erickson, "Threat Identification and Strategic Appraisal by the Soviet Union, 1930–1941," in May, *Knowing One's Enemies*, p. 380.

7. Klyatskin, *Na zaschite*, p. 429. By the mid–1920s, a variation on Vatsetis's program was eventually adopted; see David M. Glantz, "Soviet Mobilization in Peace and War, 1924–42: A Survey," *The Journal of Soviet Military Studies* 5, no. 1 (September 1992): 327–330.

8. Ibid., pp. 327–329.

9. There are several excellent studies of the intellectual ferment in the Red Army in the 1920s. Some of the most useful include Samuelson, *Soviet Defence*, pp. 58–79; Erickson, *Soviet High Command*, pp. 164–213; Rapoport and Alexeev, *High Treason*,

pp. 91–146; Kipp, *Mass, Mobility, passim*; and James J. Schneider, *The Structure of Strategic Revolution: Total War and the Roots of the Soviet Warfare State* (Novato, Calif.: Presidio Press, 1994), chaps. 5 and 6.

10. Samuelson, *Soviet Defence*, p. 39.

11. Ibid., p. 40.

12. Ibid., p. 44.

13. Ibid.

14. Ibid., p. 41.

15. Ibid., p. 43.

16. Ibid., pp. 45–46.

17. Ibid., p. 55.

18. Ibid.

19. Ibid., p. 46. Given the ideological framework of this document, and the absolute certainty with which all concerned expected an assault at some point by the forces of capitalist imperialism, I am persuaded by Samuelson's argument in *Soviet Defence*, p. 47 n. 52, to use the definitive translation *The Future War* in preference to the more generalized rendering, *Future War*, which implies a level of speculative abstraction more relevant to the work of western theorists like Basil Liddell-Hart, J.F.C. Fuller, W. Sikorski, William Mitchell, G. Douhet, and H. G. Wells.

20. Although these authors worked under the overall guidance of Tukhachevsky, a letter sent to him by Nikonov when the study was finished in the summer of 1928 clearly implies that Tukhachevsky, by that time chief of the Leningrad Military District, had not yet read it; ibid., p. 46 n. 51.

21. Ibid. For more on the impact of this study, and other intelligence estimates, on overall Soviet military and industrial planning and policy, see Samuelson's work, which has as its central theme this very problem.

22. M. N. Tukhachevsky et al., *Budushchaia Voina* (Moscow: Third Section of IV [Intelligence] Directorate of RKKA Staff, 1928), TsGASA, F. 33988, Op. 2, D. 682, pp. 1–53.

23. Ibid., D. 683, pp. 54–93.

24. Ibid., D. 654, pp. 94–229.

25. Part IV-a: Ibid., D. 685, pp. 230–275; Part IV-b: ibid., D. 686, pp. 277–574.

26. Ibid., D. 687, pp. 575–637.

27. Ibid., D. 688, pp. 638–735.

28. Ibid., D. 682, pp. 12–13.

29. Ibid.

30. Ibid., p. 14.

31. Ibid., pp. 24–26.

32. Ibid., pp. 26–28.

33. Ibid., pp. 28–29.

34. Ibid., p. 29.

35. Ibid., p. 43.

36. Ibid., p. 69. Similar data in this table is included for France, Germany, and the United States; Great Britain is conspicuously absent.

37. Ibid., p. 93.

38. Ibid., D. 685, p. 256.

39. Ibid., p. 257.

40. Ibid., pp. 257–258.

41. Ibid., D. 687, p. 578.
42. Ibid., D. 685, p. 275.
43. Ibid., p. 269.
44. Ibid., p. 274.
45. Ibid., p. 276.
46. Ibid., p. 576.
47. Ibid., p. 585.
48. Ibid., p. 593.
49. Ibid., p. 631–632.
50. Ibid., p. 606.
51. Ibid., p. 612.
52. Ibid., p. 615.
53. Ibid., p. 616.
54. Ibid., p. 621.
55. Ibid., p. 634.
56. Ibid.
57. Ibid.
58. Ibid., 636–637.
59. Ibid., D. 688, p. 642.
60. Ibid., p. 650.
61. Ibid., pp. 651–652.
62. Ibid., p. 659.
63. Samuelson, *Soviet Defence*, p. 106.
64. Tukhachevsky et al., *Budushchaia Voina*, p. 724.
65. Ibid.
66. Ibid., p. 731.
67. Ibid., p. 732.
68. Ibid.
69. Ibid., pp. 733–734.
70. Ibid., p. 734.
71. Ibid., pp. 734–735.
72. See Samuelson, *Soviet Defence*, chaps. 4–5.
73. Ibid., chaps. 3–4.
74. Ibid., p. 73.
75. Ibid., pp. 105–106. Although not explicitly identified as the work of the Fourth Department, given the chain of command and the substance of the information, it almost certainly was.
76. Ibid., p. 107.
77. Ibid., pp. 107–108.
78. Ibid., p. 108.
79. Ibid., p. 109.
80. For a discussion of these war plans, see ibid., pp. 110–111.
81. Lih, Naumov, Khlevniuk, *Stalin's Letters*, pp. 208–209, Letter 62, 1 September 1930. Stalin went on to suggest that the money to pay for the extra 700,000 reservists necessary for this expansion be raised by increasing vodka production; see ibid., p. 209.
82. It is important to note, however, that such a distinction would have been considered artificial by Marxist-Leninist analysts of the Fourth Department, for the interdependence of capabilities and intentions derives from the inevitability of armed

conflict and the influence of the correlation of forces on the policies of the ruling classes. The point argued here is that *this* view is ideologically narrow, and inevitably too restrictive for a realistic interpretation of international behavior.

83. For example, numbers used by Triandafillov for a 1927 war plan variant largely corresponded to those in U.S. War Department classified Soviet order of battle estimates; see Glantz, "Soviet Mobilization," p. 325.

84. *The Oxford Companion to World War II*, ed. by I.C.B. Dear (Oxford: Oxford University Press, 1995), p. 900.

85. Ibid., p. 957.

86. Ibid., pp. 373–374.

87. Voroshilov wrote that "whatever the conditions of war will ultimately be, we must base our calculations on the worst case"; see Samuelson, *Soviet Defence*, p. 108. Although he was specifically referring to the likelihood of a British-led wartime blockade against the USSR, this principle clearly governed RU analysis, especially in *The Future War*.

88. This is obviously a vastly simplified overview of European foreign policy in the 1920s. It does reflect, however, the fundamental picture drawn by numerous scholars over the years. For particulars, the reader is referred to Wandycz's work, *The Twilight of the French Eastern Alliances, 1926–1936: French-Czechoslovak-Polish Relations from Locarno to the Remilitarization of the Rhineland*, which, despite its title, provides a very thorough description of the policies of all the involved states.

89. Alaric Searle, "Conflict between Britain and the Soviet Union—1926," *The Journal of Soviet Military Studies* 3, no. 3 (September 1990); 513–524. p. 518.

90. Frank P. Chambers, *This Age of Conflict: The Western World—1914 to the Present* (New York: Harcourt, Brace & World, 1962), pp. 124–125.

91. Wandycz, *Twilight*, p. 108.

92. Ibid., p. 49.

93. Antony Polonsky, *Politics in Independent Poland, 1921–1939: Crisis of Constitutional Government* (Oxford: Clarendon Press, 1972), p. 200.

94. Wandycz, *Twilight*, pp. 156–157, 253–254.

95. Karski, *Great Powers*, pp. 136–138.

96. John Robert Ferris, *The Evolution of British Strategic Policy, 1919–26* (Hampshire, U.K.: MacMillan Press, 1989), p. 43.

97. Wandycz, *Twilight*, p. 50.

98. Karski, *Great Powers*, p. 128.

99. Wandycz, *Twilight*, p. 50.

100. The French ambassador to Poland in 1928, Jules Larouche, observed that "the Poles secretly despised the Romanians and had little in common with Yugoslavia. Some of these feelings were mutual"; cited in ibid., p. 118.

101. Most histories of "Enigma" and "ULTRA" contain variations of this information. See, for example, Peter Calvocoressi, *Top Secret Ultra* (New York: Ballantine Books, 1981), pp. 34–37; and Gordon Welchman, *The Hut Six Story: Breaking the Enigma Codes* (New York: McGraw-Hill, 1982), pp. 14–15.

102. This was, for example, the conclusion of a *Gosplan* report dated 24 January 1931, which observed that "a war in 1931 would from the imperialists' side, have the character of *preventive* war"; see Samuelson, *Soviet Defence*, p. 155 (emphasis in original).

Epilogue

We end our story in 1933, a year in which a number of crucial developments led the Soviet Union and the Fourth Department to dramatically reshape their policies. The Great Depression was in its third year and getting worse, with no end in sight. Radical movements on the left and right were growing, especially in France, Romania, Hungary, and Germany, where Adolf Hitler was appointed chancellor in January. Marking a revolution of a different sort was the inauguration of Franklin D. Roosevelt as president of the United States. In Japan, once again an intense and violent political struggle broke out among the military leadership, a situation that portended further aggression in Asia. Benito Mussolini cast a covetous eye toward Ethiopia, and the corrupt and exhausted monarchy in Spain would soon collapse into civil war. The "popular front" and the policies of appeasement followed.

Throughout the period covered in this work, the Soviet leadership and the Fourth Department regarded a combined attack on the western border by a coalition led by Poland and Romania and supported by France and Great Britain as the primary military threat. This scenario changed dramatically in 1933–34 with the Nazi consolidation of power and the beginning of German rearmament. Hitler's Third Reich now became the most dangerous threat, almost equaled by Japan in the Far East, with whom the Red Army came to blows almost two years before the Nazi invasion of the Soviet Union.

The RU spent the next several years preparing for the storm Berzin and others were certain would come. Red Army Intelligence became heavily involved in the Spanish Civil War, where it had a chance, like its Nazi opposite number, to observe under battlefield conditions many of the ideas and weapons explored by Russian and German officers only a few years earlier on

Soviet soil. And in Spain, Yan Berzin, erstwhile chief of the intelligence directorate, for all practical purposes commanded the Republican forces. By now a truly professional organization, the RU went about assembling espionage networks in Europe, Asia, and the United States that ultimately provided decisive intelligence in the next war, including the "Red Orchestra," Richard Sorge's "Tokyo Ring," and the American network that contained Whittaker Chambers, Elizabeth Bentley, and Alger Hiss. Their efforts significantly shaped the course of World War II and the peace that followed.

The *Razvedupr* also fell victim to a bloody assault by the secret police that all but destroyed it, as Stalin's purge of the Red Army decimated the leadership of its intelligence directorate. One result was that many of its overseas networks were taken over by the NKVD, although they continued to be "staffed" and supervised on the ground by RU personnel (a situation misunderstood by many historians of Soviet intelligence even today). In response, some members of the Fourth Department actually sought safety by transferring to the NKVD, but this only delayed the inevitable. Others decided to flee. Ignace Poretsky tried both.

Poretsky, filled with terror and rage at what was being done to his friends and associates, sent an open letter in July 1937 to the Central Committee of the CPSU. Denouncing the show trial and execution of sixteen "Old Bolsheviks," which began the purges in August 1936, Poretsky declared that "he who now keeps quiet becomes Stalin's accomplice, betrays the working class, betrays socialism." He concluded by calling for the creation of a "Fourth International" to replace the hopelessly feeble and corrupt Comintern, which was in any event now little more than Stalin's creature. Disgusted, he also returned the Order of the Red Banner which he had been awarded.[1] Poretsky and his family then retired to Switzerland, where they tried to live a normal life in the open and without any protection from the authorities. Within two months he was dead, the victim of a roadside ambush organized by the NKVD.[2]

With the example of his friend fresh in mind, Walter Krivitsky decided to defect with his wife and child to the West. At first ignored by the counterintelligence agencies of both Great Britain and the United States, officials finally took notice of him after the publication of a series of articles written by him in the *Saturday Evening Post* and his memoir, *I Was Stalin's Agent*. Thereafter he was finally interrogated by MI5 and the FBI, and even testified before the House Special Sub-Committee on Un-American Activities (HUAC). The constant strain of knowing that he was a marked man, however, wore heavily on Krivitsky, who in the course of 1940 sank ever deeper into depression, convinced that the chekists were reading his mail, following him, and tapping his phone. He was certainly aware of the fact that in August the NKVD had finally managed to kill Trotsky in Mexico City. In January 1941, the HUAC again subpoenaed him to appear on 10 February 1941. He failed to show up. Later that day, Washington, D.C. police found Krivitsky dead of an apparently self-inflicted gunshot wound. The circumstances surrounding his death remain a matter of debate.[3]

Yet as horrific as the slaughter was among the clandestine branches of the RU, it was a hundredfold worse among the officers and staffs of the Red Army's operational and tactical intelligence units. The consequences of this suicidal massacre did not begin to become apparent until the disastrous "Winter War" with Finland in 1939–40, in which poor intelligence work was a major reason for the huge casualties suffered by the Red Army. Worse by an order of magnitude, however, was the destruction visited upon the Red Army by the *Wehrmacht* during "Operation Barbarossa," when the lack of experienced intelligence officers from army group through divisional level seriously, almost fatally, weakened the ability of the Red Army to mount coherent defensive or counteroffensive operations. Somehow a cadre of experienced intelligence officers and agents nevertheless did survive the apocalypse of 1937–41, and through their hard work in the Soviet field commands on the Russian front and in the factories and governments of Europe, they played a decisive role in the eventual triumph of Soviet arms over Nazi Germany.

Even before the Red Army's tanks rolled into the outskirts of Berlin, however, Stalin had already begun to redirect the efforts of many of the GRU's men and women against the new "main enemy"—the United States—thereby setting the stage for their next great mission: to wage, and win, the Cold War.

NOTES

1. Poretsky, *Our Own People*, pp. 1–3.

2. Andrew and Gordievsky, *KGB*, p. 162. Krivitsky apparently implicated in the murder the sister of CPUSA chief Earl Browder, Margaret, who had been a long-time INO agent; see Klehr et al., *Secret World*, pp. 238–239.

3. Waldman, *Labor Lawyer*, pp. 351–353. Former NKVD assassin Pavel Sudoplatov asserted in his self-serving memoirs that although he and his "special tasks" unit had orders to "look for Krivitsky," these were merely routine, and that Krivitsky did indeed commit suicide, shooting himself "in despair as a result of a nervous breakdown"; Pavel Sudoplatov and Anatoli Sudoplatov, with Jerrold L. Schecter and Leona P. Schecter, *Special Tasks: The Memoirs of an Unwanted Witness—A Soviet Spymaster*, foreword by Robert Conquest (New York: Little, Brown and Company, 1994), p. 49.

APPENDIX A

Organizational Charts

Chart 1
The Red Army Intelligence Directorate, 1918–1930

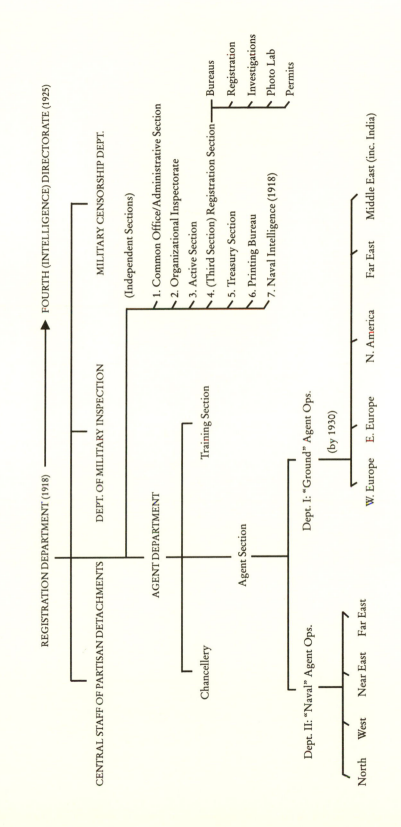

Chart 2
The Peking Military Center (PMC)

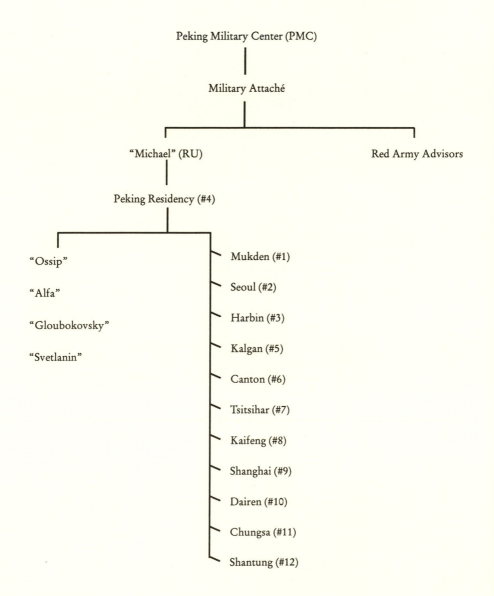

Peking Military Center (PMC)

Military Attaché

"Michael" (RU)   Red Army Advisors

Peking Residency (#4)

"Ossip"   Mukden (#1)

"Alfa"   Seoul (#2)

"Gloubokovsky"   Harbin (#3)

"Svetlanin"   Kalgan (#5)

Canton (#6)

Tsitsihar (#7)

Kaifeng (#8)

Shanghai (#9)

Dairen (#10)

Chungsa (#11)

Shantung (#12)

Chart 3
Richard Sorge's Shanghai Residency

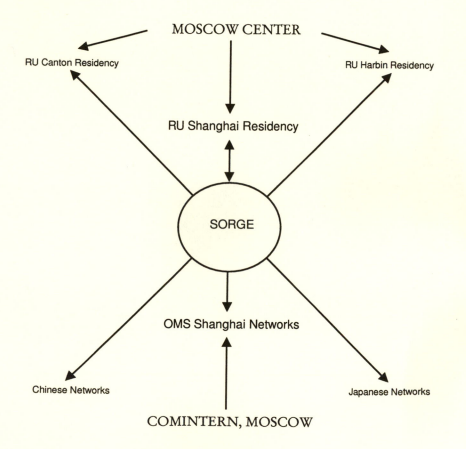

APPENDIX B

Tables

Table 1
Forces Available to Western Bordering States after Wartime Mobilization (1926 estimates)

Country	Infantry	Cavalry
Poland	60 divisions	4 divisions & 5 brigades
Romania	32 " "	3 divisions
Latvia	5 " "	2 regiments
Lithuania	4 " "	4 " "
Estonia	4 " "	2 " "
Finland	6 div., 2 brig.	1 division
TOTAL:	111 div., 2 brig.	8 div., 5 brig., 8 reg.

Source: Samuelson, *Soviet Defence,* p. 44.

Table 2
Peacetime Establishment of Armies of the Western Bordering States (*Future War* estimates)

Country	Infantry	Cavalry	Total Strength
Poland	30 divisions	7 divisions	312,000
Romania	24 " "	3.5 " "	162,000
Latvia	4 " "	1 regiment	20,000
Estonia	3 " "	1 regiment	14,000
Lithuania	2 " "	2 " "	15,000
Finland	4 " "	2 " "	33,000
TOTAL:	67 " "	11.5 divs.	556,000

Except for the Polish infantry divisions, most of these were at cadre strength; they would be expanded by prewar and wartime mobilization.

Source: Tukhachevsky et al., *Buduschchaia Voina,* d. 683, p. 54.

Table 3
Casualty Estimates for the Western Bordering Coalition in the "Future War"

Country	Strength in 1st 4–6 Months	Average Annual Losses
Poland	1.5 million	600,000
Romania	900,000	360,000
Latvia	120,000	48,000
Estonia	100,000	40,000
Lithuania	120,000	48,000
Finland	160,000	54,000

Source: Tukhachevsky et al., *Buduschchaia Voina*, d. 683, p. 92

Table 4
Estimated Correlation of Forces at Start of the "Future War"
(1928 threat assessment est.)

Forces	Enemy Coalition	Red Army
Infantry divisions	109	100
Aircraft	1,190	1,046
Tanks	401	90
Guns	5,620	7,034
Troops	3.1 million	2.66 million

Source: Samuelson, *Soviet Defence*, p. 106.

Bibliography

PRIMARY SOURCES

Unpublished documents
Microforms

Belitskii, S. M. *Operativnaia razvedka*. Moscow: Gosudarstvennoe izdatel'stvo otdel Voennoi Literatury, 1929.

Tukhachevsky, M. N., et al. *Budushchaia Voina*. Moscow: Third Section of IV (Intelligence) Directorate of RKKA Staff, 1928. TsGASA, f. 33988, op. 2, d. 682–8.

Voennyi zarubezhnik.

Archives

"*Polevoi shtab RVSR.*" TsGASA, f. 6. op. 1, L. 7–12.

U.S. National Archives. Harry S. Truman Library. Papers of Harry S. Truman, White House Central Files. Department of the Army. Confidential File, 1949–50, Box No. 4, *A Partial Documentation of the Sorge Espionage Case.*

Published Document Collections

D'yakov, Yu. D., and Bushueva, T. S. *Fashistskii mech kovalsya v USSR*. Moscow: Sovetskaya Rossiya, 1992.

————. *The Red Army and the Wehrmacht: How the Soviets Militarized Germany, 1922–33, and Paved the Way for Fascism*. New York: Prometheus Books, 1995.

Klehr, Harvey, Haynes, John Earl, and Firsov, Fridrikh Igorevich. *The Secret World of American Communism*. New Haven: Yale University Press, 1995.

Lazitch, Branko, and Drachkovitch, Milorad M. *Lenin and the Comintern*. Vol. 1. Stanford: Hoover Institution Press, 1972.

Lih, Lars T., Naumov, Oleg V., and Khlevniuk, Oleg V., Eds. *Stalin's Letters to Molotov, 1925–1936*. Trans. by Catherine A. Fitzpatrick. New Haven: Yale University Press, 1995.

Mitarevsky, N. *World Wide Soviet Plots*. Tientsin, China: Tientsin Press, n.d. (ca. 1928).

Trotsky, Leon. *How the Revolution Armed: The Military Writings and Speeches of Leon Trotsky*. Vol. 1, *The Year 1918*. Trans. and annotated by Brian Pearce. London: New Park Publications, 1979.

Wilbur, C. Martin, and Lien-ying How, Julie, Eds. *Documents on Communism, Nationalism, and Soviet Advisors in China, 1918–1927: Papers Seized in the 1927 Peking Raid*. New York: Columbia University Press, 1956.

Memoirs and Autobiographies

Agabekov, Georges. *OGPU: The Russian Secret Terror*. Trans. by Henry Bunn. New York: Brentano's, 1931.

Akhmedov, Ismail. *In and out of Stalin's GRU: A Tatar's Escape from Red Army Intelligence*. Frederick, Md.: University Publications of America, 1984.

Chambers, Whittaker. *Witness*. Washington, D.C.: Regnery Gateway, 1980.

Cherepanov, A. *Zapiski voennogo sovetnika v Kitae, 1925–1927*. Moscow: Izdatel'stvo "Nauka," 1971.

Crossman, Richard, Ed. *The God that Failed*. New York: Harper & Brothers, 1950.

Gitlow, Benjamin. *I Confess: The Truth about American Communism*. New York: E. P. Dutton & Co., 1940.

Hilger, Gustav, and Meyer, Alfred G. *The Incompatible Allies: A Memoir of German-Soviet Relations, 1918–1941*. New York: MacMillan, 1953.

Hill, Captain George A. *Go Spy the Land: Being the Adventures of I.K.8 of the British Secret Service*. London: Cassell and Company, 1936.

Krebs, Richard [Jan Valtin]. *Out of the Night*. New York: Alliance Book Corporation, 1940.

Krivitsky, Walter. *I Was Stalin's Agent*. London: The Right Book Club, 1940.

Kuusinen, Aino. *Before and after Stalin: A Personal Account of Soviet Russia from the 1920s to the 1960s*. London: Michael Joseph, 1974.

Lockhart, R. H. Bruce. *Memoirs of a British Agent*. London: MacMillan London, 1974.

Massing, Hede. *This Deception*. New York: Duell, Sloan and Pearce, 1951.

Memories of Georgi Dimitrov. Sofia: Sofia Press, 1972.

Poretsky, Elisabeth. *Our Own People: A Memoir of 'Ignace Reiss' and His Friends*. London: Oxford University Press, 1969.

Starinov, I. G. *Miny zhdut svoevo chasa*. Moscow: Voennoe izdatel'stvo Ministerstva Oborony SSSR, 1964.

———. *Over the Abyss: My Life in Soviet Special Operations*. Trans. and intro. by Robert Suggs. New York: Ivy Books, 1995.

Sudoplatov, Pavel, and Sudoplatov, Anatoli. With Jerrold L. Schecter and Leona P. Schecter. *Special Tasks: The Memoirs of an Unwanted Witness—A Soviet Spymaster*. Foreword by Robert Conquest. New York: Little, Brown and Company, 1994.

Trepper, Leopold. *The Great Game: Memoirs of the Spy Hitler Couldn't Silence*. New York: McGraw-Hill, 1977.

Visnnyakova-Akimova, Vera Vladimorovna. *Two Years in Revolutionary China, 1925–1927*. Trans. by Steven I. Levine. Cambridge, Mass.: Harvard University Press, 1971.

Waldman, Louis. *Labor Lawyer*. New York: E. P. Dutton and Company, 1944.

Werner, Ruth. *Sonya's Report*. Trans. by Renate Simpson. London: Chatto & Windus, 1991.

Wright, Peter. *Spycatcher: The Candid Autobiography of a Senior Intelligence Officer*. New York: Viking Penguin, 1987.

Yardley, Herbert. *The American Black Chamber*. Indianapolis: Bobbs-Merrill, 1931.

Miscellaneous

Neuberg, A. *Armed Insurrection*. Trans. by Quintin Hoare. London: NLB, 1970.

U.S. Congress. House. *Hearings before a Special Committee on Un-American Activities*. "Investigation of Un-American Propaganda Activities in the United States." "Testimony of Walter Krivitsky, Former Member, Soviet Military Intelligence Service, Through an Interpreter, Boris Shub." Washington, D.C.: U.S. Government Printing Office, 1939.

SECONDARY SOURCES

Aderath, M. *The French Communist Party, a Critical History (1920–84): From Comintern to 'the Colours of France'*. Manchester: Manchester University Press, 1984.

Andrew, Christopher, Ed. *Intelligence and International Relations 1900–1945*. Exeter, U.K.: Exeter University Publications, 1987.

Andrew, Christopher, and Gordievsky, Oleg. *KGB: The Inside Story of Its Foreign Operations from Lenin to Gorbachev*. New York: Harper Collins, 1990.

Angress, Werner T. *Stillborn Revolution: The Communist Bid for Power in Germany, 1921–1923*. Princeton: Princeton University Press, 1963.

Avrich, Paul. *Kronstadt 1921*. Princeton: Princeton University Press, 1970.

Barron, John. *KGB: The Secret Work of Soviet Secret Agents*. New York: Bantam Books, 1974.

Bogacki, Anatole C. J. *A Polish Paradox: International and the National Interest in Polish Communist Foreign Policy 1918–1948*. Boulder, Colo.: East European Monographs, 1991.

Borovikh, Genrikh. *The Philby Files: The Secret Life of Master Spy Kim Philby*. Ed. and intro. by Phillip Knightly. Boston: Little, Brown and Company, 1994.

Brook-Shepherd, Gordon. *The Storm Petrels: The First Soviet Defectors, 1928–1938*. London: Collins, 1977.

Brown, Anthony Cave, and MacDonald, Charles B. *On a Field of Red: The Communist International and the Coming of World War II*. New York: G. P. Putnam's Sons, 1981.

Calvocoressi, Peter. *Top Secret Ultra*. New York: Ballantine Books, 1981.

Chambers, Frank P. *This Age of Conflict: The Western World—1914 to the Present.* New York: Harcourt, Brace & World, 1962.

Chan, F. Gilbert, and Etzold, Thomas H., Eds. *China in the 1920s.* New York: New Viewpoints, 1976.

Cienciala, Anna M., and Komarnicki, Titus. *From Versailles to Locarno: Keys to Polish Foreign Policy, 1919–1925.* Lawrence: University Press of Kansas, 1984.

Conquest, Robert. *The Harvest of Sorrow: Soviet Collectivization and the Terror-Famine.* New York: Oxford University Press, 1986.

———. *The Great Terror: A Reassessment.* New York: Oxford University Press, 1990.

Corson, William R., and Crowley, Robert T. *The New KGB: Engine of Soviet Power.* New York: William Morrow and Company, 1985.

Costello, John. *Mask of Treachery: Spies, Lies and Betrayal.* New York: Warner Books, 1989.

Craig, Gordon A. *The Politics of the Prussian Army, 1640–1945.* New York: Oxford University Press, 1964.

Crow, Duncan, and Robert J. Icks. *Encyclopedia of Tanks.* New York: Chartwell Books, 1975.

Dallin, David J. *The Rise of Russia in Asia.* New Haven: Yale University Press, 1949.

———. *Soviet Russia and the Far East.* London: Hollis & Carter, 1949.

———. *Soviet Espionage.* New Haven: Yale University Press, 1955.

Deacon, Richard. *A History of the Russian Secret Service.* London: Frederick Muller, 1972.

Dirlik, Arif. *The Origins of Chinese Communism.* New York: Oxford University Press, 1989.

Draper, Theodore. *The Roots of American Communism.* New York: Viking Press, 1957.

———. *American Communism and Soviet Russia.* New York: Viking Press, 1960.

Dziak, John. *Chekisty: A History of the KGB.* New York: Ivy Books, 1988.

Ehrt, Adolf. *Bewaffneter Aufstand: Enthüllungen über den kommunistischen Umsturzversuch an Vorabend der nationalen Revolution.* Berlin-Leipzig: Eckart-Verlag, 1933.

Erickson, John. *The Soviet High Command, a Military-Political History.* London: St. Martin's Press, 1962.

Evans, Stanley G. *A Short History of Bulgaria.* London: Lawrence & Wishart, 1960.

Ferris, John Robert. *The Evolution of British Strategic Policy, 1919–26.* Hampshire, U.K.: MacMillan Press, 1989.

Fischer, Ruth. *Stalin and German Communism: A Study in the Origins of the State Party.* Preface by Sidney B. Fay. Cambridge: Harvard University Press, 1948.

Fuller, William C. *Strategy and Power in Russia, 1600–1914.* New York: The Free Press, 1992.

Germanis, Uldis. *Oberst Vacietis und die lettischen Schuetzen im Weltkrieg und in der Oktoberrevolution.* Stockholm: Almquist & Wiksell, 1974.

Getzler, Israel. *Kronstadt, 1917–1921: The Fate of a Soviet Democracy.* Cambridge: Cambridge University Press, 1983.

Glantz, David. "Soviet Mobilization in Peace and War, 1924–42: A Survey." *The Journal of Soviet Military Studies* 5, 3 (September 1992): 323–362.

Golyakov, S., and Ponizovskii, V. *"Nachal'nik razvedki." Komsomol'skaya pravda* (13 November 1964): 4.

Gorchakov, Ovidii. "*Yan Berzin: sud'ba komandarma nevidimovo fronta.*" *Novaya i noveishaya istoriya*, no. 2 (March–April 1989): 131–159.

Groehler, Olaf. *Selbstmörderische Allianz: Deutsch-russische Militärbeziehungen, 1920–1941*. Berlin: Vision Verlag, 1992.

Haigh, R. H., Morris, D. S., and Peters, A. R. *German-Soviet Relations in the Weimar Era: Friendship from Necessity*. Aldershot, Engl.: Gower Publishing Company, 1985.

Hammer, Armand. With Neil Lyndon. *Hammer*. New York: G. P. Putnam's Sons, 1987.

Harries, Meirion, and Harries, Susie. *Soldiers of the Sun: The Rise and Fall of the Imperial Japanese Army*. New York: Random House, 1991.

Heller, Mikhail, and Nekrich, Aleksandr. *Utopia in Power: The History of the Soviet Union from 1917 to the Present*. Trans. by Phyllis B. Carlos. New York: Summit Books, 1986.

Hofman, George F. "The United States' Contribution to Soviet Tank Technology." *Journal of the Royal United Services Institute for Defence Studies* 125, no. 1 (March 1980): 63–68.

Höhne, Heinz. *Codeword Direktor*. New York: Berkley, 1970.

Jay, Martin. *The Dialectical Imagination: A History of the Frankfurt School and the Institute of Social Research, 1923–1950*. Boston: Little, Brown & Company, 1973.

Johnson, Chalmers. *An Instance of Treason: Ozaki Hotsumi and the Sorge Spy Ring*. Stanford: Stanford University Press, 1990.

Kahn, David. *The Code-Breakers*. London: Sphere Books, 1973.

Karski, Jan. *The Great Powers and Poland, 1919–1945: From Versailles to Yalta*. Lanham, Md.: University Press of America, 1985.

Kipp, Jacob W. *Mass, Mobility, and the Red Army's Road to Operational Art, 1918–1936*. Ft. Leavenworth, Kans.: Soviet Army Studies Office, U.S. Army Combined Arms Center, 1987.

———. *Lenin and Clausewitz: The Militarization of Marxism, 1914–1921*. Ft. Leavenworth, Kans.: Soviet Army Studies Office, U.S. Army Combined Arms Center, 1988.

Klehr, Harvey, and Haynes, John Earl. *The American Communist Movement: Storming Heaven Itself*. New York: Twayne, 1992.

Klyatskin, S. M. *Na zashchite Oktyabrya: organizatsiya regulyarnoi armii i militsionnoe stroitel'stvo v Sovetskoi Respublike, 1917–1920*. Moscow: "Nauka," 1965.

Koch, Stephan. *Double Lives: Spies and Writers in the Secret Soviet War of Ideas against the West*. New York: The Free Press, 1994.

Kolesnikov, M. *Takim byl Rikhard Zorge*. Moscow: Voennoe izdatl'stvo Ministerstva Oborony SSSR, 1965.

Korzun, L. "*Razvedka v russkoi armii v pervoi mirovoi voine.*" *Voennoe istoricheskiy Zhurnal*, no. 4 (April 1981): 60–71.

Krastynya, Ya. P., Ed. *Istoria latyskskikh strelkov*. Riga: Izdatl'stvo "Zinatne," 1972.

Leggett, George. *The Cheka: Lenin's Political Police*. Oxford: Clarendon Press, 1981.

Leonard, Raymond W. "Studying the Kremlin's Secret Soldiers: A Historiographical Essay on the GRU, 1918–1945." *The Journal of Military History* 56, no. 3 (July 1992): 403–421.

Les Migrations Internationales de la Fin du XVIIIe Siècle à Jours. Paris: Éditions du Centre National de la Recherche Scientifique, 1980.

MacKinnon, Janice R., and MacKinnan Stephen R. *Agnes Smedley: The Life and Times of an American Radical*. Berkeley: University of California Press, 1988.

Mäder, Julius. *Dr. Sorge Report*. Berlin: Militärverlag der Deutschen Demokratischen Republik (VEB), 1984.

Mangulis, Visvaldis. *Latvia in the Wars of the 20th Century*. Princeton Junction, N.J.: Cognition Books, 1983.

May, Ernest R., Ed. *Knowing One's Enemies: Intelligence Assessment before the Two World Wars*. Princeton: Princeton University Press, 1984.

McCord, Edward A. *The Power of the Gun: The Emergence of Modern Chinese Warlordism*. Berkeley: University of California Press, 1993.

McIntyre, Robert J. *Bulgaria: Politics, Economics and Society*. London: Pinter Publishers, 1988.

Menning, Bruce W. *Bayonets before Bullets: The Russian Imperial Army, 1861–1914*. Bloomington: Indiana University Press, 1992.

Mikhailov, I. M., Ed. *Vstretimsya posle zadaniya*. Moscow: Izdatel'stvo DOSAAF, 1973.

Miller, Nathan. *War at Sea: A Naval History of World War II*. New York: Scribner, 1995.

Mortimer, Edward. *The Rise of the French Communist Party, 1920–1947*. Part 1. London: Faber and Faber, 1984.

Nollau, Gunther. *International Communism and World Revolution: History and Methods*. Foreword by Leonard Shapiro. London: Hollis & Carter, 1961.

The Oxford Companion to World War II. Ed. by I.C.B. Dear. Oxford: Oxford University Press, 1995.

Perrault, Gilles. *The Red Orchestra*. Trans. by Peter Wiles. New York: Schocken Books, 1969.

Peterson, Virgil W. *The Mob: 200 Years of Organized Crime in New York*. Ottawa, Ill.: Green Hill Publishers, 1983.

Polmar, Norman. *Aircraft Carriers: A Graphic History of Carrier Aviation and Its Influence on World Events*. Garden City, N.Y.: Doubleday & Company, 1969.

Polonsky, Antony. *Politics in Independent Poland, 1921–1939: Crisis of Constitutional Government*. Oxford: Clarendon Press, 1972.

Ponizovskii, V. *Soldatskoe pole: geroicheskie biografii*. Moscow: Izdatel'stvo vse-soyuznovo ordena krasnovo znameni dobrovol'novo obshchestvo sodeistviya armii, aviatsii i flotu, 1971.

Powers, Richard Gid. *Not without Honor: The History of American Anticommunism*. New York: The Free Press, 1995.

Prange, Gordon. With Donald M. Goldstein and Katherine V. Dillon. *Target Tokyo: The Story of the Sorge Spy Ring*. New York: McGraw-Hill, 1984.

Rapoport, Vitaly, and Alexeev, Yuri. *High Treason: Essays on the History of the Red Army, 1918–1938*. Trans. by Bruce Adams. Ed. by Vladimir G. Treml. Durham: Duke University Press, 1985.

Reissner, Larrisa. *Hamburg at the Barricades, and Other Writings on Weimar Germany*. Trans. and ed. by Richard Chappell. London: Pluto Press, 1977.

Romerstein, Herbert, and Levchenko, Stanislav. *The KGB against the "Main Enemy."* Lexington, Mass.: D. C. Heath and Company, 1989.

Samuelson, Lennart. *Soviet Defence Industry Planning: Tukhachevskii and Military-Industrial Mobilisation, 1926–1937*. Stockholm: Stockholm Institute of East European Economies, 1996.

Schneider, James J. *The Structure of Strategic Revolution: Total War and the Roots of the Soviet Warfare State*. Novato, Calif.: Presidio Press, 1994.

Scott, Harriet Fast, and Scott, William F. *Soviet Military Doctrine*. Boulder, Colo.: Westview Press, 1988.

Searle, Alaric. "Conflict between Britain and the Soviet Union—1926." *The Journal of Soviet Military Studies* 3, no. 3 (September 1990): 513–524.

Shipley, Peter. *Hostile Action: The KGB and Secret Soviet Operations in Britain*. London, Pinter, 1989.

Shumelev, I. I., Ed. *Soldaty nevidimykh srazhenii: rasskazy o podvigakh chekistov*. Moscow: Voennoe izdatel'stvo Ministerstva Oborony SSSR, 1968.

Simpkin, Richard. *Deep Battle: The Brainchild of Marshal Tukhachevskii*. London: Brassey's Defence Publishers, 1987.

Sinclair, Andrew. *The Red and the Blue: Intelligence, Treason and the Universities*. London: Weidenfeld and Nicolson, 1986.

Solonitsyn, G. "*Nachal'nik sovetskoi razvedki*." *Voennoe istoricheskiy Zhurnal*, no. 11 (November 1979): 92–94.

Suvorov, Viktor. *Inside Soviet Military Intelligence*. New York: Macmillan, 1984.

———. *Spetsnaz: The Inside Story of the Soviet Special Forces*. Trans. by David Floyd. New York: W. W. Norton & Company, 1987.

Swearingen, Rodger, and Langer, Paul. *Red Flag in Japan: International Communism in Action, 1919–1951*. Westport, Conn.: Greenwood Press, 1968.

Theoharis, Athan, Ed. *From the Secret Files of J. Edgar Hoover*. Chicago: Ivan R. Dee, 1991.

Tiersky, Ronald. *French Communism, 1920–1972*. New York: Columbia University Press, 1974.

Toledano, Ralph de. *J. Edgar Hoover: The Man in His Time*. New Rochelle, N.Y.: Arlington House, 1973.

Villemarest, Pierre de. *GRU: Le plus secret des services sovietiques, 1918–1988*. Paris: Editions Stock, 1988.

Volkogonov, Dmitri. *Stalin: Triumph and Tragedy*. Trans. by Harold Shukman. New York: Grove Weidenfeld, 1991.

———. *Trotskii: politicheskii portret*. Vol. 2. Moscow: Novosti, 1992.

———. *Lenin: A New Biography*. Ed. and trans. by Harold Shukman. New York: The Free Press, 1994.

Wandycz, Pyotr. *The Twilight of the French Eastern Alliances, 1926–1936: French-Czechoslovak-Polish Relations from Locarno to the Remilitarization of the Rhineland*. Princeton: Princeton University Press, 1988.

Watt, Donald Cameron. "Who Plotted against Whom? Stalin's Purge of the Soviet High Command Revisited." *The Journal of Soviet Military Studies* 3, no. 1 (March 1990): 46–65.

Weissburg, Alex. *Conspiracy of Silence*. Trans. by Edward Fitzgerald. London: Hamish Hamilton, 1952.

Welchman, Gordon. *The Hut Six Story: Breaking the Enigma Codes*. New York: McGraw-Hill, 1982.

West, Nigel. *MI5: British Security Service Operations, 1909–1945*. London: The Bodley Head, 1981.

Whaley, Barton. *Covert German Rearmament, 1919–1939: Deception and Misperception*. Frederick, Md.: University Publications of America, 1984.

Whitney, R. M. *Reds in America*. New York: The Beckwith Press, 1924.

Wilbur, C. Martin. *The Nationalist Revolution in China, 1923–1928*. Cambridge: Cambridge University Press, 1983.

Williams, Robert Chadwell. *Klaus Fuchs, Atom Spy*. Cambridge: Harvard University Press, 1987.

Willoughby, Maj. Gen. Charles. *Shanghai Conspiracy: The Sorge Spy Ring*. New York: E. P. Dutton & Company, Inc., 1952.

Wohl, Robert. *French Communism in the Making, 1914–1924*. Stanford: Stanford University Press, 1966.

Wollenberg, Erich. *The Red Army: A Study in the Growth of Soviet Imperialism*. London: Seeker & Warburg, 1940.

Woytak, Richard A. *On the Border of War and Peace: Polish Intelligence and Diplomacy in 1937–1939 and the Origins of the ULTRA Secret*. Boulder, Colo.: East European Quarterly, 1979.

Subject Index

Name Index

Absalymov, Minzakir, 1
Adam, Wilhelm, 155
Adamczik, Willi, 146
Agabekov, Georges, xiv, 25, 44, 88, 102
Akhmedov, Ismail, xiv
Albert. *See* Muraille
"Alex," 124
Alexandrovski, 142
Amanullah, Amir of Afghanistan, 43–44
Aralov, Simon Ivanovich, 10, 14–15, 23, 167
"Ausem," 138–139

Barbé, Henri, 91–92
Baranov, P. I., 157
Barion, Hans, 146
Batcha Sakao (the "Water Carrier"), 44–45
Bazarov, Boris, 147, 160
Bentley, Elizabeth, 110, 192
Beria, Lavrenti, xiii
Berkowitz, Benjamin, 95–96
Bernstein, Abraham. *See* Uzdanski-Yelenski
Bertrand, Gustave, 186
Berzin, Y. K., 9, 18, 19, 29, 34, 48, 57, 78, 80, 87, 89, 90, 92–93, 103, 111–112, 118, 124, 127–128, 165, 191; biography of, 11–13, 23; and counterfeiting, 114–116, 130; and *Reichswehr*, 135, 138, 151, 154, 156–158, 162–163; and reorganization of RU, 9–10; in Spain, 53, 192; and threat assessment and analysis, 137, 170–171, 181, 185–186
Bir, Izaia, 93–96
Blomberg, Werner von, 154
Blücher, V., 38–39, 48
Blunt, Anthony, 77. *See also in subject index* Cambridge Spy Ring
Boissonas. *See* Muraille
Boky, Gleb, 90
"Boris" (Bulgarian RU agent), 50, 59
Borodin, M., 38–39
Borovich, Alex, 17
Borsig, Conrad von, 30
Botzenhard, Hans, 60, 143–144
Brandler, Heinrich, 29
Brauchitsch, Walter von, 161
Brockdorff-Rantzau, Count U. von, 28
Browder, Earl, 41, 52
Bukharin, N., 37, 52
Bulow, Count Enrique von, 115
Burde, Fritz, 148–149, 160